Earthkeepers

OBSERVERS AND PROTECTORS OF NATURE

Earthkeepers

OBSERVERS AND PROTECTORS OF NATURE

ANN T. KEENE

OXFORD UNIVERSITY PRESS

NEW YORK · OXFORD

This book is for Charles.

Oxford University Press
Oxford New York Toronto
Delhi Bombay Calcutta Madras Karachi
Kuala Lumpur Singapore Hong Kong Tokyo
Nairobi Dar es Salaam Cape Town
Melbourne Auckland Madrid
and associated companies in Berlin Ibadan

Copyright © 1994 by Ann T. Keene

Published by Oxford University Press, Inc.,
200 Madison Avenue, New York, New York 10016

Library of Congress Cataloging-in-Publication Data

Keene, Ann T.
Earthkeepers: observers and protectors of nature / by Ann T. Keene
p. cm.
Includes bibliographical references and index.
Summary: Profiles men and women who have been prominent in the field of natural history. Includes a list of organizations promoting conservation and nature study.
ISBN 0-19-507867-5
1. Naturalists—Biography—Juvenile literature. 2. Conservationists—Biography—Juvenile literature. 3. Nature conservation—Juvenile literature.
[1. Naturalists 2. Conservationists 3. Nature conservation] I. Title.
QH26.K43 1994

508'.092'2—dc20
[B]

93-18126
CIP
AC

1 3 5 7 9 8 6 4 2
Printed in Singapore
on acid-free paper

On the cover: (clockwise from top left)
Jane Goodall, Louis Agassiz, Rachel Carson, and Theodore Roosevelt
Frontispiece: Naturalist John Muir on a hike through California's Yosemite Valley in 1907. Largely because of Muir's efforts, the U.S. government established Yosemite National Park in 1890.

Design: Sandy Kaufman
Layout: Loraine Machlin

Contents

Preface

One definition of "keeper" is "a person responsible for the care and well-being of something valuable." "Earthkeeper" is not found—yet—in any dictionary, although perhaps someday it might be. It is a word I use to describe men and women, past and present, who have had an enormous curiosity about the natural world in which we live, and who have made major contributions to our understanding of nature.

Many Earthkeepers have called themselves naturalists. Some were scientists who studied plants (botanists), animals (zoologists), fossils (paleontologists), and rock formations (geologists). Others were self-trained amateurs who pursued nature study as a hobby. Since the late 19th century, Earthkeepers have been politically active as preservationists, conservationists, ecologists, and environmentalists.

On the following pages you will meet a variety of Earthkeepers, men and women who have been prominent in the field of natural history. In chronological order, 46 Earthkeepers are profiled in extended essays; many others are identified in the section called "More Earthkeepers to Remember" that follows each of the four parts of the book.

Of course, this volume cannot tell the story of every Earthkeeper who has ever lived; there are thousands, perhaps millions of them. Today the growing environmental movement includes Earthkeepers in cities, towns, and villages throughout the world. At a time when Earth is besieged by many negative results of industrialization, and when numerous plant and animal species are threatened with extinction, we need an abundance of Earthkeepers, male and female, young and old, committed to caring for nature.

Ann T. Keene
Westport, Connecticut

A note to the reader:

You may want to know more about some of the Earthkeepers you meet on these pages. Further Reading, which begins on page 213, offers a list of books about many of them, as well as other books and articles about nature and the environment that are available at your school or local library. There is also a Further Reading list at the end of each Earthkeeper's profile. Beginning on page 208, you will find a list of organizations promoting conservation and nature study; write to them for further information about their activities.

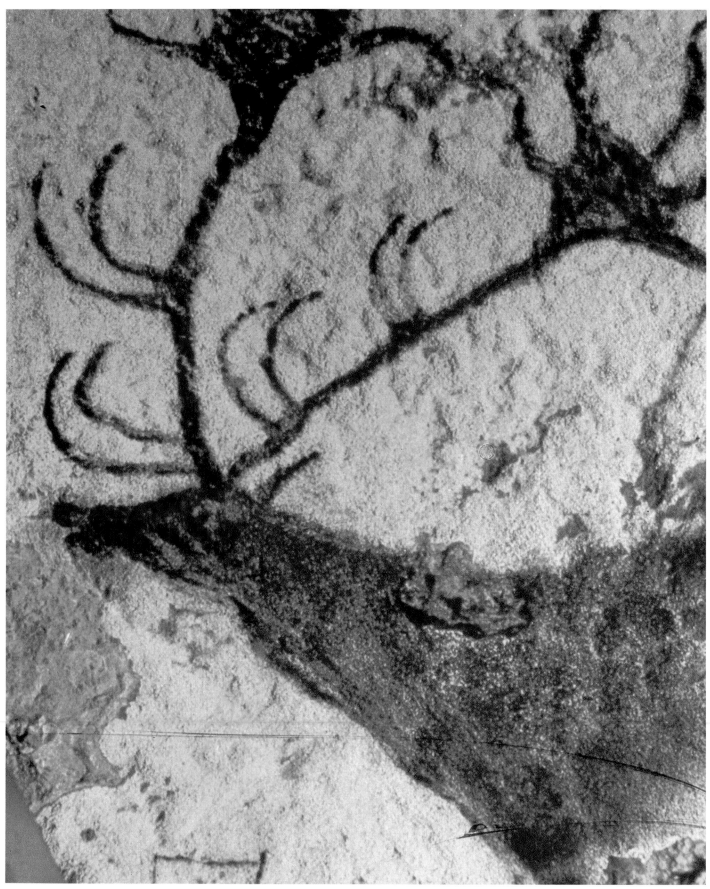

Since prehistoric times human beings have recorded their responses to nature. More than 20,000 years ago, a resident of what is now southwestern France decorated the walls and ceiling of a cave called Lascaux with paintings of animals, including this stag.

1 A Search for Meaning and Order

Men and women have probably been fascinated by the natural world since our species, *Homo sapiens*, first walked upon the Earth some half a million years ago. That fascination has expressed itself in different ways over the centuries, however. To our earliest ancestors, much of nature—dangerous plants, threatening animals, fierce tides and storms, strange lights that moved in the heavens—must have seemed a collection of frightening forces to be confronted and overcome in order to obtain food, medicine, shelter, and clothing, and to ensure personal safety and survival. This view of the natural world as an enemy to be conquered has persisted: only in the late 20th century have peoples throughout the world come to share the realization that humankind can live in harmony with nature.

Long before human beings created written languages, they expressed their responses to the natural world in art. The earliest known artistic depictions of nature, which survive in Europe, the Near and Middle East, and Asia, represent the hunting of animals. Cave drawings and carvings that may date as far back as 20,000 B.C. have been found in Spain and France. Egyptian tomb decorations portraying hunting were made as early as 2400 B.C. Ornamental bronze jars made about 500 B.C. in China also show scenes of combat between men and beasts.

Explanations for the existence of nature were the basis of ancient cultural and religious traditions throughout the world, transmitted orally long before they appeared in written form. Creation stories dating back thousands of years have been found in every culture on Earth, from the ancient civilizations of the Middle East and Asia to the Native Americans of North America. Myths of the Greeks and Romans and the Norsemen relate imagined origins of plant and animal life. Animal stories that taught as they entertained also have a long history: the *Fables* of Aesop, for example, date from about 600 B.C., and the great Hindu collection of fables, the *Panchatantra*, and the Buddhist *Jataka* tales are thousands of years old.

Motivating all these ancient attempts to explain the natural world was a desire to make some sense of what could be observed—to establish order amid the seeming chaos of nature. Natural history, or the scientific study of nature—which today we call botany, zoology, and mineralogy—originated in ancient Greece with the philosopher Aristotle (384-322 B.C.), who divided the universe into two parts, the animate (plants and animals) and the inanimate (minerals). Most of his nature writings concentrate on the study of animals—what we now call zoology.

In his *History of Animals* and several other works, Aristotle described different forms of animal life (the word *history* comes from a Greek word meaning "investigation") and classified them according to their method of reproduction. Although many of his conclusions about their relationships and structures were eventually rejected as false, his arrangement of animals into two groups, those with red blood and those without, is reflected in the modern zoological classification of vertebrates (those with backbones) and invertebrates (those without backbones).

Aristotle believed that nature had a purpose, and that every structure within nature had its place on a so-called ladder of life. This important aspect of Aristotle's thought was taken a step further in the writings of two early Romans, the philosopher and dramatist Seneca (who was born around 4 B.C. and died in A.D. 65), and the scholar Pliny the Elder (A.D. 23-79), which became influential during the so-called Dark and Middle Ages. Seneca's book *Natural Questions* was mostly an account of known information about natural history, but its significance lay in Seneca's belief that nature had been created by God to serve mankind. This view was shared by leaders of the Christian church and has persisted in the Western world for several thousand years.

Pliny expressed a similar view in his 37-volume *Natural History*; its entertaining but inaccurate accounts of animals were adapted by early Christian writers to create stories with religious themes. These collections, known as bestiaries, were popular during the Middle Ages. They included known European animals as well as imaginary creatures such as unicorns and dragons. They fancifully depicted real animals that early travelers to the Far East, including Marco Polo (1254-1324), had reported seeing.

While animal studies slipped into the fanciful and imaginary for nearly 2,000 years following the death of Aristotle, plants were the continued focus of scientific study. Theophrastus (who was born around 372 B.C. and died about 287 B.C.), another Greek philosopher, followed Aristotle's method of classification in his botanical writings (*Inquiry into Plants* and *Causes of Plants*). In the first century A.D., a Greek army doctor named Dioscorides wrote the first work of applied science, *Materia Medica* (*On Medical Matters*), a systematic account of the uses of plants in medical treatment. During the following thousand years monks made numerous copies of Dioscorides' treatise and illustrations and they also made Arabic and Latin translations.

During the late Middle Ages, new accounts of the medicinal uses of northern European plants and roots, called "herbals," appeared. The invention of printing around 1450 gave rise to the creation of many printed herbals lavishly illustrated with woodcut prints. The German naturalist Otto Brunfels (1488-1534) is credited with producing the first printed work on botany that relied solely on observation: *Living Portraits of Plants* (1530-36). His countryman Leonhard Fuchs (1501-66) produced another important herbal, *The History of Plants* (1542). Botanical manuals were also being written in China in the 16th century; the best known was *Ben Zao Gang Mu* (*Great Pharmacopoeia*; 1583), by Li Shi-Zhen (born 1518).

During the Renaissance, the discovery and exploration of the New World were matched by the rediscovery of the thought of the ancient world, especially the writings of Aristotle, which inspired scholars to make new studies of both plants and animals. The Italian Andreas Cesalpino (1519-1603) and the Swiss Caspar Bauhin (1560-1624) are remembered today for their extensive catalogs of plants. Several animal encyclopedias were written, including the *History of Animals* (published about 1550) by the Swiss Konrad von Gessner (1516-65); Gessner's work is considered the starting point of modern zoology. The Italian Ulissi Aldrovandi (1522-1605) and the

The Roman naturalist Pliny the Elder was killed while investigating the eruption of Mt. Vesuvius in A.D. 79. Vesuvius has been active more than 50 times since then; this watercolor depicts an eruption in the early 19th century.

Frenchmen Guillaume Rondelet (1506-66) and Pierre Belon (1517-64) also contributed major zoological studies.

The need for an orderly classification, or taxonomy, of plants and animals increased dramatically as explorers began bringing back from the New World thousands of specimens never before seen in Europe. In Aristotle's time and for many centuries afterward, the number of known kinds of living organisms had totaled no more than 1,000; by the 16th century many times that amount had been discovered. Scholars hastened to make sense of them all, devising many conflicting, "artificial" systems, based on superficial resemblances rather than on extensive similarities, and giving different Latin names to the same species. For example, animals might be arranged in one system according to whether they were useful or harmful; in another, by habitat, or where they lived (one scholar grouped beavers with fish, because they both lived in the water); and in still another, according to familiarity (farm animals such as cows and horses in one group, "foreign" apes and lions in another). The state of plant classification was just as chaotic, although the artificial system devised by the French botanist Joseph Pitton de Tournefort (1656-1708)—which grouped plants according to similarities in flower petals–was widely adopted and replaced other artificial systems.

An important factor in the emergence of so-called natural classification—a system that took into account all characteristics of an organism—was the invention and gradual refinement of the microscope in the second half of the 17th century. The microscope made possible the examination of small units of organic matter, called cells. (The concept of the cell was advanced by the English scientist Robert Hooke [1635-1703] in 1665.)

An illustration from a medieval German book shows both real and imaginary animals paying homage to a lion, revered as "the king of beasts" since antiquity.

The English botanist and herbalist John Ray (1627-1705), who devised the first natural system of classification, is considered the father of modern taxonomy. Ray wrote about insects, birds, and fish as well as plants; his zoological taxonomy, *Synopsis methodica animalium* (1693), based on a study of comparative anatomy, or the examination of the different parts that make up an animal's body, was the first classification of animals based upon anatomical structures. Ray's major contribution to botany was the division of plants into monocotyledons (plants with single-seed leaves) and dicotyledons (plants with double-seed leaves).

The modern system of plant and animal classification is hierarchical; that is, groups are ranked at certain levels within other groups. According to this system, a particular group is called a taxon (plural: taxa), and the level at which it is ranked is called a category. By the early 18th century, three categories, or levels, were in common use—kingdom, genus, and species—and three kingdoms—animal, plant, and mineral—were recognized. Later taxonomists, beginning with the Swedish naturalist Carl Linnaeus (1707-78), added other levels—family, order, class, and division or phylum—between genus and kingdom.

The discoveries and contributions of Linnaeus are an important chapter of natural history. The story of Earthkeepers begins, however, with a man born at the very end of the 17th century, eight years before Linnaeus. John Bartram was a poor farmer, self-educated, neither scholar nor scientist, yet he is remembered today as the first native American naturalist.

John Bartram

William Bartram

"A GREAT INCLINATION TO PLANTS"

T he lives of John Bartram, once described as "the greatest natural botanist in the world," and his son William, whose own explorations in the field of natural history were important to both science and English literature, were closely intertwined with the early life of the American nation. Father and son together spanned a remarkable three centuries and counted among their friends virtually every prominent figure in colonial America. Generations of scientists, farmers, and gardeners continue to benefit from their efforts to discover and preserve the New World's natural bounty.

John Bartram was born in 1699 in a rural area near Philadelphia to a poor Quaker farmer and his wife. His parents, involved in a religious dispute with the local Friends Meeting, moved to North Carolina when John was a small child, leaving him behind to be raised on his grandparents' farm. (The senior Bartram was later killed in an Indian massacre.) John Bartram had no formal education but as he grew into manhood proved to be a natural farmer as well as an adept student of plant life. He wrote much later that from the age of 10 he had "a great inclination to plants and knew all that I once observed by sights though not their proper names, having no person nor books to instruct me." From friendly Indians he learned various botanical "cures" that he used to treat his neighbors, all the while increasing his yields of grain and hay by draining his fields along the Schuylkill River and rotating crops.

A hunger to learn more about the natural world led him to buy several books about botany and to find a schoolteacher in Philadelphia who taught him basic Latin. Around 1730 he began collecting plants from the area and laid out what would eventually become the best-known botanical garden in the New World. He attracted the attention of several learned men in

Self-taught naturalist John Bartram founded one of the earliest plant nurseries in the United States at his farm near Philadelphia.

An elderly William Bartram sat for this portrait by a friend, Philadelphia artist Charles Willson Peale, in the early 19th century.

John Bartram

BORN

May 23, 1699
Delaware County, Pennsylvania

DIED

September 22, 1777
Kingsessing, near Philadelphia,
Pennsylvania

EDUCATION

Self-educated

MAJOR INTEREST

Botany

ACCOMPLISHMENTS

First native American botanist;
established Bartram's Gardens, one
of the first botanical gardens in
America; performed experiments
with cross-fertilization and hybridiza-
tion, developing new varieties of
flower and plant seeds

HONORS

Founding member of the American
Philosophical Society (1743);
appointed botanist to King George
III of England (1765); elected to the
Swedish Royal Academy

Philadelphia, who opened their own libraries and gardens to him as he continued to educate himself. One, a botanist associate of William Penn named John Logan, was an especially helpful tutor and showed Bartram how to use a microscope.

A London merchant and fellow Quaker named Peter Collinson, who was also an avid gardener, heard about Bartram's work and hired him to collect native specimens for shipment to England. Bartram gathered box after box of plants growing in and around his farm and sent them to the delighted Collinson, who paid him well. In 1736 several English gardeners joined with Collinson and commissioned Bartram to provide them with regular shipments, paying him an annual fee. Certain now of adequate compensation for his "hobby," John Bartram began making collecting trips farther afield, venturing up the Schuylkill and into the wilderness areas of the Rattlesnake and Blue Mountains; north into the Catskills and beyond, into the region around Lake Ontario; and as far south as Virginia. He also gathered small birds and mammals, which he preserved and shipped to naturalists abroad.

Over the years John Bartram's fame spread as his specimens attracted the attention of scientists throughout the colonies and in Europe who sought his expertise, including American naturalists John Clayton and Cadwallader Colden, the Dutchman Johann Friedrich Gronovius, and the Swede Carl Linnaeus. Benjamin Franklin became his friend, and both men were among the founding members of the Philadelphia-based American Philosophical Society. (Later, when Bartram was troubled by failing eyesight, Franklin fitted him with one of his numerous inventions, bifocal glasses.)

For many years John Bartram traveled alone on his expeditions, leaving behind a wife and a family that eventually grew to include nine children. But by the early 1750s one of his sons had developed a strong interest in his father's collecting and was old enough to be taken along. William Bartram had been born in the family's farmhouse in 1739. Beginning in childhood "little Billy" showed his father's "great inclination to plants," as well as a strong aptitude for drawing. Though he had educational opportuni-ties unavailable to his father, William Bartram was happier learning from John, and as a teenager regularly accompanied him on collecting trips into the wilder-ness, drawing much of what he observed. But the senior Bartram, concerned that his son find a proper livelihood, first had him study printing and engraving. When William did not show a particular inter-est in pursuing either trade, he was ap-prenticed to a merchant in Philadelphia.

During the years when the French and Indian War (1754-63) restricted wilderness travel, John Bartram made several major trips within colonial borders, including an expedition south from Pittsburgh down the Ohio River, and a long journey through the Carolinas during which he discovered the insect-eating plant that was later named Venus's-flytrap. When the war ended, the frontier became relatively safe all the way west to Mississippi, and Florida, now a possession of the British, could also be explored. Bartram, now in his 60s, was eager to visit the far Southeast while his health permitted. To finance the trip, Benjamin Franklin secured an appoint-ment for Bartram as the official botanist to King George III at an annual salary of £50.

In 1765 John and his son William, now a novice merchant in North Carolina, headed south to Georgia and Florida, where they explored the St. Johns River, producing an accurate survey of the main stream and its branches as well as noting "the situation and quality of the soil, the vegetables, and the animal production"—and accumulating a large collection of plants that was duly shipped off to King George.

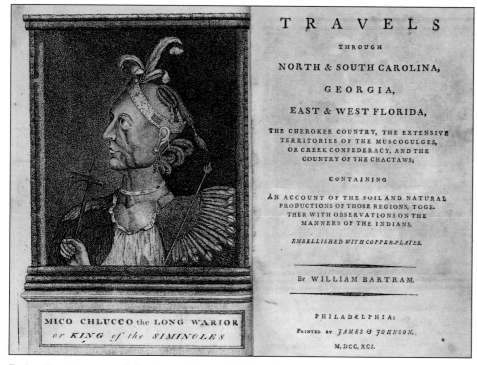

Facing the title page of the first edition of William Bartram's *Travels* is a drawing he made of Mico Chlucco, a Seminole chief. Bartram's book is valued for its accounts of Native American culture as well as for its scientific observations.

William Bartram

BORN

April 20, 1739
Kingsessing, near Philadelphia, Pennsylvania

DIED

July 22, 1823
Kingsessing

EDUCATION

Learned botany from his father, John Bartram; several years of secondary instruction at the Philadelphia Academy; self-taught artist

MAJOR INTERESTS

Botany; botanical illustration; natural history

ACCOMPLISHMENTS

First naturalist to provide reliable descriptions of the reptiles and amphibians of Florida, and to compile a catalog of American birds; appointed professor of botany, University of Pennsylvania (1782); author of *Observations on the Creek and Cherokee Indians* (1789) and *The Travels of William Bartram* (1791)

Two years later John published his journal of the trip as *A Description of East Florida*; it sold so well that two more editions were printed, in 1769 and 1774.

Meanwhile, William seemed no closer to establishing what his father hoped would be a "respectable" livelihood. Despite his obvious talents as an observer and illustrator of nature, his father still believed that such a calling would not provide his son with stability. William continued to draw—through the efforts of Collinson, his illustrations of American plants and animals were in great demand in England—but was having no success as a merchant. He briefly attempted life as a planter on the St. Johns River, but when that failed, he returned to Philadelphia to work as a farm laborer. John Bartram, Jr., four years younger than William and the businessman in the family, ran Bartram's Gardens, which had now become a profitable nursery, providing plants and seeds to gardeners throughout the colonies. (Thomas Jefferson was one of its customers.)

When Peter Collinson died in 1768, his place as a valued friend and mentor to the Bartrams was soon taken by a well-to-do English Quaker physician, John Fothergill. Dr. Fothergill had a wide-ranging interest in the natural and physical sciences and maintained a renowned garden at his estate in Essex. He requested both specimens and drawings from the Bartrams, increasingly relying upon William as John became less active. Fothergill was particularly interested in obtaining plants from what he called "the back parts of Canada," but William wanted to return to southeastern America and stubbornly refused. Fothergill finally gave in, arranging for him to be paid £50 a year for his services. William Bartram sailed from Philadelphia on March 20, 1773, and did not return home until nearly four years later, shortly after New Year's Day, 1777.

William Bartram's journey took him through the Carolinas, Georgia, much of the northern half of Florida, and westward through Alabama to Baton Rouge.

William Bartram drew the blossom and fruit of the *Franklinia,* or Franklin tree, which the Bartrams first found in Georgia in 1765. William rediscovered the tree in 1776, named it after Benjamin Franklin, and saved it from extinction by cultivating specimens at his nursery.

> *"This world, as a glorious apartment of the boundless palace of the sovereign Creator, is furnished with an infinite variety of animated scenes, inexpressibly beautiful and pleasing…."*
>
> —William Bartram, *The Travels of William Bartram* (1791)

Bartram kept a journal in which he recorded extensive descriptions of animal and plant life and Indian culture, collected hundreds of specimens, and produced numerous drawings. During his years in the wilderness, the American Revolution began. He learned of the Battle of Lexington while traveling among the Cherokees in the Carolinas, and for a while served with a group of colonial volunteers in Georgia near the Florida border when the British threatened to invade St. Augustine.

He returned home to find his father ill and feeble, and worrying—unnecessarily, it turned out—over the possible threat to the safety of his gardens from marauding British troops. John Bartram died the following September, and his son William settled permanently at the farm. A lifelong bachelor, he enjoyed the company of his brothers' families while he tended the famous gardens and entertained distinguished visitors, including Franklin, George Washington,

and fellow naturalists André Michaux, Alexander Wilson, and Thomas Nuttall. In 1782 he was appointed professor of botany at the University of Pennsylvania, a largely honorific post that left him free to remain at the farm, where he began to write about his experiences. His first book was *Observations on the Creek and Cherokee Indians*, an enlightened and objective report completed in 1789 but not printed until 1815.

To raise funds for publication of his second book, an extensive account of his longest trip, Bartram solicited subscriptions from 1,000 contributors, among them then-Secretary of State Jefferson, President Washington, and Vice President John Adams. The book that would become a classic of natural history was published in Philadelphia in 1791, under the ungainly title *Travels Through North and South Carolina, Georgia, East and West Florida, the Cherokee Country, the Extensive Territories of the Muscogulges, or Creek Confederacy, and the Country of the Chactaws; Containing an Account of the Soil and Natural Productions of Those Regions, Together with Observations on the Manners of the Indians*. In later editions the title was abbreviated to *The Travels of William Bartram*.

The reception of Bartram's *Travels* in America was lukewarm, but in Europe the book became an astounding success. By 1801 it had appeared in nine foreign editions and became a major inspiration to the Romantic poets William Wordsworth and Samuel Taylor Coleridge, both of whom used images from Bartram's book in their own works. As a work of science, Bartram's *Travels* proved to be remarkably accurate, as later generations of natural historians have

verified. Bartram is also credited with being a reliable ethnologist, a scholar who studies human cultures: his accounts of Indian culture, which include the only known contemporary account of Seminole music, continue to be studied and valued.

In his later years, William Bartram focused his attention on ornithology, eventually compiling a catalog of 200 American birds—the first such list in the New World. As an old man, he still worked in the family gardens, wearing old clothes and accompanied by a pet crow named Tom, who reportedly helped his master with weeding.

FURTHER READING

Bartram, John, and William Bartram. *John and William Bartram's America: Selections from the Writings of the Early American Naturalists*. Edited by Helen Gere Cruickshank. 1957. Reprint. Greenwich, Conn.: Devin-Adair, 1990.

"Bartram, John." In *Dictionary of American Biography*. Vol. 1. New York: Scribners, 1964.

Bartram, William. *The Travels of William Bartram*. 1791. Reprint. Irvine, Calif.: Reprint Services Corporation, 1991.

"Bartram, William." In *Dictionary of American Biography*. Vol. 1. New York: Scribners, 1964.

Berkeley, Edmund, and Dorothy S. Berkeley. *The Life and Travels of John Bartram*. Gainesville: University Press of Florida, 1990.

Carl Linnaeus

"THE LITTLE BOTANIST"

One of the many fascinating stories about Carl Linnaeus concerns his surname. In Sweden, until the late 17th century, only members of the country's nobility had family names. Other Swedes called themselves after their fathers' Christian names—thus Linnaeus's father was Nils Ingemarsson, meaning "Nils, son of Ingemar." But in the late 1600s more and more Swedes began using family names. Nils, a Lutheran pastor with a passionate love of flowers, chose Linnaeus, a Latinized form of *linn*, the word for the linden tree. The linden was one of the few flowering trees in Sweden, and according to local folklore it was sacred. The appropriately named Carl Linnaeus—he later Latinized his first name to Carolus—grew up to be the greatest naturalist of his time and made the naming of plants his life's work.

Carl Linnaeus was born in a farm cottage near South Råshult, in the south of Sweden, in 1707. He was introduced in infancy to the beauty and delights of nature: according to another story, his father would set him in the grass near the parsonage and place a flower in his hand, and the baby would

In this portrait Carl Linnaeus is dressed in the costume of a native Laplander, which he wore during his collecting expedition in Lapland. In his hand is a sprig of *Linnea borealis,* the flowering plant that bears his name.

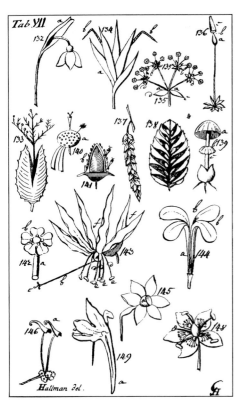

Linnaeus drew these flower types and parts to illustrate his book *Philosophia botanica (Botanical Philosophy)*, which was published in 1751.

"I would gladly write in verse; however, I was not born a poet, but a botanist instead."

—note from Linnaeus that accompanied his first manuscript, a gift to his patron, Olaf Celsius (1730)

remain contented with his treasure for hours. Soon Nils was taking his son on walks through the woods and meadows of his parish and around the shore of nearby Lake Möckeln, teaching him the names of plants. By the age of eight, Carl was himself so well-versed in the subject that he was nicknamed "the little botanist."

Carl's parents assumed that he would grow up to become a clergyman, like his father. But at the school the boy attended in Växjö—near his father's new parish in Stenbrohult—he showed no aptitude for theology, or for learning Greek or Hebrew, preferring instead the study of plants. One of his teachers suggested a career in medicine—a field in which his knowledge and inclination might be put to use, since physical illness at that time was treated with remedies made from plants. Accordingly, he was sent for a year to the University of Lund, which proved inadequate, and then, in 1728, to the University of Uppsala, north of Stockholm.

Uppsala was thought to be Sweden's finest university, and of special interest to Carl was its famous botanical garden. When he arrived at the school, however, he found it run down and the garden in disarray, the victims of Sweden's costly involvement in foreign wars. To make matters worse, his father had been able to give him only enough money to pay his entrance fees. So the poor student lined his worn shoes with paper and trudged around the town begging university officials for a small scholarship, until at last they gave in.

Dr. Olaf Celsius, a dean of the university and an amateur botanist, became the young man's benefactor, inviting Linnaeus to live at his house and helping him to secure a position as a lecturer at the botanical garden. The grateful Linnaeus presented his first manuscript, a study of plant reproduction, to Celsius on New Year's Day, 1730.

Seeking a way to make himself more widely known, Linnaeus went on an extensive collecting trip to the largely unexplored region of northern Scandinavia, known as Lapland, in 1732, supported by a grant from the Swedish Royal Society. He returned to Uppsala at the end of the year with plant and animal specimens, a thick journal, and several manuscripts recording his observations. But what little interest there was in his trip was created by Linnaeus himself, who turned his rooms into a small museum and dressed in a Lapp costume when he gave his lectures at the university.

During the next several years, Linnaeus developed and wrote about his major interest: plant classification. He still needed a medical degree, however, if he was to earn a living, and found a university in Holland, at Harderwijk, that granted such degrees without extensive study. The wealthy father of a fellow student agreed to pay for the trip abroad if Linnaeus would accompany the man's son. Thus Linnaeus journeyed to Holland in 1734, a quickly written thesis in hand—as well as a collection of his botanical manuscripts—and was promptly given the necessary degree in exchange for a small fee.

But Linnaeus was still reluctant to settle down to the life of a village doctor in Sweden. Intent on establishing his reputation in botany, he traveled on to the more prestigious University of Leiden, where he showed his manuscripts to Johann Friedrich Gronovius (1690-1760), a prominent botanist who owned a well-known herbarium. Gronovius was so impressed with the work that he paid for the publication of *Systema naturae (System of Nature,* 1735), in which Linnaeus classified plants according to the structures of their reproductive parts. This so-called artificial system of classification was the basis for all of Linnaeus's later work in botany.

Soon Linnaeus's fortunes began to change for the better. He was given a job cataloging plants at the botanical garden in Amsterdam, and then obtained a position as both physician and botanist-in-residence on an estate near Leiden. Other publications followed, including the *Genera plantarum* (*Plant Groups*) and *Flora Lapponica* (*Plants of Lapland*; both 1737). During the years he spent abroad (1734-38), Linnaeus changed from a poverty-stricken student into a respected man of science, and was welcomed as a visitor in London, Oxford, and Paris, where he explained and promoted his system of classification.

Linnaeus returned to Sweden in 1738, married the daughter of a physician, and settled in Stockholm, establishing a small medical practice while he continued to study and classify plants. In 1741 he was appointed to the medical faculty at the University of Uppsala, and the following year achieved what he had been seeking for many years: a professorship in botany. He soon became a popular and sought-after teacher, and attracted many students and disciples.

During the second half of his life, Linnaeus continued his work in classification, devising systems for both the animal and mineral kingdoms, and published numerous books. He also restored the university's botanical garden, once again making it famous in both Europe and the New World, and even added a small zoo, thanks to generous donations from the royal family for the purchase of exotic animals (Linnaeus was especially fond of monkeys and parrots). In 1761 he was elevated to the nobility, and at court adopted the name Carl von Linné. His home life was reportedly less pleasant: his wife was quarrelsome, and none of his five children shared his interest in nature.

Linnaeus's artificial classification scheme was the one most widely used in botany between 1737 and 1810, but by the middle of the 19th century it had been replaced by so-called natural systems based on the work of French botanist Antoine Laurent de Jussieu. However, another of Linnaeus's contributions to the study of nature is still used today: binomial nomenclature, the standardized Latin "two-name naming" of plants and animals. According to this system, the scientific name of a species consists of two parts: its genus name plus an adjective.

Linnaeus introduced binomial nomenclature into his written works gradually, beginning in 1745. He first applied it to the entire known plant kingdom (at that time around 6,000 species) in *Species plantarum* (*Plant Species*; first edition, 1753), the basis for most plant names today. Animal nomenclature is based on the 10th edition (1758) of his *Systema naturae*, in which the term for modern man, *Homo sapiens*, first appears.

After Linnaeus's death in 1778, his widow sold most of his collections to an Englishman, J. E. Smith, a founder of the Linnean Society of London; following Smith's death, they were given to the society, where they remain today. Other artifacts from Linnaeus's life and work are displayed at the Botanical Museum and the Zoological Museum in Uppsala and the Natural History Museum in Stockholm.

FURTHER READING

Adams, Alexander B. "Order Replaces Chaos." In *Eternal Quest: The Story of the Great Naturalists*. New York: G. P. Putnam, 1969.

Blunt, Wilfrid. *The Compleat Naturalist: A Life of Linnaeus*. New York: Viking, 1971.

Frangsmyr, Tore, ed. *Linnaeus: The Man and His Work*. Berkeley: University of California Press, 1983.

Linnaeus, Carl. *Miscellaneous Tracts Relating to Natural History*. 1762. Reprint. Salem, N.H.: Ayer, 1978.

Carl Linnaeus

BORN

May 23, 1707
South Råshult, Sweden

DIED

January 10, 1778
Uppsala, Sweden

EDUCATION

Universities of Lund and Uppsala

MAJOR INTERESTS

Botany; classification of plants and animals; medicine

ACCOMPLISHMENTS

Devised the system of binary nomenclature for classifying plants and animals; author of more than 180 works, including *Systema naturae* (1735); *Genera plantarum* (1737); *Philosophia botanica* (1751); and *Species plantarum* (1753); professor of medicine (1741-42) and botany (1742-78), University of Uppsala

HONORS

Awarded noble rank, 1761

Georges Buffon

A SCIENTIST AT THE FRENCH COURT

As a boy, Georges Buffon, the son of a wealthy landowner and government official in the town of Dijon, was both brilliant and fun-loving. He was talented in mathematics and reportedly would interrupt whatever game he was playing to solve a math problem. However, young Georges was restless, and though he studied law to please his father, he resisted settling down after receiving his diploma. Instead, he went on a pleasure tour of Europe.

Buffon enjoyed the sights and the merriment, but the serious, intellectual side of him was attracted to something else: the different land formations he encountered in his first venture beyond Dijon. Why were there glaciers in some parts of the continent and volcanic rocks in others? he wondered. That question would persist in Buffon's mind until his death more than half a century later, and it caused a permanent change in the young man's attitude: by the time he returned to Montbard, the family estate, his desire for pleasure had been replaced by a burning curiosity about natural history.

But Buffon needed to conquer his tendency toward laziness, he realized, if he were going to amount to anything.

For nearly 50 years Georges Buffon worked daily on his *Histoire naturelle*, always dressed in his most elegant clothes and never without his wig.

Georges Buffon

BORN

September 7, 1707
Montbard, Côte-d'Or, France

DIED

April 16, 1788
Paris, France

EDUCATION

Law diploma from the College of Dijon

MAJOR INTEREST

Natural history

ACCOMPLISHMENTS

Head of the Jardin du Roi, Paris; author of *Histoire naturelle* (44 volumes, 1749-1804), first modern comprehensive work on natural history

HONORS

Elected to the Académie Française, the Académie des Sciences; fellow, Royal Society (London)

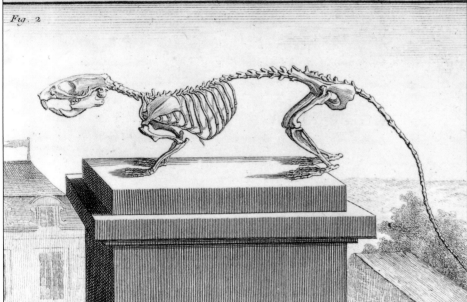

An illustration from Buffon's *Histoire naturelle* shows a *surmulot* (French for "brown rat") and its skeleton. In an attempt to include every known example of animal and plant life, Buffon paid collectors for specimens gathered throughout the world.

Years later, he told the story of how that had been accomplished. He paid one of his servants to make him get up before 6:00 A.M. by throwing a pitcher of cold water on him as he lay sleeping.

Seeking to establish his reputation as a learned man, the newly industrious Buffon focused his attention on science. He studied gardening and forestry methods, applying what he learned to the improvement of his estate, and wrote papers on mechanics and mathematics that were published by the Académie des Sciences. Visiting England as a scientist during the early 1730s, Buffon so impressed his scholarly hosts that they secured his appointment as a fellow of the Royal Society. Back at Montbard, in 1735 he translated into French a little-known but important English work about plant growth, Stephen Hales's *Vegetable Staticks* (1727), which enhanced his growing reputation as a botanist. He also continued independent research on the growth and conservation of trees that helped maintain the royal forests and earned him the recognition of the king.

The ambitious Buffon was eager to achieve a position of prestige that would gain him wider recognition throughout Europe. When he learned that the superintendency of the Jardin du Roi (the King's Garden, renamed the Jardin des Plantes, or Garden of Plants, after the French Revolution) was available, he successfully schemed to secure it for himself. Louis XV's appointment of the 35-year-old Buffon in 1742 marked a turning point in the career of the amateur scientist, who now had a professional post.

During the next decade Buffon transformed the Jardin and its museum from a small, seedy collection of neglected plants and dusty display cases into a renowned center for the study of botany. This astounding accomplishment was the result not only of Buffon's scientific knowledge but also of his charming personality: when the king would not give him any money to repair the garden, Buffon flattered wealthy Frenchmen into becoming patrons, granting them fancy made-up titles in exchange. He obtained specimens from scientists and collectors throughout Europe and the New World by promising fame and glory for their contributions.

Secure in his position, Buffon now turned his enormous energy to another project: writing a book about the natural world in its entirety, beginning with the Earth's creation and including information on all its known animals, plants, and minerals. This vast project, which eventually filled 44 volumes, was the famous *Histoire naturelle* (*Natural History,* 1749-1804), the first work since antiquity to gather together all known information about natural history.

Beginning in the mid-1740s, and for

"In nature there are only individuals; genera and orders and classes exist only in our imagination."

—from *Histoire naturelle* (1749-1804)

the remainder of his life, Buffon worked daily on the *Histoire,* dividing his time between Montbard and Paris. He rose promptly at six, dressed in elaborate court costume (including a wig and ruffles, numerous rings, and all his awards and decorations), and wrote continuously for eight hours, usually standing.

The *Histoire* is elegantly written, more an entertaining nature guide than a textbook. The tone is set in the famous opening sentence: "One should begin by seeing much, and coming back for a second look." As for classification, Buffon had no interest in offering long lists of categories. He had only contempt for Linnaeus, who, he said, had reduced the wonders of nature to a series of tedious lists. Buffon was equally contemptuous of the physicist and entomologist René Réaumur (1683-1757) and his six-volume study of insects. Dismissing the work, he wrote, "A bee should not occupy more space in the head of a naturalist than it does in nature."

But the most controversial aspect of Buffon's *Histoire* was its assertion that the world was not, as Christians then believed, 6,000 years old. All the planets, Buffon said, had been created thousands and thousands of years earlier when a comet collided with the sun. He then offered an account of Earth's development as a series of catastrophic changes, from a time when the seas covered most of it (seashell fossils had been found on top of the Alps in Switzerland), to the creation of the continents by volcanic upheavals and a period of tropical warmth through much

of the world, followed by the appearance of various flora and fauna, and ultimately man. Buffon's insight foreshadowed the theories of Charles Darwin and Alfred Russel Wallace in the 19th century, but pressure from the church-connected professors at the Sorbonne, France's esteemed university in Paris, forced Buffon to recant in a later volume of the *Histoire* anything he had said about the origins of the Earth that seemed at odds with the teachings of the Bible.

Thirty-six volumes of Buffon's masterwork were published before his death in 1788; the remaining eight were completed by an associate. Buffon had hoped that his surviving son, also named Georges, would follow in his footsteps, and arranged for Georges to be tutored by the naturalist Jean Baptiste Lamarck. However, Georges, never a scholar, was more interested in pursuing pleasure, as his father had been many years before. He survived the elder Buffon by barely five years, dying on the guillotine at the age of 30 in 1793, a victim of the French Revolution.

FURTHER READING

Adams, Alexander B. "A Broader View." In *Eternal Quest: The Story of the Great Naturalists.* New York: G. P. Putnam, 1969.

Buffon, Georges. *The Natural History of Oviparous Quadrupeds and Serpents.* 1802. Reprint. 2 vols. Salem, N. H.: Ayer, 1978.

Lyon, John, and Philip Sloan, eds. *From Natural History to the History of Nature: Readings from Buffon and His Critics.* South Bend, Ind.: University of Notre Dame Press, 1981.

Jean Baptiste Lamarck

THE "PROFESSOR OF
INSECTS AND WORMS"

ike Georges Buffon, who would one day be his
employer, Jean Baptiste Lamarck reportedly had
little interest in nature during his youth. Nor
were there many resources to encourage such an
interest. As the last of 11 children of a former
army officer and small landowner, Lamarck's destiny seemed
likely to be that of the younger sons of all large families in
18th-century France: the priesthood. Struggling to support his
large household, Lamarck's father sent the adolescent Jean
Baptiste to a seminary in Amiens where he could receive free
schooling.

The young Lamarck did well enough at his studies but was
eager to be a soldier, like his older brothers. In 1761, after his
father's death, he left the seminary and joined a company of
the French army, then engaged in the Seven Years' War
(1756-63). Distinguishing himself in battle, Lamarck was
commissioned as an officer. He spent seven years with a
French garrison, first in Toulon and then in Monaco, where
many long walks in the countryside awakened in him an
interest in the natural world.

Illness forced Lamarck to resign his commission and go to
Paris for treatment. Eventually cured but with little means

Jean Baptiste Lamarck was the first scientist to name and study
invertebrates (animals without backbones). He also invented the
word *biology* and devised an early theory of evolution.

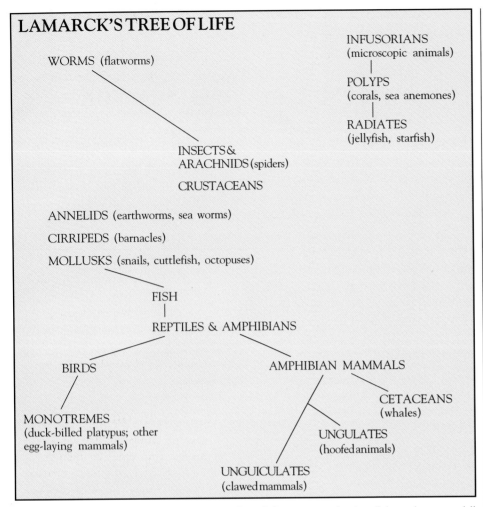

LAMARCK'S TREE OF LIFE

WORMS (flatworms)

INFUSORIANS
(microscopic animals)

POLYPS
(corals, sea anemones)

RADIATES
(jellyfish, starfish)

INSECTS &
ARACHNIDS (spiders)

CRUSTACEANS

ANNELIDS (earthworms, sea worms)

CIRRIPEDS (barnacles)

MOLLUSKS (snails, cuttlefish, octopuses)

FISH

REPTILES & AMPHIBIANS

BIRDS

AMPHIBIAN MAMMALS

CETACEANS
(whales)

MONOTREMES
(duck-billed platypus; other
egg-laying mammals)

UNGULATES
(hoofed animals)

UNGUICULATES
(clawed mammals)

Lamarck, an early theorist of evolution, believed that man and other "clawed mammals" had descended from other species; he illustrated that progression in the chart above.

beyond a small army pension, Lamarck found work as a bank clerk while he dreamed of becoming a scientist, perhaps a physician or a botanist, or a specialist in meteorology (the study of weather). There seemed no likelihood, however, that he could afford the training for a new profession. But a turning point in his life came when, during one of his frequent walks along the River Seine, he met the philosopher Jean Jacques Rousseau, who also had an amateur interest in botany. The two men talked, Rousseau was impressed, and through the philosopher's connections Lamarck received an introduction to the scientific world of Paris in the early 1770s.

For a time Lamarck studied medicine, then took courses in botany at the Jardin de Roi under the direction of Bernard de Jussieu, the uncle of Antoine

Laurent de Jussieu. Jussieu was trying to reclassify the Jardin's collection, and Lamarck was such an excellent student that he became the older man's assistant. Eager to prove himself, Lamarck wrote *Flore française* (*French Flora*), a guidebook to French plants. Buffon, superintendent of the Jardin, was so impressed that in 1778 he arranged to have the book published. A year later Lamarck was elected to the Académie des Sciences.

Despite this apparent success, however, Lamarck—who by this time had a family of his own to support—was still struggling to earn a living. In 1781 Buffon tried to help his protégé—and himself—by hiring Lamarck as a tutor to his son Georges and sending them on a European tour. However, the boy was so disagreeable during the journey—even

as an old man, Lamarck still remembered how young Georges had once poured a bottle of ink on him—that they were both soon back in Paris. Buffon may have blamed the tutor for the failings of his son, for he never offered Lamarck a permanent post at the Jardin de Roi.

For several years Lamarck earned his living by writing a botanical dictionary. Then, a year after Buffon's death in 1788, he at last achieved what promised to be a permanent position as keeper of plants at the Jardin. The French Revolution soon began, but Lamarck managed to survive amid the upheaval…it was his suggestion to change the name of the Jardin de Roi to Jardin des Plantes, thus eliminating the reference to the deposed king (*roi*). Further reorganization by the new government and maneuvering by Lamarck led to a new appointment in 1793 as professor of zoology at the Jardin (which despite its name, included animal specimens as well as plants), with specific responsibilities for "insects and worms."

Lamarck knew nothing at all about zoology, much less "insects and worms," the phrase Linnaeus had used to describe "leftover" creatures that could not be identified as birds, mammals, reptiles, or fish. Amazingly, no one had yet even bothered to classify them, although they made up an enormous 90 percent of the animal kingdom. In fact, Lamarck had been given the appointment because no one cared about them. But given the unstable political situation, Lamarck welcomed the job. Over the next nine years he worked steadily, arranging and classifying these creatures that he named invertebrates—those without backbones—to distinguish them from the vertebrates, animals *with* backbones.

In *Système des animaux sans vertèbres* (*Invertebrate Systems*), his first book about his new interest, published in 1802, Lamarck made the bold assertion that all species, including man, are descended from other species. No one paid much

"Men with small vision can concentrate only on small objects, and yet they are the majority. . . . must we always evade considering the larger questions just to busy ourselves incessantly gathering all the little facts that are discovered without ever trying to find general truths?"

—from *Hydrogéologie* (1802)

attention to him then, but seven years later, when he refined his concept of "progression"—what later became known as evolution—in *Philosophie zoologique (Zoological Philosophy)*, he drew the scorn of other scientists, who ridiculed him and dismissed his theories as rubbish. (Unlike Buffon, whose theories about the Earth's origins had antagonized the Catholic church, Lamarck was not pressured into denying his assertions, for the church had been stripped of much of its authority during the revolution.)

According to Lamarck, evolution is the consequence of two forces: the inheritance of acquired characteristics, and the striving upward of every living creature from a simple to a more complex form. The first supposition has been disproved by modern genetics: characteristics acquired in the course of an organism's life are not passed on to the next generation. But the second—that complex life forms evolve from simpler forms—is the basis for the modern theory of evolution advanced later in the 19th century by Charles Darwin and Alfred Russel Wallace.

Despite a lack of recognition,

Lamarck continued to labor at the Jardin, reclassifying the "insects and worms" as crustaceans (shellfish), arachnids (spiders), and annelids (worms), and writing the multivolume *Histoire naturelle des animaux sans vertèbres (Natural History of Invertebrates*; 1815–22), in which he introduced the word "biology." Lamarck also wrote about meteorology and tried to develop a method of long-range weather forecasting. But no one paid much attention to him or his "department of debris," as some of his colleagues called it. Ironically, the man who became his greatest opponent was the anatomist Georges Cuvier—whose invitation to study at the Jardin had been strongly supported by Lamarck himself back in 1795.

Lamarck spent his last years in poverty. His eyesight declined and eventually he became totally blind. When he died at the age of 85, he was buried in a temporary grave—there was not enough money for a permanent burial. Five years later, the body was removed, but no one knows where it was taken. Today the final resting place of the man who gave the world the words "invertebrates" and "biology" and offered the basis for one of the most significant theories in the history of science is a mystery.

FURTHER READING

Adams, Alexander B. "A Glimpse of a Truth." In *Eternal Quest: The Story of the Great Naturalists*. New York: G. P. Putnam, 1969.

Jordanova, L. J. *Lamarck*. New York: Oxford University Press, 1984.

Lamarck, Jean Baptiste. *Zoological Philosophy*. 1809. Reprint. Translated by Hugh Elliot. Chicago: University of Chicago Press, 1984.

Peattie, Donald Culross. "A Chevalier in Science: Lamarck." In *Green Laurels: The Lives and Achievements of the Great Naturalists*. New York: Simon & Schuster, 1936.

Jean Baptiste Lamarck

BORN
August 1, 1744
Picardy, France

DIED
December 18, 1829
Paris, France

EDUCATION
Studied medicine and botany in Paris

MAJOR INTERESTS
Botany; zoology

ACCOMPLISHMENTS
First to distinguish between vertebrate and invertebrate animals (introduced the term *Invertebrata*); first to establish the invertebrate classes of Crustacea (shellfish) and Arachnida (spiders) and the phylum Annelida (worms); botanist and later professor of zoology at the Jardin de Roi, Paris; early theorist of evolution; author of six books, including *Philosophie zoologique* (1809) and *Histoire naturelle des animaux sans vertèbres* (1815–22); first to use the word "biology"

HONORS
Elected to the Académie des Sciences

Alexander Wilson

THE ORIGINAL
BIRD MAN

The name most people associate with North American birds is John James Audubon—but before Audubon there was Alexander Wilson, the real father of American ornithology.

More unlikely origins for a naturalist are difficult to imagine. Born to a poor family in Paisley, Scotland, Wilson left school at the age of 10 to be apprenticed to a weaver. (For many centuries Paisley has been a weaving center.) His father was also a weaver, although the elder Wilson earned an additional livelihood as a smuggler. (Some of Alexander Wilson's biographers believe that he helped his father in this illicit trade.) Alexander completed his apprenticeship successfully, but chose to become a peddler of fabrics rather than a weaver while he secretly pursued his real interest: writing verse.

It was Wilson's career as a poet that inadvertently turned him into a naturalist. In his verse Wilson criticized the harsh working and living conditions of the weavers and satirized the men for whom they worked. One of the overseers charged Wilson with libel (making unjustified negative statements about him), won the suit, and had Wilson sent to jail when he could not pay the fine. When he finished his sentence of

Alexander Wilson, America's pioneering ornithologist, was a weaver, poet, and perhaps even a smuggler in his native Scotland before immigrating to the United States in 1794.

nearly two years, Wilson was compelled to burn his poems. Impoverished and bitter, he left Scotland for America and a new life in 1794.

Landing in Philadelphia, Wilson spent the next eight years in Pennsylvania, New Jersey, and Virginia, trying his hand at printing, surveying, peddling, and finally schoolteaching. As he tramped about the countryside, he began collecting specimens of colorful birds and making careful notes of their nests and habits. Hesitantly at first, he also started to draw what he had collected.

By the early 1800s Wilson had established himself as a schoolmaster not far from Bartram's Gardens near Philadelphia. He became acquainted with the Bartram family and eventually the entire Bartram circle, which included the Peale family and other prominent men of learning in the city. Noting Wilson's interest in birds and his skill in observing them, William Bartram encouraged his young friend to abandon teaching and take up bird study full time. The ambitious Wilson responded by declaring that he would produce an illustrated catalog of all the birds of North America.

Wilson, of course, needed some means of support to undertake such a project, which would require extensive travel. Help came in 1807 in the form of an offer from a prominent publisher, Samuel Bradford, whose sons were Wilson's students and who had heard about Wilson's ambition: he would be paid $900 a year to edit a new encyclopedia, but those duties would be light enough to enable him to work on his bird book, which Bradford would also publish.

During the next six years Wilson traveled throughout the eastern United States, from the Georgia-Florida border north to Maine, and as far west as New Orleans, always searching for new birds to write about and sketch. He proved himself to be a clever salesman as well as a naturalist, perhaps using the persuasive skills he had acquired as a peddler: as he

Wilson traveled thousands of miles through the American wilderness to sketch birds in their natural habitats. Sometimes, however, he used stuffed specimens to illustrate *American Ornithology*; the originals of these birds were collected by his friend Meriwether Lewis on the famous Lewis and Clark expedition.

journeyed in search of specimens, he sold hundreds of subscriptions at $120 each to what he and his publisher had decided would be a 10-volume work called *American Ornithology*. Among those who bought subscriptions were Thomas Jefferson and Revolutionary War hero Thomas Paine.

Not everyone Wilson approached agreed to buy his book, however. During

"I am . . . a volunteer in the cause of Natural History, impelled by nobler views than those of money."

—from a letter to William Bartram

Alexander Wilson

BORN

July 6, 1766
Paisley, Scotland

DIED

August 23, 1813
Philadelphia, Pennsylvania

EDUCATION

Attended grammar school until the age of nine

MAJOR INTEREST

Ornithology

ACCOMPLISHMENTS

Author of *American Ornithology* (9 volumes, 1808-29), the first encyclopedia of North American birds; considered the father of American ornithology

HONORS

Elected to the American Philosophical Society and the Philadelphia Academy of Natural Sciences

a visit to Louisville, Kentucky, in the spring of 1810, Wilson asked a young storekeeper named John James Audubon to become a subscriber. Audubon could not afford the high fee but surprised Wilson by showing him some of his own bird drawings, then helped Wilson gather specimens in the surrounding countryside. Audubon later wrote about the incident, and reported that he had felt resentful of Wilson's project. Neither man knew then, of course, that the unknown young Frenchman would one day become more widely celebrated than Wilson for his beautiful paintings of birds.

Predictably, Wilson had little time to work on Bradford's encyclopedia and had to give up its editorship, but his success in selling subscriptions to *American Ornithology* supported him. Seven volumes appeared between 1808 and 1813, the year of his sudden death, from dysentery; two additional volumes were later published. Wilson's work was popular during the early 19th century and was reprinted several times. Although his portraits are unremarkable by today's standards—especially when compared to those in Audubon's *Birds of America*—they provided the first glimpses of America's rich array of birds to a wide audience. Readers were especially charmed by Wilson's accompanying essays on bird life and lore.

Wilson was proud of his work, which he saw as a patriotic celebration of the natural beauty of his adopted country. He apparently had only two other interests: poetry and music. He never married, although he was engaged at the time of his death, and a sister and cousin living in New York State were the only members of his family in the New World. Wilson relaxed by sitting under a tree and playing the flute; composing verses was a form of relaxation, too.

Wilson had continued to write and publish poetry after emigrating to America—his subject was now nature,

not social criticism—but these efforts did not receive much recognition. One exception was his long poem *The Foresters* (1805), an account of a walking trip he took in 1804 from Philadelphia to Niagara Falls, which was reprinted several times. Wilson's collected poems were published in a single volume in London three years after his death.

Today Alexander Wilson and his pioneering work on American birds are largely forgotten. One story survives, however, that should earn him new respect as a conservationist. In Philadelphia in the early 1800s, robins were a sought-after delicacy, and thousands of them were shot for food. To stop this slaughter, Wilson submitted an anonymous article to several local newspapers claiming—falsely—that the robins' diet of pokeberries made their flesh "unwholesome." The demand for the birds dropped sharply, and their killing virtually ended.

FURTHER READING

Adams, Alexander B. "The Collectors." In *Eternal Quest: The Story of the Great Naturalists*. New York: G. P. Putnam, 1969.

Cantwell, Robert. *Alexander Wilson: Naturalist and Pioneer*. Philadelphia: Lippincott, 1961.

Hunter, Clark. *The Life and Letters of Alexander Wilson*. Philadelphia: American Philosophical Society, 1983.

Kastner, Joseph. "A Peddler of Birds." In *A Species of Eternity*. New York: Knopf, 1977.

Peattie, Donald Culross. "Wilderness Birdsmen: Wilson and Audubon." In *Green Laurels: The Lives and Achievements of the Great Naturalists*. New York: Simon & Schuster, 1936.

"Wilson, Alexander." In *Dictionary of American Biography*. Vol. 10. New York: Scribners, 1964.

Georges Cuvier

THE BONE DETECTIVE

The history of scientific discovery is filled with many ironies—outcomes often contrary to what is expected. One of the greatest ironies of all is that Georges Cuvier, anatomist, paleontologist, and an enemy of the theory of evolution, discovered the fossil evidence that was later used to support that very theory. It is a further irony that Cuvier and Lamarck, the man Cuvier so enjoyed ridiculing for his ideas about evolution, stand together as the scholarly "fathers" of the study of both divisions of the animal kingdom—vertebrates and invertebrates respectively.

Like Lamarck, Cuvier was the son of a retired army officer; unlike Lamarck, Cuvier was an only child and the focus of his mother's undivided attention. Virtually from the moment of his birth in 1769, she saw that he received the best education possible, including a thorough grounding in Latin and access to good books. Cuvier especially liked to look through volumes of

French paleontologist Georges Cuvier poses with a fossilized fish and a magnifying glass. Cuvier studied fossils throughout his life; he became so skilled in identifying prehistoric animals that he could reconstruct an entire specimen from only a few bone fragments.

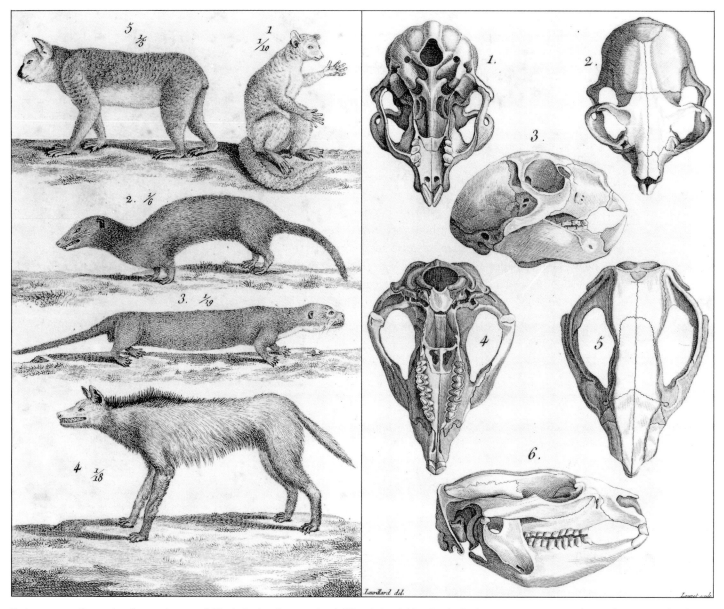

Facing pages from the first volume of Cuvier's *Le règne animal (The Animal Kingdom)* depict an assortment of vertebrates—animals with backbones—and their skulls. Cuvier classified the animal kingdom into four divisions (vertebrates, mollusks, articulates, and radiates); he believed that each had been created independently.

Buffon's *Histoire naturelle* and reproduce the drawings he found there; later, as his reading improved, he pored over the text and drew pictures of species that were not illustrated. Pliny's *Natural History* was another favorite book of the young Cuvier.

An excellent student in the local schools of Montbéliard—a small town in northeastern France then under the control of the German Duke of Wurtemburg—Cuvier received a scholarship to the university-level

Caroline Academy, founded by the duke in Stuttgart. There he studied the sciences as well as public administration, and graduated in 1788. Cuvier was disappointed when the duke did not offer him employment, but he quickly found a position in Caen, in northwestern France near the English Channel, as tutor to the son of the Count d'Héricy.

In Caen young Cuvier was introduced to the social and intellectual life of the French nobility and was able to pursue his growing interest in science at the local botanical gardens. He read and reread Linnaeus and Buffon, and roamed about the countryside observing birds and collecting fossils and plant specimens. He also corresponded with scientists in other parts of France and grew increasingly interested in comparative anatomy.

Cuvier was able to continue this idyllic life with the count and his family through the early years of the French Revolution, moving with them from the town of Caen to a small village to avoid entanglement in the conflicts in Paris. By 1795, however, as the political situation became more stable, he was eager to find employment in the French capital.

Helped by the recommendations of scientist friends he had met through his association with the d'Héricys—and the encouragement of the aging Lamarck—the 25-year-old Cuvier was appointed professor of anatomy at the Jardin des Plantes. Here he found what he later described as great piles of fossil bones; "how to restore these monuments of the past and make sense of them" soon became his mission. Thus the field of vertebrate paleontology—the scientific study of the fossils of animals with backbones—was born. Cuvier, with his extensive knowledge of anatomy and zoology, would become an expert in constructing the entire forms of extinct animals on the basis of only a few bone fragments.

The brilliant Cuvier did not, however, neglect comparative anatomy, the subject he had been hired to teach. His first book, *Tableau élémentaire de l'histoire naturelle des animaux (Elementary Table of the Natural History of Animals)*, published in 1798, was his earliest classification of the animal kingdom. This was followed by *Leçons d'anatomie comparée (Lessons in Comparative Anatomy)* in 1800, with its central idea that function and structure in animal organs depend upon each other.

In addition to his scientific work Cuvier assumed administrative duties with the French department of educa-

tion, at the request of the emperor, Napoleon, and also agreed to serve as secretary of the Académie des Sciences. Throughout his life Cuvier was sought after for his scientific and administrative ability as well as his great personal charm: the years with the count had enabled him to polish his social skills as well as refine his intellect. He was widely respected; his lectures were heavily attended; his views were solicited by the monarch of his country.

The introduction to his third published work, *Recherches sur les ossements fossiles de quadrupèdes (Investigations of Fossil Bones*; 1812), contains Cuvier's first speculations on the origins of the Earth and the role of fossils in understanding its development. Buffon, solely on the basis of seashell fossils discovered in the Alps, had offered a theory of Earth's creation as the result of a collision between a comet and the sun, followed by the gradual evolution of various forms of life. The church had made him publicly recant this heresy but, like Galileo a century earlier, he still believed in his heart that his theory was correct. (After agreeing to withdraw his assertion that the Earth rotated around the sun, Galileo is supposed to have muttered to himself, "Still, it moves.")

Cuvier, who had amassed fossil evidence for Buffon's theory on a far grander scale than Buffon could have dreamed of, drew a different conclusion. A Lutheran who believed in the literal truth of the Bible and thought that the Earth's age was no greater than 6,000 years, Cuvier decided that extinct animals had died out as a result of a series of isolated catastrophes, and were replaced by new forms of life that moved into each region. The most recent such "catastrophe," he believed, had been the biblical Flood, which man had survived. The very thought of evolution was nonsense to Cuvier.

Classification, however, was another matter. In *Le règne animal (The Animal Kingdom*; 1817) Cuvier divided the

Georges Cuvier

BORN

August 23, 1769
Montbéliard, Wurtemburg (now France)

DIED

May 13, 1832
Paris, France

EDUCATION

Caroline Academy, Stuttgart

MAJOR INTERESTS

Comparative anatomy; paleontology

ACCOMPLISHMENTS

Considered the father of comparative anatomy and vertebrate paleontology; author of *Tableau élémentaire de l'histoire naturelle des animaux* (1798), *Leçons d'anatomie comparée* (1800), *Recherches sur les ossements fossiles de quadrupèdes* (1812), *Le règne animal* (1817; revised 1829–30), *Histoire naturelle des poissons* (1828–31)

HONORS

Member of the Institut Française, the Académie Française, the Académie des Sciences, the Légion d'Honneur; elevated to noble rank (1818; henceforth known as Baron Cuvier)

"The least bit of bone . . . has a character determined in relation to the class, order, genus, and species to which it belongs to such an extent that every time one has only the extremity of a well-preserved bone, one can . . . determine all those points as assuredly as if one had the entire animal."

—from *Recherches sur les ossements fossiles de quadrupèdes* (1812)

animal kingdom into four types: vertebrates, mollusks, articulates (crustaceans and insects), and radiates (starfish and jellyfish). He gave credit to Lamarck for his work on "shells and corals," but denied any possible connection among the four animal groups: each, he felt, had been created, and therefore existed, independently.

In his last years Cuvier continued to work hard, publishing a revised edition of *Le règne animal* (1829-30) and the eight-volume *Histoire naturelle des poissons* (*Natural History of Fish;* 1828-31), which described 5,000 species of fish and which Cuvier had worked on for 30 years. He received many honors, including elevation to noble rank and election to the prestigious Académie Française.

Other leading scientists of his day called upon Cuvier, among them Louis Agassiz, Alexander von Humboldt, and Charles Lyell. John James Audubon visited Cuvier during his trip to Paris in 1728, and recorded a memorable description in his journal: "age about 65 [in fact he was 59]; size corpulent, five feet five . . . head large; face wrinkled and brownish; eyes gray, brilliant and sparkling; nose aquiline, large and red; mouth large, with good lips; teeth few, blunted by age, excepting one on the lower jaw, measuring nearly three-quarters of an inch square."

But despite the adulation, these years were not entirely happy. Cuvier's last surviving child died (he had been married since 1804 to a widow with four children; they had had four more). Political turmoil resumed in Paris. And a prominent botanist named E. Geoffroy Saint-Hilaire, who had helped Cuvier obtain his position at the Jardin in 1795, wrote a paper 36 years later upholding Lamarck's views about the interrelatedness of animal species and attacking Cuvier for

refusing to acknowledge the evidence. Cuvier counterattacked and, as a more persuasive debater—discussions on the matter were held in an open forum at the Académie des Sciences—eventually drubbed his former benefactor into silence with his astonishing command of facts.

The victory was short-lived: Cuvier died not long afterward, on May 13, 1832. He was mourned throughout France and received a state funeral, during which he was eulogized by Geoffroy Saint-Hilaire. He left behind a body of work that would, in the very near future, help to establish the truth he had tried so hard to refute.

FURTHER READING

Adams, Alexander B. "Reconstructing the Past." In *Eternal Quest: The Story of the Great Naturalists.* New York: G. P. Putnam, 1969.

Coleman, William R. *Georges Cuvier, Zoologist.* Cambridge: Harvard University Press, 1964.

Cuvier, Georges. *The Class Mammalia: The Animal Kingdom Arranged in Conformity with Its Organization.* 1827. Reprint. 5 vols. Salem, N.H.: Ayer, 1978.

Outram, Dorinda. *Georges Cuvier: Vocation, Science, and Authority in Post-Revolutionary France.* Manchester, England: Manchester University Press; New York: St. Martin's, 1988.

More Earthkeepers to Remember

Nicolaus Steno (1638-86), a Danish naturalist and physician, made major contributions to early geological theory. He was among the first to recognize that fossils were remains of organisms; he also described the formation of mountains and volcanoes.

Mark Catesby (about 1679-1749) was an English naturalist who traveled in the southern American colonies, collecting plants and writing about native flora and fauna. He wrote and illustrated *The Natural History of Carolina, Florida, and the Bahama Islands* (1731-48). Catesby was the first naturalist to study American bird migration; he also wrote about New World trees and shrubs and introduced many species into European gardens.

The Exhumation of the Mastodon, painted by Charles Willson Peale in 1806-8, commemorated the excavation of mastodon (prehistoric elephant) bones near Newburgh, New York, in 1801. Peale himself, aided by some of his 17 children, dug the pit and built the bucket chain to remove seeping water. His friend Thomas Jefferson provided tents so that workers could sleep at the site.

John Clayton (about 1685-1773), botanist, was born in Fulham, England, and emigrated to Virginia in 1705. He traveled throughout the colony collecting specimens for his own botanical garden and for shipment to Carl Linnaeus, Peter Collinson, and Johann Friedrich Gronovius. Clayton's research was the basis for Gronovius's *Flora Virginica* (*Plants of Virginia*, 1743; second edition, 1762), an important early classification of American plants.

Cadwallader Colden (1688-1776), a physician, emigrated from Ireland to Philadelphia in 1710, and eight years later settled in New York, where he became a colonial official. Colden was also an amateur physicist, astronomer, chemist, and botanist. Using Linnaeus's system, he classified all of the plants on his extensive New York estate. Linnaeus praised Colden's work and had it published.

Peter Kalm (1715-79), a Swedish botanist, was a friend of Linnaeus and traveled in North America collecting plants during the years 1748-51. Upon his return to Sweden, he wrote *Travels in North America* (three volumes, 1753-61), which includes numerous observations about natural history.

Gilbert White (1720-93) was an English country parson who never traveled beyond England and spent most of his life within a few miles of his home in Selborne. His personal observations about local flora and fauna, originally written as a series of letters to a friend, were published in book form as *The Natural History of Selborne* in 1788. One of the most popular books of all time, it has appeared in dozens of editions and translations throughout the world.

Cadwallader Colden's daughter, **Jane Colden** (1724-66), was America's first woman botanist. Working closely with her father, she collected, classified, and illustrated numerous species, and was known throughout the colonies and Europe for her knowledge of plants. Her volume of botanical drawings was rescued during the Revolutionary War by a Hessian soldier; today it resides in the British Museum.

James Hutton (1726-97), an amateur Scottish geologist, formulated the so-called uniformitarian principle, which stated that natural agents at work on and within the Earth had been operating in the same manner for many years. Hutton's theory was publicized by his associate John Playfair in *Illustrations of the Huttonian Theory* (1802).

Thomas Pennant (1726-98), a Welsh naturalist, is considered the most important British zoologist between John Ray and Charles Darwin (1809-82). The author of *British Zoology* (1766) and other studies of animals, Pennant also wrote a series of travel books that include descriptions of natural history in the British Isles and Europe. Most of Gilbert White's *The Natural History of Selborne* was written as a series of letters to Pennant.

The aromatic white hedge plant of the American South called the gardenia (*Gardenia jasmoides*) was named in honor of **Alexander Garden** (1730-91), a Scottish naturalist and physician who emigrated to South Carolina as a young man. Garden studied the flora and fauna of the colony, and corresponded with Linnaeus, Peter Collinson, Johann Friedrich Gronovius, Cadwallader Colden, John Bartram, and other eminent naturalists, for whom he also collected specimens, including the first electric eels sent to Europe. His support for Linnaean classification led to his election to the Royal Society of Uppsala.

J. Hector St. John de Crèvecoeur (1735-1813), a Frenchman who emigrated to America, settled on a farm in what is now Orange County, New York. An amateur botanist, he included among his friends his neighbor Cadwallader Colden and both Bartrams. Crèvecoeur's series of essays on American life and natural history, collected and first published in London in 1782 as

Naturalist, explorer, and scientific patron Sir Joseph Banks assembled one of the largest plant collections in the world at his renowned herbarium in England. Banks's specimens, together with his library of rare books on natural history, are now owned by the British Museum.

Letters from an American Farmer, received wide acclaim from many, including Georges Buffon, and have appeared in numerous translations.

Charles Willson Peale (1741-1827), a leading American painter, was also a prominent amateur naturalist. In 1786 he opened Peale's Museum in Philadelphia to exhibit his enormous collection of "the wonderful works of nature," which later included the first complete skeleton of an American mastodon. Peale's was the first successful natural history museum in the United States.

The German naturalist **Peter Simon Pallas** (1741-1811) studied fossils and geological formations. Appointed professor of natural history at the Imperial Academy of Sciences in St. Petersburg in 1768, he undertook a six-year expedition through Russia and Siberia collecting mammoth and rhinoceros fossils. He published his major findings in *Reise durch verschiedene Provinzen des russischen Reichs (Journey Through Various Provinces of the Russian Empire*; three volumes, 1771-76).

Sir Joseph Banks (1743-1820) was a British explorer and naturalist who accompanied Captain James Cook on his voyage around the world (1768-71); Banks returned with many plant specimens for his renowned herbarium. A large personal fortune enabled Banks to be a major patron of science, financing agricultural research and sponsoring collecting trips in many countries. Banks was honorary director of the Royal Botanic Gardens at Kew, England, and president of the Royal Society of London.

Thomas Jefferson (1743-1826), author of the Declaration of Independence, ambassador to France, and third president of the United States, was also an amateur naturalist. He collected and classified plants, animals, and fossils, and had experimental gardens at his country home, Monticello. During his years in France (1785-89) he knew many of the leading scientists in Paris, including Georges Buffon. As president, Jefferson sponsored the Lewis and Clark expedition, which brought back a variety of plant and animal life from the newly acquired Louisiana Territory west of the Mississippi River.

André Michaux (1746-1802), a leading French botanist, collected plant specimens in Europe, the Middle East, and North America for the French government. During his years of travel in the New World (1785-97) he identified many new plants and established tree nurseries in New Jersey and South Carolina. Michaux enjoyed the patronage of many eminent Americans, including George Washington and Thomas Jefferson. Many of his specimens were lost in a shipwreck during his return to France, but Michaux was still able to compile *Flora Boreali-Americana*, a catalog of plant species used as a guide by later botanists in North America.

Antoine Laurent de Jussieu (1748-1836) was the most prominent member of a French family of botanists remembered for their work in identifying plant species. His *Genera plantarum* (*Plant Groups*, 1789) is considered the basis of modern plant classification.

Abraham Werner (1750-1817), a German geologist, was the founder of the so-called Neptunist School, which advanced the theory that Earth's rocks had been formed from water. He was opposed by the Plutonists, who claimed that rocks had been created by heat from within the Earth. Although the Neptunists were convincingly refuted by James Hutton and others, Werner made a lasting contribution to the science of geology by demonstrating the chronological succession of rocks.

William Maclure (1763-1840) was born in Scotland but emigrated to the United States, where he became known as the father of American geology. In 1809 MacLure published the first geological map of the United States, along with a memoir entitled *Observations on the Geology of the United States Explanatory of a Geological Map*. Maclure was one of the founders of New Harmony, Indiana, along with naturalist Thomas Say.

Samuel Latham Mitchill (1764-1831), a well-known figure in U.S. intellectual and political circles in the early 19th century, was a physician and chemist as well as a professor of botany at Columbia University in New York City. The learned Mitchill, who was called "a living encyclopedia" by his contemporaries, published numerous scientific writings in scholarly journals, including a botanical history of North and South America and a geological study of the banks of the Hudson River.

Mitchill also contributed notes on American animals to the U.S. edition (1804) of the *General History of Quadrupeds*, originally published in England in 1790 by **Thomas Bewick** (1753-1828). Bewick was the foremost wood engraver of his time, and was well-known for his illustrations of birds and animals. His most famous work is the *History of British Birds* (Vol. 1, *Land Birds*, 1797; Vol. 2, *Water Birds*, 1804).

William Smith (1769-1839) is considered the father of English geology. Nicknamed "Strata Smith," he was the first to use fossils to identify the relative ages of different geological strata. In 1815 he published *A Delineation of the Strata of England and Wales, with Part of Scotland*, the first large-scale geological map in the world.

After five months of digging, Peale and his fellow workers uncovered the bones of three mastodons, which were later reassembled. The largest skeleton—11 feet high and 30 feet long—was installed at Peale's Museum, where it opened to public view on Christmas Eve 1801 as "The Ninth Wonder of the World." The famous skeleton is visible behind the curtain that Peale raises in his self-portrait *The Artist in His Museum*, completed in 1822. Other mastodon bones lie in the right foreground of the painting.

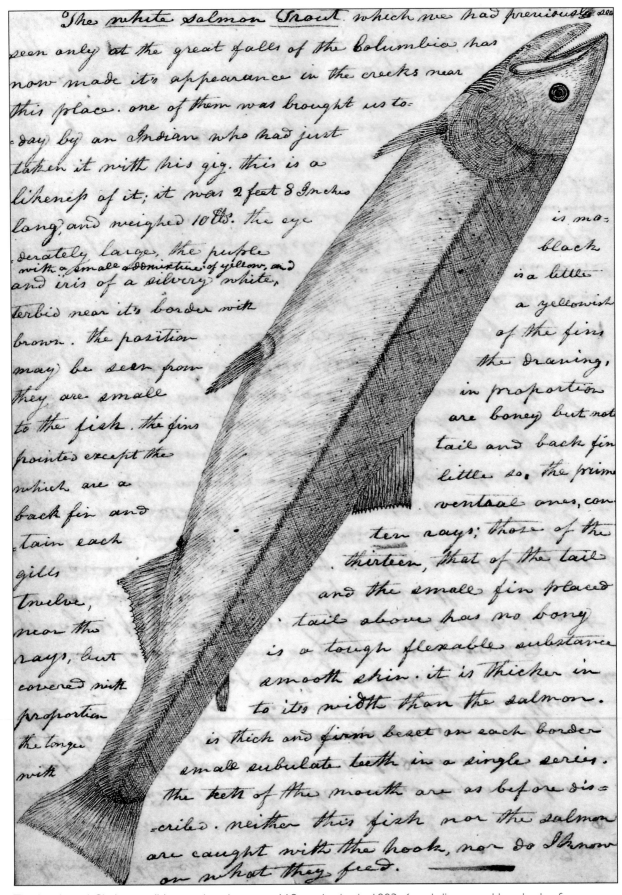

The white salmon Trout which we had previously seen only at the great falls of the Columbia has now made its appearance in the creeks near this place. one of them was brought us to-day by an Indian who had just taken it with his gig. this is a likeness of it; it was 2 feet 8 Inches long, and weighed 10 lbs. the eye is moderately large, the pupil black with a small admixture of yellow, and and iris of a silvery white, a little terbid near its border with a yellowish brown. the position of the fins may be seen from the drawing, they are small in proportion to the fish. the fins are boney but not pointed except the tail and back fin which are a little so. the back fin and ventral ones, contain each thirteen, that of the tail gills and the small fin placed twelve, tail above has no bony near the is a tough flexable substance rays, but smooth skin. it is thicker in covered with to its width than the salmon. proportion is thick and firm beset on each border the tongue small subulate teeth in a single series. with the teeth of the mouth are as before described. neither this fish nor the salmon are caught with the hook, nor do I know on what they feed. ———

The Lewis and Clark expedition explored western U.S. territories in 1803–6 and discovered hundreds of new animals and plants, including this coho, or silver salmon, which Clark sketched in his journal.

2 An Era of Growth and Discovery

 As the 18th century gave way to the 19th, a new age of discovery unfolded as naturalists began traveling into unexplored regions of the Western Hemisphere. Streams of Europeans combed the mountains and jungles of South America in search of hitherto unknown specimens. North of the equator, as the frontier of the recently independent United States pushed farther west, naturalists clamored to be taken along on government-sponsored expeditions to explore newly acquired territory, beginning with the journey of Meriwether Lewis (1774-1809) and William Clark (1770-1838). By mid-century, naturalists were also probing the biological mysteries of the Arctic and Antarctic and penetrating the African interior.

Discoveries during the 19th century in the field of natural history revolutionized human understanding of the origins of the Earth and the life it supports. New studies of glaciers, rock formations, and fossils gave birth to the science of modern geology and confirmed the suspicions of Georges Buffon that Earth was far older than the 6,000 years claimed by biblical scholars. As naturalists discovered thousands of new plants and animals, they moved closer to Lamarck's belief that species had evolved over time rather than being created in a single instant.

Part 2 of *Earthkeepers* begins with the story of Alexander von Humboldt, whose long professional life started in the closing years of the 18th century and ended as Charles Darwin was writing the final chapters of his landmark masterwork, the *Origin of Species*.

Alexander von Humboldt

A NATURALIST OF
MANY TALENTS

Baron Alexander von Humboldt, explorer, scientist, and one of the most accomplished men of his time, is also remembered as one of the world's greatest naturalists. He was born in Berlin in 1769 to a noble family. His father, who had served with distinction in the army of Frederick the Great of Prussia, died when the boy was 10 years old, and Alexander and his elder brother, Wilhelm, were raised by their mother, a French Huguenot (Protestant) who believed strongly in education.

Both Humboldt sons were privately tutored in the classics, mathematics, the physical sciences, languages, and economics, for their mother hoped that they would become important public officials. Wilhelm fulfilled her wish, and more, distinguishing himself as a diplomat, language scholar, philosopher, and educational reformer. Alexander's journey to renown was somewhat more circuitous, but eventually he became more celebrated than his brother.

While Wilhelm went on to the University of Jena and remained there to complete his studies, Alexander studied economics in Frankfurt for a year, then engineering and

A mining engineer and mineralogist turned naturalist, Humboldt spent five years exploring South America and published a 30-volume account of his discoveries.

> "*The earth is loaded with plants, and nothing impedes their free development. An immense layer of mold indicates the uninterrupted action of organic powers. The crocodiles and the boas are masters of the river; the jaguar, the peccary, the tapir, and the monkeys pass through the forest without fear and without danger. . . . This aspect of animated nature, in which man is nothing, has something in it strange and sad.*"

—from *Voyage de Humboldt et Bonpland* (describing a tributary of the Orinoco River, in the South American interior; 1805-34)

Alexander von Humboldt

BORN

September 14, 1769
Berlin, Prussia (now Germany)

DIED

May 6, 1859
Berlin

EDUCATION

University of Frankfurt an der Oder;
University of Göttingen; Freiburg
School of Mines (Saxony)

MAJOR INTERESTS

Natural history; magnetism;
meteorology

ACCOMPLISHMENTS

Made extensive scientific explorations of South America, including the Orinoco River and the Andes Mountains; made major discoveries about the Earth's magnetic field and its weather; concluded from studies of volcanoes that Earth's crust had been formed by a series of eruptions; major writings include *Voyage de Humboldt et Bonpland* (30 volumes, 1805–34); *Asie Centrale* (3 volumes, 1843); and *Kosmos* (5 volumes, 1845–62)

HONORS

Humboldt Current, ocean current off the western coast of South America, named after him

botany in Frankfurt an der Oder, followed by mineralogy and geology at the University of Göttingen. Botany excited him, and he dreamed of traveling in other parts of the world to gather exotic plants. But mineralogy also beckoned him, and in 1790 he enrolled for further study in that field at the School of Mines in Freiburg, founded in 1766 as the first such institution in the world. For two years he vigorously pursued a daily schedule of classes and trips into the local mines; his evenings were devoted to botany.

In 1792 Humboldt left the school for full-time employment with the Prussian department of mines. Characteristically, the energetic Humboldt involved himself in every aspect of mining, not only managing and supervising, but also inventing a miner's lamp, improving safety conditions, and—with his own funds—establishing a technical school for young miners. His duties also called for frequent travel as a representative of the Prussian government to inspect mines in other parts of Europe.

During these years Humboldt also widened his interest in science, particularly in chemistry, electricity, and magnetism, and he performed numerous experiments. After his mother died in 1796, he felt free to pursue the dream he had been nurturing for many years: to explore a remote land. He tried to join private and government-sponsored scientific expeditions abroad, but these were canceled because of the Napoleonic Wars. The frustrated Humboldt and a friend, a botanist named Aimé Bonpland, decided to travel on their own to Spanish colonies in the New World.

In Madrid they approached the Spanish government through officials at the German embassy for permission to travel "in the interests of science" in Central and South America. At first they had no luck, but in an audience with King Charles IV himself, Humboldt and Bonpland were so persuasive and their knowledge so impressive that the trip was approved. There would be no financial assistance from the government—but this was not a problem, since Humboldt had inherited a considerable amount of money upon his mother's death.

On June 5, 1799, Humboldt and Bonpland sailed on the packet boat *Pizarro* from the port of La Coruña. Humboldt brought with him more than 40 scientific instruments, including barometers, sextants, a quadrant, hygrometers (which measured humidity), thermometers, a telescope, a rain gauge, a microscope, a chronometer, and devices that measured Earth's magnetism. The first leg of the voyage was

Among the plates in Humboldt's *Voyage* was this illustration of a species of South American monkey, *Simia satanas*.

ments, collected marine specimens, made astronomical observations, and calculated the *Pizarro*'s position (his determinations of longitude and latitude were more accurate than the captain's).

When the two men left the ship upon its arrival in Cumaná, Venezuela, in the late summer of 1799, they lingered there for a few months observing an eclipse of the sun and experiencing an earthquake before beginning an arduous journey that would last five years. In the first year they traveled inland by foot and canoe through wilderness, battling insects, torrid heat, and heavy rains, to the Orinoco River and discovered that the Casiquiare River linked the Amazon and Orinoco river systems. Returning to Cumaná in July 1800, they sailed to Havana, Cuba, and remained there until March 1801, when they embarked on another trip to the South American continent, this time to the Andes.

For nearly two years Humboldt and Bonpland explored the mountains, again under the most primitive conditions and without the benefit of any climbing equipment. Bonpland concentrated on gathering plants while Humboldt, who had developed a particular interest in volcanoes, climbed several active peaks. His ascent of Chimborazo, in Ecuador, to more than 19,000 feet (just 1,300 feet short of the summit) was the highest any man had ever climbed; Humboldt's record stood for 30 years. The climb was all the more remarkable because it was done without additional oxygen, a mainstay of modern ascents; Humboldt, in fact, was the first person to observe that so-called mountain sickness was due to a lack of oxygen at high altitudes.

Toward the end of 1802, Humboldt and Bonpland sailed from Lima, Peru, north to Guayaquil, Ecuador, on the Pacific coast, en route to Mexico. Humboldt was able to observe the oceanic current off the west coast of South America, which he named the Peruvian Current; later it was renamed

dangerous: Spain was at war with Great Britain, and British ships patrolled the Spanish and Portuguese coasts. After two weeks dodging enemy vessels, the *Pizarro* landed at Tenerife, off the African coast in the Canary Islands. There the two scientists spent several days exploring the volcanic mountain Pico de Teide before continuing across the Atlantic on the *Pizarro*. Back aboard ship, Humboldt busied himself with his various instru-

the Humboldt Current in honor of its "discoverer," although the modest Humboldt protested that the current had been known to generations of local fishermen long before his arrival.

The two men spent a year exploring Mexico, then traveled to the United States in the spring of 1804, where they visited Philadelphia and were received at the White House by President Thomas Jefferson before sailing for home. By the end of the summer Humboldt was back in Europe with his instruments, journals, and 42 boxes of plant, animal, and geological specimens. He settled in Paris, a center of intellectual and scientific activity, and for the next 23 years assembled the South American data he had collected into a series of books— *Voyage de Humboldt et Bonpland (Voyage of Humboldt and Bonpland)*—that eventually totaled 30 volumes (1805-34). He paid for their publication himself, as well as engravings of illustrations made for them by artists and mapmakers he had hired. For a decade he was aided by Bonpland, but in 1816 the botanist accepted a position in Buenos Aires as a professor of natural history and remained in South America for the rest of his life. Humboldt then turned to others for aid, including Cuvier, who helped him with sections in the books on zoology and comparative anatomy.

Humboldt's research in South America and later experiments in Europe greatly influenced our understanding of the Earth and its origins, and he is rightfully considered the founding father of the sciences of physical geography and geophysics. His meticulously recorded meteorological data—temperatures, rainfall, barometric pressure—were the basis for the science of comparative climatology. His experiments with magnetism led to his discovery that Earth's magnetic force decreases from the poles to the equator. Humboldt's studies of volcanoes offered evidence that the crust of the Earth had been formed by a series of eruptive forces.

In 1827, nearly out of money, Humboldt was forced to return to Berlin to earn his living at the court of King Frederick William III as a chamberlain and tutor to the crown prince. But he still made time for science: he became active in several scientific societies, organizing international conferences for the exchange of ideas and persuading the Russian and British governments to establish observatories in their various possessions throughout the world to measure variations in the Earth's magnetic field. At the invitation of the Russian czar he toured Central Asia—then largely unexplored—for six months in 1829, making geological observations, collecting data for his isothermal world map (a map that showed bands of equal temperature), and visiting gold and platinum mines in the Ural Mountains, where he discovered diamonds. His three-volume account of the trip, *Asie Centrale (Central Asia)*, was published in 1843.

In his later years Humboldt became interested in making the knowledge of scientific discoveries available to as wide an audience as possible. To this end, he gave public lectures on geography that were attended by thousands; he also wrote *Kosmos (Cosmos)*, a five-volume popular explanation of the physical world that he finished only a few weeks before his death in May 1859, at the age of 89.

Humboldt was without question an intellectual giant, not only of the 19th century but for all time. His many scientific accomplishments were made possible, however, not only by his enormous intelligence and physical robustness but also because of his ability to get along with others—a skill especially necessary at a time when Europe was in a state of political upheaval. Contemporary accounts relate that he was a charming man, genuinely interested in others. He gave advice and financial support to many young scientists, including the Swiss-American

Humboldt returned to Europe with hundreds of zoological, botanical, and geological specimens he collected in South America, including *Inga fulgens,* a plant he described and illustrated in the *Voyage.*

Louis Agassiz; in fact, Humboldt was so generous that he died virtually penniless.

Another aspect of Humboldt's life should be mentioned, although it has no direct bearing on his contributions to the field of natural history. He was an outspoken opponent of slavery and a staunch supporter of democratic ideals. When the young Simón Bolívar, who later became known as the Great Liberator of South America, was in Paris in the early 1800s, Humboldt befriended him. Many historians credit Humboldt with inspiring Bolivar's return to South America to liberate its people from colonial rule.

FURTHER READING

Adams, Alexander B. "A Noble Privilege." In *Eternal Quest: The Story of the Great Naturalists.* New York: G. P. Putnam, 1969.

Botting, Douglas. *Humboldt and the Cosmos.* New York: Harper & Row, 1973.

De Terra, Helmut. *The Life and Times of Alexander von Humboldt.* New York: Knopf, 1955.

Gaines, Ann. *Alexander von Humboldt, Colossus of Exploration.* New York: Chelsea House, 1991.

Kellner, L. *Alexander von Humboldt.* New York: Oxford University Press, 1963.

Von Hagen, Victor Wolfgang. "Alexander von Humboldt." In *South America Called Them: Explorations of the Great Naturalists.* New York: Knopf, 1945.

John Chapman (Johnny Appleseed)

THE ORCHARD PLANTER

Yes, there really was a Johnny Appleseed, although he exists more in legend than fact. The man celebrated in American folk tradition for more than a century as a friend of nature was born John Chapman in Leominster, Massachusetts, in 1774. Little is known about the circumstances of his birth, although his father later fought in the Revolutionary War and was discharged for mismanaging military supplies. Chapman's boyhood is a mystery; he would say in later life only that he had enjoyed wandering in the countryside, searching for birds and flowers.

In 1797 Chapman appeared in western Pennsylvania, at the edge of the frontier, and began collecting apple seeds from local cider presses. By 1801 he had planted thousands of seeds and established apple tree nurseries in the wilderness from the Allegheny River to central Ohio. He is known to have lived off and on in a cabin in Ashland County, Ohio, near Mansfield, until about 1828 with his half-sister and her family. When Indians, incited by the British, threatened to attack settlements near Mansfield in 1812, Chapman traveled as far west as Mt.

John Chapman, the legendary Johnny Appleseed, is shown with an apple seedling and a pruning knife in this detail of a 19th-century engraving. Chapman, who combined tree planting with religious preaching, usually traveled with a Bible tucked in his pants.

John Chapman (Johnny Appleseed)

BORN

September 26, 1774
Leominster, Massachusetts

DIED

March 10, 1845
Fort Wayne, Indiana

EDUCATION

Unknown

MAJOR INTEREST

Planting apple orchards

ACCOMPLISHMENTS

Established apple orchards from western Pennsylvania to northern Indiana; encouraged pioneers to plant apple trees

---

*"And
A boy
Blew west,
And with prayers and incantations,
And with 'Yankee Doodle Dandy,'
Crossed the Appalachians,
And was 'young John Chapman,'
Then
'Johnny Appleseed, Johnny Appleseed.' "*

—from *"In Praise of Johnny Appleseed,"*
by Vachel Lindsay (1925)

Vernon, Ohio, on the Indiana border, warning homesteaders of their approach.

During his years in Ohio, Chapman became a familiar sight and acquired the nickname "Johnny Appleseed" as he tramped hundreds of miles planting and tending his orchards and tree nurseries, which eventually reached as far west as northern Indiana. He was an eccentric figure who often stopped bystanders to preach from the Bible and from the works of Emanuel Swedenborg, a Swedish religious philosopher, but the popular legend that he went barefoot, dressed in a coffee sack, and wore a tin pot for a hat has never been substantiated. A more reliable account suggests that Chapman's bizarre outbursts of preaching followed his heartbreak at the death of his wife, a Choctaw Indian, and their baby. According to this story, Chapman searched in vain for dogfennel, known as "fever-weed," when she fell ill with malaria; tea made from this weed was a folk remedy for the disease. After her death, he is supposed to have planted dogfennel seed wherever he went.

Chapman settled in the area near Fort Wayne, Indiana, in the early 1830s and established more apple nurseries and orchards. At his death in 1845, he was a successful businessman who owned 22 properties totaling near 1,200 acres.

Chapman did not, as popularly believed, establish the first American apple orchards; these had existed for at least two generations before his time. He did, however, distribute thousands of free seedlings to pioneers, thus encouraging the growth of orchards farther and farther west.

"Johnny Appleseed" has been celebrated in popular culture since the late 19th century in verse, songs, drama, and even the movies, as a gentle folk hero who revered nature and taught others to respect it. In the late 20th century his legend is still taught to American schoolchildren as a symbol of concern for the Earth.

FURTHER READING

Dorson, Richard. "Johnny Appleseed." In *American Folklore*, 232-36. Chicago: University of Chicago Press, 1959.

Hunt, Mabel Leigh. *Better Known as Johnny Appleseed*. Philadelphia: Lippincott, 1950.

Price, Robert. *John Chapman: A Bibliography of "Johnny Appleseed" in American History, Literature and Folklore*. Paterson, N.J.: Swedenborg Press, 1944.

———. *Johnny Appleseed: Man and Myth*. Bloomington: Indiana University Press, 1954.

John James Audubon

PAINTER OF BIRDS
AND ANIMALS

John James Audubon is probably the most famous naturalist in the world. Schoolchildren are introduced at an early age to his paintings of American birds, often because of the educational efforts of the National Audubon Society, a U.S.-based organization that promotes the study of nature. Many twists and turns occurred in Audubon's life, however, before his most famous work, *The Birds of America* (1827-38), established his reputation as a naturalist.

There were both notable similarities and curious differences between Audubon and Alexander Wilson, the other founding father of American ornithology. The young French storekeeper who somewhat warily greeted Wilson in Louisville on a spring morning in 1810 had come to America seven years earlier to try to earn a living, not to study nature. But Wilson, who had known only poverty in Scotland, had emigrated on his own; Audubon, on the other hand, had been sent by his wealthy father, who was exasperated with his son's indolence and sought to keep him from serving in Napoleon's army. Although both Audubon and Wilson had little formal education and were self-taught in both drawing and natural history, Wilson seems to

John James Audubon began drawing birds as a teenager in France, but he did not earn his living as a painter of wildlife until he was in his 40s.

PLATE 96.

Columbia Jay.
GARRULUS ULTRAMARINUS.

Audubon's hand-colored engraving of a pair of Columbia jays appears as Plate 96 of *The Birds of America*, his celebrated four-volume collection of bird illustrations.

have been the more observant naturalist. Audubon, however, is considered the world's greatest painter of birds and other wildlife.

Audubon was born in 1785 on the island of Santo Domingo in the Caribbean. His father, Jean, was a wealthy merchant and planter, his mother a local Creole who died soon after his birth. The younger Jean, as Audubon was then called, and a younger half-sister born to another Creole woman were taken back to France by their father in 1789, and adopted formally by the elder Audubon and his legal wife, who had him baptized as Jean Jacques. Young Audubon was doted on by his new stepmother, who found it difficult to force him to do his lessons. By the age of 15, Audubon still had only the rudiments of an education but had become interested in Buffon's *Histoire naturelle* and began to make drawings of French birds.

Audubon was sent to America in 1803 and early in the following year settled at Mill Grove, an estate near Philadelphia owned by his father. Audubon was supposed to interest himself in a lead mine on the property, but instead he lived the life of a sportsman and country gentleman, hunting wildlife but also continuing to draw birds. During this time he performed the first bird-banding experiment in America: in the spring of 1804 he tied thread to the legs of two newly hatched peewees and the following spring observed that they had returned to nest near their birthplace.

When Audubon's father sold Mill Grove, young Jean—who had Americanized his name to John James—was forced to earn his living. He worked for a while for a New York merchant but was restless in the city and longed to return to the countryside. That opportunity came in the late summer of 1807, when he and a friend, Ferdinand Rozier, went west to open a general store. They settled in Louisville for three years but did not prosper, and shortly after

Wilson's visit moved downriver to Henderson, Kentucky, accompanied by Audubon's wife, Lucy, an Englishwoman living on an estate in neighboring Mill Grove whom he had returned East to marry in 1808.

Audubon's business fortunes did not improve. Rather than storekeeping, he preferred forays into the wilderness, hunting animals and meeting local characters, including the elderly frontiersman Daniel Boone, who became a close friend. His partnership with Rozier soon dissolved, and he involved himself in a series of enterprises that were financial disasters. The last venture to fail was a grist and lumber mill, and Audubon was forced to declare bankruptcy in 1819. He was jailed briefly for indebtedness, then supported his growing family by doing crayon portraits and taxidermy.

By 1820, Audubon decided to pursue full-time the interest he enjoyed most: illustrating birds. He traveled down the Ohio and Mississippi rivers to New Orleans, looking for birds to draw and painting portraits to pay expenses. Lucy soon joined him, and in the early 1820s worked as a governess for a wealthy family while her husband taught music and dancing at a local school, accompanying students on his violin. In 1824 Audubon traveled to Philadelphia to find an engraver for his growing collection of bird drawings and was advised to go abroad.

After a time of scrimping and saving, and largely supported by Lucy's funds, Audubon sailed for Europe in the summer of 1826. Beginning in Liverpool and then continuing on to Edinburgh and London, Audubon sold subscriptions to his planned book to raise funds for its engraving and printing; he continued to pay his personal expenses through portraits, but now he was making oil paintings of birds, not people, and they sold quickly. Presenting himself as an "American Woodsman," Audubon delighted acquaintances with

John James Audubon

BORN

April 26, 1785
Les Cayes, Santo Domingo

DIED

January 27, 1851
New York City

EDUCATION

Private tutoring

MAJOR INTEREST

Natural history illustration

ACCOMPLISHMENTS

Illustrator of *The Birds of America* (4 volumes, 1827–38), and author, with William MacGillivray, of its accompanying text, *Ornithological Biography* (5 volumes, 1831–39), and index, *A Synopsis of the Birds of North America* (1839); illustrator of *Viviparous Quadrupeds of North America* (3 volumes, 1845–48), and author, with John Bachman, of its accompanying text (3 volumes, 1846–53)

HONORS

Elected a member of the Royal Society of Edinburgh (1827) and a fellow of the American Academy (1830)

In his later years Audubon illustrated mammals as well as birds. This engraving of a gray fox was included in Audubon's last work, *Viviparous Quadrupeds of North America.*

accounts—some fictitious—of life in the wilderness.

In Edinburgh he was warmly received, meeting many of the city's famous residents, including the poet and novelist Sir Walter Scott, and was honored with election to the Royal Academy in 1827. In London, Audubon sold more subscriptions, including one to the English queen, Adelaide, an amateur naturalist (King George IV declined), and also found an engraver to begin work on his book. During this stay abroad he also journeyed briefly to Paris, where he was warmly greeted by Georges Cuvier, who pressed his guest for details about American wildlife.

The first volume of Audubon's *Birds of America* was published in 1827; during the next 11 years three more volumes appeared. The series included 435 hand-colored engravings of Audubon's drawings. In 1830 Lucy joined him in Edinburgh, where he began work on a separate text to accompany *The Birds of America,* aided by an ornithologist named William MacGillivray; the resulting five volumes were published between 1831 and 1839 in Edinburgh as *Ornithological Biography.*

The books were an immediate success and made Audubon famous throughout Europe. Praise came from leading scientists on the Continent, including Cuvier, who called Audubon's

> *"A century hence . . . Nature will have been robbed of many brilliant charms, the rivers will be tormented and turned astray from their primitive courses, the hills will be leveled with the swamps."*

—from an entry in Audubon's journal

drawings "the most magnificent monument that art has raised to science." By 1829, articles about him had begun to appear in scientific and scholarly journals in America, and in 1830 he was honored by election as a fellow of the American Academy. When he returned to the United States in 1831 he was celebrated as the leading naturalist of his day. For the next three years Audubon traveled on several expeditions in North America, accompanied by family members and naturalist friends, first to the Texas coast, then to Florida, and finally to Labrador, where the large-scale slaughter of birds and seals evoked from him a loud protest.

Audubon spent the years 1834-39 in both North America and Great Britain. In Edinburgh he completed work on the *Ornithological Biography* and also wrote and published—again with MacGillivray's help—an index to the larger works entitled *A Synopsis of the Birds of North America* (1839). In America he continued to draw birds, traveling as far west as Galveston, Texas, in search of new species to illustrate. By 1841 Audubon had settled permanently in the United States, on an estate on the Hudson River in upper Manhattan called Audubon Park.

Audubon spent the last decade of his life preparing a smaller edition of *The Birds of America* and working on an ambitious series of drawings that eventually numbered 150 and were published as *Viviparous Quadrupeds of North America* (three volumes, 1845-48). Helping him with this latter project—a study of mammals—were his two sons as well as the naturalist John Bachman, who had become a close friend and who wrote the accompanying three-volume text (1846-53).

Initially Audubon used skins and stuffed specimens as models for his mammal drawings; later (in 1843) he traveled west to Fort Union, on the upper Missouri River, in search of subjects. During this journey he participated in a buffalo hunt in order to obtain specimens to illustrate, but later complained about the wholesale slaughter of these animals.

At his death in January 1851 Audubon was mourned as the greatest naturalist of his time, but it is important to remember that his reputation rests on his exceptional artistic abilities. Although Audubon made many written observations of wildlife that were included in his books, the credit for their scientific accuracy goes to his collaborators MacGillivray and Bachman. Ironically, the man whose name is synonymous with the study of American birds was not an ornithologist but a gifted draftsman and painter.

FURTHER READING

Adams, Alexander B. "The Collectors." In *Eternal Quest: The Story of the Great Naturalists*. New York: G. P. Putnam, 1969.

————. *John James Audubon*. New York: G. P. Putnam, 1966.

Audubon, John James. *The Audubon Reader*. Edited by Scott Sanders. Bloomington: Indiana University Press, 1986.

————. *The Birds of America*. 4 vols. 1827-38. Reprint (2 vols.). New York: Dover, 1967.

————. *John James Audubon: The Watercolor Paintings for "The Birds of America."* New York: Villard, 1993.

"Audubon, John James." In *Dictionary of American Biography*. Vol. 1. New York: Scribners, 1964.

Audubon, Lucy. *The Life of John James Audubon, the Naturalist*. New York: G. P. Putnam, 1902.

Audubon, Maria, ed. *Audubon and His Journals*. 2 vols. 1897. Reprint. New York: Dover, 1986.

Chancellor, John. *Audubon: A Biography*. New York: Viking, 1978.

DeLatte, Carolyn E. *Lucy Audubon: A Biography*. Baton Rouge: Louisiana State University Press, 1982.

Peattie, Donald Culross. "Wilderness Birdsmen: Audubon and Wilson." In *Green Laurels: The Lives and Achievements of the Great Naturalists*. New York: Simon & Schuster, 1936.

Thomas Nuttall

THE BRILLIANT FOOL

homas Nuttall began life in poverty in England and retired there more than 50 years later as the genteel owner of a country estate. His professional life, however, was spent entirely in North America, where he transformed himself from a penniless printer with a passion for natural history into a distinguished faculty member at Harvard University.

Unlike his contemporary John James Audubon and the older Scottish émigré Alexander Wilson, Nuttall knew for certain even as a young boy that the study of natural history would be his life's work, and that North America would be his "laboratory." Born to a poor rural family, Nuttall had no formal education but somehow learned to read and write and teach himself about animals, plants, and minerals in his native Yorkshire. As a young boy he was apprenticed to his uncle, and he worked until the age of 22 as a printer in Liverpool, using every spare moment for study and saving money for passage to America. His long-held dream came true in 1808, when he arrived in Philadelphia. The city had become widely known in both Europe and America, thanks to the Bartrams and their circle, as an unofficial "home" to New World naturalists.

Immediately upon landing, Nuttall went out into the countryside looking for plants and soon found his way to the home of Dr. Benjamin Smith Barton, a professor at the Univer-

Self-educated Englishman Thomas Nuttall explored North America, became a celebrated author and lecturer on natural history, and taught at Harvard University.

"I prefer the wilds of America a thousand times."

—from a letter to a friend, after Nuttall's return to England

sity of Pennsylvania who had written the first American botany text, *Elements of Botany*, some years later. Barton must have been impressed with the young man's zeal, for he readily agreed to be his teacher. Soon Nuttall was going on collecting trips for Barton along the Delaware coast.

Within two years of his arrival, Nuttall embarked on a western collecting expedition sponsored by Barton, traveling via the Great Lakes to Detroit. (Nuttall was supposed to be paid eight dollars a month by his benefactor, but apparently never bothered to collect his salary.) Barton had wanted Nuttall to continue on from Detroit to Winnipeg, but the dual presence of British troops and unfriendly Indians led him to accept the invitation of an American surveyor to accompany him in his canoe to what is now Mackinac Island, in northern Lake Huron.

Mackinac was the gathering place of fur trappers and traders who worked for John Jacob Astor's American Fur Company; the presence of Nuttall—described by all who knew him as absent-minded, incompetent in practical matters, and somewhat naïve—among this rowdy, boisterous group was recorded for posterity in a book called *Astoria*, by American author Washington Irving. It was in Mackinac that Nuttall acquired his derisive nickname, "Le Fou" (French for "The Fool"), by which he became known among both trappers and Indians.

Despite ridicule, primitive and often hostile surroundings, and repeated attacks of malaria, Nuttall persisted single-mindedly in searching out unusual plant, animal, and fossil specimens as he accompanied traders on to St. Louis and up the Missouri River, and then down the Mississippi. Nuttall's seemingly miraculous survival of near disasters—he continued to be plagued by malaria, often became lost, and came close to dying in severe storms—was as noteworthy as the collection of specimens he amassed and shipped back to Dr. Barton in Philadelphia. (Not everything survived the journey: Indians often broke open the jars containing animal specimens and drank the alcohol used to preserve them. This setback was not unique to Nuttall, however; writings of many naturalists in North America in the 18th and 19th centuries complain of the same problem.)

In the fall of 1811 Nuttall arrived in New Orleans, concluding the first expedition into the new American West by a professional botanist. After sending off the last of Dr. Barton's shipments, he sailed for England with more plants, seeds, and bulbs, which he sold there. Nuttall remained in his native country for more than three years, preparing a catalog of the plants he had discovered on his Western journey and also working on his journals. Interestingly, the cataloged plants were claimed as the discoveries of a German botanist living in London named Frederick Pursh, who had also appropriated and took credit for specimens collected by Lewis and Clark on their expedition; the modest Nuttall, a scientist who sought no fame, seems to have made no objection. As for Nuttall's journals, they were not published until 140 years later (*Travels into the Old Northwest*, 1951).

Returning to the United States in 1815, Nuttall embarked on further collecting expeditions. First he ventured into the American Southeast, where William Bartram had explored, and then west as far as Cincinnati and central Kentucky. Two years later Nuttall was

EARTHKEEPERS

Thomas Nuttall

BORN

January 5, 1786
Yorkshire, England

DIED

September 10, 1859
Lancashire, England

EDUCATION

No formal schooling

MAJOR INTERESTS

Botany; ornithology; mineralogy

ACCOMPLISHMENTS

During a long residence in the United States studied the natural history of North America; author of numerous works, including *The Genera of North American Plants, and a Catalogue of the Species, to the Year 1817* (1818); *A Journal of Travels into the Arkansa Territory* (1821); and *A Manual of the Ornithology of the United States and Canada* (1832), the first popular bird guide in America; instructor in natural history, Harvard University; curator, Harvard Botanical Garden

HONORS

Elected a fellow of the Linnean Society of London, member of the American Philosophical Society, and correspondent of the Philadelphia Academy of Natural Sciences

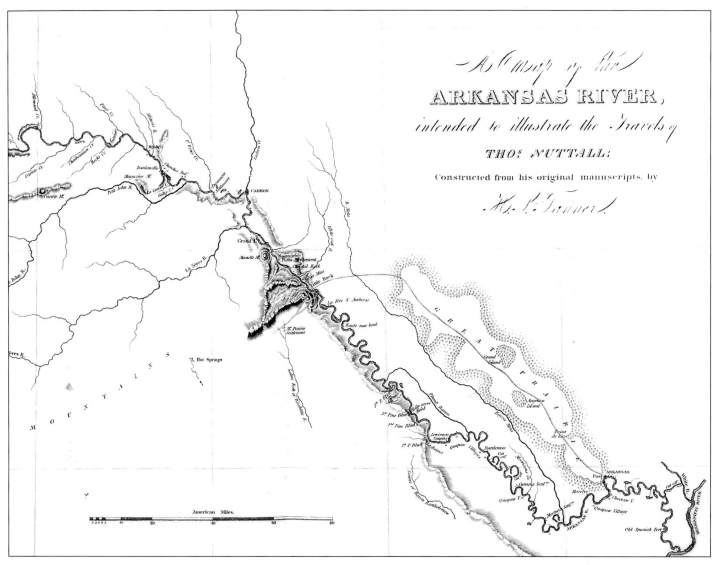

This map illustrated Nuttall's second book, *Journal of Travels into the Arkansa Territory*, which was a best-seller in both America and Europe. It included accurate observations of plants and animals, weather, and Indian tribes.

back in Philadelphia, writing the *Genera of North American Plants and a Catalogue of Species to 1817*, which he published in 1818 at his own expense. The *Genera*, which included all the botanical discoveries made to date by Nuttall and his predecessors, was for many years considered the most reliable guide to American plants. Curiously, it was more well-received abroad than in the New World—despite the fact that it used the old-fashioned Linnean system of classification rather than the so-called natural method that was becoming increasingly popular in England and Europe.

During 1818–19 Nuttall ventured west again, first to Pittsburgh and Cincinnati and eventually down the Mississippi to the Arkansas River, which he followed into what is now Oklahoma. Nuttall had his usual mishaps—he suffered from malaria; encountered unfriendly Indians, poisonous snakes, and inhospitable terrain; and got lost more than once—but he had his usual luck, too, surviving catastrophe to return home with numerous outstanding specimens, dozens of them not yet classified. He sold some of them, but gave away many to fellow naturalists, including Thomas Say and the Frenchman Charles Le Sueur. Another benefit of the trip was Nuttall's journal, published in 1821 as *A Journal of Travels into the Arkansa [sic] Territory*. The *Journal*, which includes valuable information on Indian tribes and Nuttall's meteorological observations, became popular in both America and Europe, and is still read for its reliable account of frontier life.

Despite his shy manner, Nuttall became a sought-after speaker, first in a series of public lectures at Philadelphia's Academy of Sciences and then to audiences farther afield, including students at Yale University. His growing fame led to his appointment in 1822 as a lecturer in natural history at Harvard University (because of Nuttall's lack of formal education, he was denied the title of "professor") and as curator of the Harvard Botanical Garden, at a salary of $500 a year (a few years later it was doubled). Finally able to live in some comfort, Nuttall remained at Harvard for 10 years, becoming a popular teacher and transforming the botanical garden into a first-rate institution by donating his own specimens and attracting contributions from naturalists throughout the world.

During his decade at Harvard, Nuttall wrote a text for his botany class, *An Introduction to Systematic and Physiological Botany* (1827), and continued to expand his scientific knowledge as he classified and wrote papers about animal and mineral specimens. A suggestion by a friend led Nuttall to write a book that made him even more famous: a popular bird guide entitled *Manual of Ornithology of the United States and Canada*, first published in 1832 and reprinted many times throughout the century. Unlike the large, expensive bird books of Wilson and Audubon, Nuttall's smaller, low-priced guide was designed to be carried into the countryside by amateur bird watchers.

Nuttall went on several short collecting trips in the eastern United States while he taught at Harvard, but he dreamed of making an extended exploration of the American Far West. Invited in 1832 to join a western-bound expedition led by Philadelphia entrepreneur and explorer Nathaniel Jarvis Wyeth, Nuttall resigned from the Harvard faculty. The two men, accompanied by a young American naturalist named John Kirk Townsend, made their way to Independence, Missouri, and then to the West Coast and the mouth of the Columbia River along a route that later became the Oregon Trail, collecting still more specimens.

Nuttall went on to Hawaii—he apparently made several visits there during his years in the West—and then, in 1835, to California, where he traveled as far south as San Diego. There, embarking on a return journey to Boston around Cape Horn, he encountered one of his former students at Harvard, Richard Henry Dana. Dana, who had left college to work as a sailor on a passenger ship, later recorded their meeting in his classic sea narrative, *Two Years Before the Mast* (1840; 1859): Nuttall, he wrote, "was strolling about — in a sailor's pea-jacket, with a wide straw hat, and barefooted, with his trousers rolled up to his knees, picking up stones and shells. Just as we were about to shove off from the beach, he came down to the boat with his shoes in his hand, and his pockets full of specimens."

Returning to Boston, Nuttall continued to classify his huge collections. Still popular as a lecturer, he gave a series of talks on natural science that attracted 12,000 requests for tickets. Among his many visitors was John James Audubon, who had come to see Nuttall during his years at Harvard; this time Audubon received information about new western bird species identified by Nuttall and Townsend, and later acknowledged their assistance.

In 1842, 56-year-old Thomas Nuttall returned reluctantly to England to live on a country estate near Liverpool willed to him by a well-to-do uncle. For the last 17 years of his life, the humbly born printer who had trained himself to be a scientist, naturalist, and explorer lived quietly as a country gentleman, breeding rhododendrons that he had introduced into Europe from Asia.

FURTHER READING

Graustein, Jeanette E. *Thomas Nuttall, Naturalist: Explorations in America, 1808-1841*. Cambridge: Harvard University Press, 1967.

Nuttall, Thomas. *A Journal of Travels into the Arkansa Territory During the Year 1819*. 1821. Reprint. Norman: University of Oklahoma Press, 1980.

———. *A Manual of Ornithology of the United States and Canada*. 1832. Reprint. Salem, N.H.: Ayer, 1974.

"Nuttall, Thomas." In *Dictionary of American Biography*. Vol. 7. New York: Scribners, 1964.

Thomas Say

THE FATHER OF AMERICAN ENTOMOLOGY

It would have been surprising if Thomas Say had *not* become at least an amateur naturalist, given his family's interest in natural history. On his mother's side he was a great-grandson of John Bartram and a grand-nephew of William Bartram, and he grew up as a member of the Bartrams' extended family circle, which included Alexander Wilson, André Michaux, and a number of members of the Peale family. Benjamin Say, Thomas's physician father and one of Philadelphia's leading citizens, was also a horticulturist (a plant expert).

Thomas Say's formal education ended with his graduation from a Quaker secondary school near his birthplace. He chose not to go on to college; as an older man, he spoke with regret of not having university training, which he felt could have helped him with his zoological studies. His interest in plants and their medicinal uses led him to study pharmacy with his father and to open an apothecary shop, but the business eventually failed. Encouraged by Wilson and his uncle William Bartram, Say broadened his interest in natural history to include insects and started a large collection of beetles and butterflies. He began spending time with other young naturalists at their gathering place, Peale's Museum, and in 1812 joined with them to found the Philadephia Academy of Natural Sciences, an organization to further the study of natural history. By 1816 Say had decided to make entomology his life's work: he would write a book that included descriptions of all known American insects.

When Thomas Nuttall returned to Philadelphia in 1817 to write the *Genera of North American Plants* and renewed his relationship with the natural history community of that city, he and Say became good friends. Both men were said to have had similar personalities: thoroughly absorbed in their work and indifferent to hardships. They often spent the night on the floor of Peale's Museum, taking turns sleeping under Charles Willson Peale's celebrated mammoth skeleton.

In 1818 Say traveled to Georgia and Florida with several other academy members, using a copy of William Bartram's *Travels* as their guide. The group apparently made few discoveries, although Say noted that Florida was "abounding in insects." The following year Say was invited—on Nuttall's recommendation—to be the zoologist on the U.S. Army-sponsored Long expedition to explore the Arkansas River and the Rocky Mountains. Despite hardships as severe as those Nuttall was experiencing in his separate western journey (Nuttall had proposed himself as botanist on the Long expedition but was not chosen), Say returned with an enormous collection of specimens, including thousands of insects that he classified for his ongoing study of American entomology.

Thomas Say

Entomologist Thomas Say, wearing his uniform from the first Long expedition, in an 1819 portrait by his friend Charles Willson Peale. An expert on North American insects, Say also published a pioneering study of shells.

BORN

June 27, 1787
Philadelphia, Pennsylvania

DIED

October 10, 1834
New Harmony, Indiana

EDUCATION

Westtown Friends' School

MAJOR INTERESTS

Insects; shells

ACCOMPLISHMENTS

Considered the father of American entomology (insect studies); author of *American Entomology* (3 volumes, 1824–28) and *American Conchology* (6 volumes, 1830–34); cofounder, Philadelphia Academy of Natural Sciences (1812); professor of natural history, University of Pennsylvania; curator, American Philosophical Society; cofounder, New Harmony, Indiana

HONORS

Elected a fellow of the Linnean Society of London

"[Florida is] a promised land not flowing with milk and honey but abounding in insects which are unknown . . . if they remain unknown I am determined it shall not be my fault."

—from a letter to a friend

Back in Philadelphia, Say's professional reputation was now established. He and Nuttall lectured together at the academy on their collecting travels, and in 1821 Say was made curator of the American Philosophical Society. The following year the two friends went their separate ways as Nuttall joined the faculty at Harvard while Say was appointed a professor of natural history at the University of Pennsylvania, where his uncle William Bartram had been named professor of botany 40 years earlier.

Say left Philadelphia briefly in 1823 to join a second Long expedition, this time to the upper Minnesota River, and then returned to complete work on the first volume of *American Entomology; or Descriptions of the Insects of North America*, which was published in 1824; the second volume appeared in 1825, the third in 1828. As the title suggests, Say's work was descriptive, not analytical: he named and described the insect forms he had collected, but did not offer

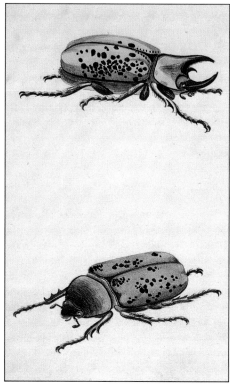

Artist and naturalist Charles Le Sueur illustrated Say's *American Entomology,* which included these engravings of a butterfly (left) and beetles.

any accounts of their habits or life histories, perhaps because of his limited formal education. Nevertheless, *American Entomology* stands as a pioneering work in insect studies and was praised by later generations of zoologists for its accuracy.

In 1825 Say, along with two fellow academy members, geologist William Maclure and French naturalist Charles Le Sueur, joined the British reformer Robert Owen in establishing the community of New Harmony, Indiana. Here he completed *American Entomology* and also worked on another pioneering book, *American Conchology* (six volumes, 1830-34), a study of shells. Charles Le Sueur engraved the illustrations for *Conchology,* which were drawn by another member of the community, Lucy Way Sistaire, who became Say's wife.

Say spent the remainder of his life in New Harmony, leaving only to travel in Mexico with Maclure in early 1828. He had always been sickly and after the Mexican trip was continually in poor health until his death in 1834. Lucy Say donated her husband's vast collections to the Academy of Natural Sciences, which elected her its first woman member in 1841.

FURTHER READING

Say, Thomas. *The Complete Writings of Thomas Say on the Entomology of North America.* 1859. Reprint. Salem, N.H.: Ayer, 1978.

"Say, Thomas." In *Dictionary of American Biography.* Vol. 8. New York: Scribners, 1964.

Stroud, Patricia Tyson. *Thomas Say, New World Naturalist.* Philadelphia: University of Pennsylvania Press, 1992.

Weiss, Harry B., and Grace M. Ziegler. *Thomas Say, Early American Naturalist.* Springfield, Ill.: Charles Thomas, 1931.

Charles Lyell

A STORY FOUND IN ROCKS

Geologist Charles Lyell made important discoveries about the origins of the Earth that helped his friend Charles Darwin formulate his theory of evolution.

Around the time that Thomas Say began collecting beetles and butterflies in the Pennsylvania countryside, a small boy in England, 10 years his junior, was also discovering the world of insects. Lying in a sickbed for three months during 1808, young Charles Lyell turned for distraction to his father's books on entomology and discovered a hobby that he pursued throughout his youth. Only as a young man, on holiday with his family, did he find a subject that interested him even more than bugs: the study of geology.

Lyell had been born in 1797 on his father's estate in Scotland, the eldest of a family that grew to include 10 children. When Lyell was still an infant, his father leased another estate in the south of England, near Southampton and adjacent to New Forest, where Lyell and his brothers and sisters had, as he later wrote, an idyllic upbringing. Young Lyell was sent to several private schools but did not excel in his studies; he preferred capturing insects and pressing them between the pages of his schoolbooks.

Lyell included engravings of shell fossils, which he examined to determine the age of the Earth, in his *Principles of Geology*.

As he matured, however, Charles Lyell began to read the books he had formerly used to preserve beetles and butterflies, and by 1816 he had learned enough to be admitted to Oxford University, where he concentrated on classical literature. Family trips during school vacations to remote areas of the British Isles inspired him to change his hobby: instead of looking for bugs he now paid close attention to the different rock formations he saw. During his first European tour, in 1818, he was intrigued—like the young Buffon, nearly a century before—by Earth's geological variations, particularly in Switzerland, where he made extensive notes on glaciers.

Back at Oxford, Lyell pursued both his degree and his interest in geology. Upon graduation in 1819, he had established such a reputation as an amateur geologist that he was elected a fellow of both the Geological Society and the Linnean Society. Nevertheless, Lyell still did not consider geology as a career. He remained at Oxford to receive a master's degree in classics, then moved to London to study law.

Lyell might have abandoned his time-consuming hobby if his eyesight had not been poor. He suffered from severe eyestrain, however, and doctors recommended that he alternate his heavy reading schedule with travel, thus giving him opportunities to continue his geological investigations. He traveled widely in Britain and on the Continent, talking with leading scientists, including Humboldt and Cuvier. By the time Lyell was admitted to the bar, in 1825, he was beginning to write scientific papers and reviews for publication in scholarly journals.

Through his reading, Lyell had become familiar with the theories of Lamarck, James Hutton, and William Smith. He dismissed Lamarck's ideas of human evolution, but did believe that "the earth is quite as old as he supposes." Lyell also agreed with Hutton and Smith that Earth had formed as a continuous series of geologic actions that were still in progress, rather than—as Buffon had believed—an ancient succession of catastrophes.

Lyell devoted more and more time to his scientific hobby. In 1828, assured of a modest but sufficient income from his well-to-do family, he gave up his law practice to pursue the study of geology full time and to write a book. In May of that year Lyell embarked on an expedition through Europe with an older Scottish friend, Sir Roderick Murchison, and Murchison's wife.

Traveling through France, Switzerland, and Italy, Lyell made geological observations while Murchison handled the details of their travel; Mrs. Murchison, an artist, made sketches and labeled specimens that Lyell collected.

"I hope and believe that the discovery and propagation of every truth, and the dispelling of every error, tends to improve and better the condition of man, though the act of reforming old opinions and institutions causes so much bitter pain and misery."

—from *Life, Letters and Journals of Sir Charles Lyell* (1881)

During the nine-month trip, which included extensive explorations of Alpine glaciers and Italy's volcanoes, Lyell determined that his book would set forth the *principles* of geology, not merely describe geological formations. The basis of those principles was his belief that Earth was in a continuous process of change.

Lyell returned to London in February 1829 and began writing the book that he entitled *Principles of Geology*; he also became an active participant in meetings of the Geological Society. There he found supporters of his theory and argued against other members who still clung to versions of Buffon's notion of successive catastrophes. The first volume of the *Principles* was published in July 1830 and was so successful that a second edition was issued at the same time as the second volume in December 1831; the third and final volume was published in April 1833.

In Lyell's own words, the *Principles* offered "a systematic account . . . of the operations of inorganic causes, such as rivers, springs, tides, currents, volcanoes, and earthquakes; the effects of all being particularly considered, with a view to illustrate geological phenomena." By studying the natural forces on Earth today, Lyell argued, we could explain what had happened in the past. But geological changes occurred slowly, over time. The evidence of layers of geological formations could mean only that Earth was far, far older than anyone had yet imagined—a conclusion that was applauded by many but still denied by those who adhered to the orthodox beliefs of the Christian church, including many faculty members and clergy at Oxford and Cambridge universities. Reconciling scientific discoveries with religious beliefs would become the leading intellectual issue of the 19th century.

Despite his detractors, Lyell, only in his mid-30s, was regarded as a distinguished member of the scientific community, in Europe and North America—where the *Principles* had been favorably reviewed—as well as Great Britain. As each edition of his work sold out, Lyell revised the text, so that the *Principles* became an up-to-date encyclopedia of geological knowledge. To gather material for revisions, Lyell traveled widely, often accompanied and assisted by his wife, Mary, whose father was also a geologist. His second book, *Elements of Geology*, a handbook of paleontology (the scientific study of past geological periods through their fossil remains), was published in 1838; like the *Principles*, it was also published in revised editions, six during Lyell's lifetime.

In 1841–42 Lyell made his first visit to North America at the invitation of the Lowell Institute in Boston. There he gave a series of lectures so popular that he was asked to repeat them. Lyell traveled extensively in the United States and Canada, visiting major cities as well as studying geological formations and taking extensive notes.

The material Lyell collected on this first North American trip became the basis for a dozen scientific papers and a two-volume work called *Travels in North America*, which included Lyell's comments on the continent's natural

Charles Lyell

BORN

November 14, 1797
Forfarshire, Scotland

DIED

February 22, 1875
London, England

EDUCATION

B.A., M.A., Oxford University; studied law in London

MAJOR INTEREST

Geology

ACCOMPLISHMENTS

During extensive travels in Europe and North America, made geological studies showing that Earth's surface changed over time; laid groundwork for Darwin's theory of evolution; books include *Principles of Geology* (3 volumes, 1830–33), *Elements of Geology* (1838), *Travels in America* (2 volumes, 1845), and *The Geological Evidences of the Antiquity of Man* (1863)

HONORS

Fellow, Royal Society of London; member, French Institute; knighted (1848) and made a baronet (1864) by Queen Victoria; recipient of the Copley Medal, highest award of the Royal Society (1858)

wonders as well as its cities and people. (Among other observations, he found Niagara Falls "more beautiful than I had expected," marveled at the cleanliness of New York City compared to London, and praised Americans for their courtesy to women.) The *Travels* was a popular success upon its publication in 1845, and in that same year he returned to North America for a second tour. That trip also resulted in a book, *A Second Visit to the United States of North America* (1849), written as a travel guide; it sold even more copies than *Travels*.

The success of his books enabled Lyell to live comfortably with his wife in England and to continue pursuing his geological research without the pressures of earning a living. He traveled regularly throughout Britain and on the Continent collecting data to update new editions of the *Principles* and *Essentials*, and made two brief return trips to North America; he also served several terms as president of the Geological Society, and actively participated in educational reform at Oxford, freeing it from church influence. In 1858 he received the Royal Society's highest award, the Copley Medal. Acclaimed as one of England's leading citizens, Lyell was knighted by Queen Victoria in 1848 and 16 years later was made a baronet.

Lyell congratulated Charles Darwin when his controversial *Origin of Species* was published in 1859; Darwin had drawn heavily on Lyell's geological discoveries in his book. But Lyell was cautious about giving full approval to the idea of evolution, and Darwin's work prompted him to do his own investigations into human origins. Now in his early 60s, he traveled through England, Belgium, and France, gathering data for the study he published in 1863 as *The Geological Evidence of the Antiquity of Man*, in which he appeared to be in limited agreement with Darwin on the principle of natural selection. Two years

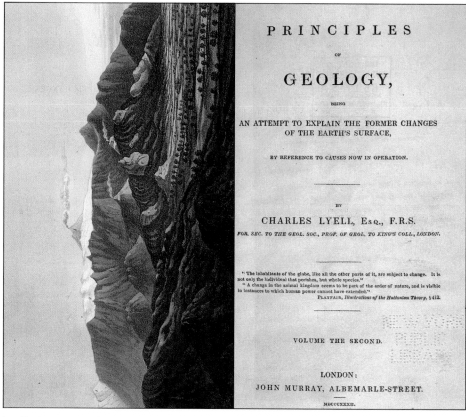

Lyell's *Principles of Geology* was one of the most influential books of the 19th century and was frequently reprinted during his lifetime. This is the first edition.

later, in a major revision of the *Principles of Geology*, he gave wholehearted approval to Darwin's theory and argued strongly for its acceptance—a bold act in the face of criticism that raged about Darwin's work.

Throughout his life, Lyell drew invaluable personal and professional assistance from his much younger wife, Mary. When she died suddenly in 1873, he was devastated. He died two years later, still revising the *Principles*, and was honored with burial in Westminster Abbey. There were many tributes to this amateur scientist who had become the most eminent geologist in the world, but Lyell would probably have been pleased the most by Darwin's: "The great merit of the *Principles*," he wrote, "was that it altered the whole tone of one's mind, and therefore . . . when seeing a thing never seen by Lyell, one yet saw it partially through his eyes."

FURTHER READING

Adams, Alexander B. "Reading the Earth's Story." In *Eternal Quest: The Story of the Great Naturalists*. New York: G. P. Putnam, 1969.

Bailey, E. B. *Charles Lyell*. New York: Doubleday, 1963.

Lyell, Charles. *Principles of Geology*. 3 vols. 1830-33. Reprint. Chicago: University of Chicago Press, 1991.

Lyell, Katherine M., ed. *Life, Letters, and Journals of Sir Charles Lyell, Bart.* 2 vols. 1881. Reprint. New York: AMS Press, 1983.

Wilson, L. G. *Charles Lyell: The Years to 1841*. New Haven: Yale University Press, 1972.

———, ed. *Sir Charles Lyell's Scientific Journals on the Species Question*. New Haven: Yale University Press, 1970.

George Perkins Marsh

A PROPHETIC VOICE FOR CONSERVATION

As a child in rural Vermont, George Perkins Marsh lived with a constant reminder of man's effect on nature: shortly before his birth, a forest fire had destroyed a large woods on a mountaintop near his home, and Marsh grew up watching trees slowly grow back amid the ashes. But the man who is now regarded as the father of the conservation movement in the United States did not really discover the natural world until middle age—and living in the Middle East, not New England.

In fact, from earliest childhood Marsh preferred books to outdoor play. His father, a lawyer, was among the leading citizens of Woodstock, Vermont; both of his parents were descendants of New England's earliest English settlers. Young

MAN AND NATURE;

OR,

PHYSICAL GEOGRAPHY

AS MODIFIED BY HUMAN ACTION.

BY

GEORGE P. MARSH.

"Not all the winds, and storms, and earthquakes, and seas, and seasons of the world, have done so much to revolutionize the earth as MAN, the power of an endless life, has done since the day he came forth upon it, and received dominion over it."—H. BUSHNELL, *Sermon on the Power of an Endless Life.*

NEW YORK:
CHARLES SCRIBNER, 124 GRAND STREET.
1864.

Marsh's prophetic book *Man and Nature* warned against human destruction of the environment in the name of "progress." Its readers included a young John Muir, who took Marsh's warnings seriously and became a celebrated conservationist.

George Perkins Marsh, shown here at work at his villa in Italy, was a celebrated diplomat and scholar who spoke at least 20 languages. Today he is revered as the founder of the modern conservation movement in the United States.

George was frail and spent hours in the family library, reading encyclopedias and teaching himself Greek and Latin. At 15 he entered Dartmouth College, having had only a few months of formal schooling, and graduated four years later at the top of his class. During his college years and into adulthood, Marsh taught himself both modern and ancient languages; in the course of his lifetime, he became fluent in at least 20.

After a few years of teaching at a local academy, Marsh studied law with his father and was admitted to the bar in 1825. He established a law practice in Burlington, Vermont, married, and tried his hand at several businesses, but nothing seemed to go well during his early years of adulthood. His businesses failed, his wife and older son died, and he found the legal profession boring. Marsh was really a scholar at heart, and perhaps as a way to heal the crushing disappointments of his life he devoted as much time as he could to philology, the study of languages.

Marsh's fortunes improved somewhat when he was appointed to the Vermont governor's executive council in 1835. During the late 1830s he also remarried happily and published his first book, an Icelandic grammar, which gained him national recognition as a scholar of Scandinavian languages. Serving on the governor's council gave Marsh a chance to use his intelligence in a political setting, and his success in this post was instrumental in getting him elected to the U.S. House of Representatives on the Whig ticket in 1842.

Marsh served two terms in the House (1843–47); his fellow congressmen included former President John Quincy Adams, with whom he had long discussions about the role of the federal government in resource preservation. As a member of Congress, Marsh opposed slavery and the Mexican War—as well as the acquisition of new western territories by the United States. Like his Vermont constituents, Marsh feared that these

undeveloped lands would prove financial burdens to the industrial East. One effort that he did support was a congressional act in 1846 that established the Smithsonian Institution, a U.S. government-sponsored organization "for the increase and diffusion of knowledge." The Smithsonian became the country's leading sponsor of scientific research, and its collections of animal, plant, and mineral specimens, as well as art objects and cultural artifacts, now number in the millions.

Marsh supported the Whig candidate Zachary Taylor in his successful bid for the U.S. Presidency in 1848, and Taylor rewarded him with an appointment as American ambassador to Turkey the following year. At the embassy in Constantinople, Marsh ably performed his professional duties despite limited funds and the political tensions that later erupted in the Crimean War (1853–56); he also had time to pursue scholarly interests.

During his years in the Middle East Marsh traveled throughout the region, from Cairo across the Sinai Desert to Jerusalem, studying its flora and fauna, its geology and weather. He shipped hundreds of specimens to the Smithsonian and also made a study of camels that led the U.S. Army to import the animals for use in its western campaigns.

The ruins of ancient civilizations that Marsh encountered again and again also drew his attention. Here he began to think about the ways in which human beings had changed the natural world to their own ends, but nearly a decade would pass before he began to assemble these reflections on paper.

When Franklin Pierce, a Democrat, was elected President in 1852, Marsh was forced to resign his ambassadorship. Back in Burlington, he found himself bankrupt; he had used his own funds to finance most of his expenses abroad, and his business ventures at home failed. Despite his desperate situation, Marsh

George Perkins Marsh

BORN

March 15, 1801
Woodstock, Vermont

DIED

July 23, 1882
Vallombrosa, Italy

EDUCATION

B.A., Dartmouth College

MAJOR INTERESTS

Law; diplomacy; philology; conservation

ACCOMPLISHMENTS

Member of U.S. Congress (1843–47); U.S. ambassador to Turkey (1849–52) and Italy (1861–82); fluent in 20 languages; his books include *The Origin and History of the English Language* (1862) and *Man and Nature* (1864), a pioneering work on conservation

HONORS

Received honorary doctorates from Harvard, Dartmouth, and the University of Delaware; elected to a number of learned societies, including Italy's scientific organization, Reale Accademia dei Lincei (1876)

doggedly forged ahead, paying his debts by teaching philology at the Lowell Institute in Boston and at Columbia University in New York, and turning his lectures into two books, *Lectures on the English Language* (1860) and *The Origin and History of the English Language* (1862), which became standard texts in the field.

Marsh also earned his living through two additional state appointments, serving on both the railroad and fish commissions. He spoke out sharply against monopoly (the control of an industry by a single company) and wrote a report about environmental abuses that had decreased the numbers of game fish in Vermont's lakes and rivers.

Marsh had joined the Republican party in 1856 and was a strong supporter of Abraham Lincoln in the 1860 presidential election. He was rewarded with another ambassadorship—this time to Italy, where he served for the remainder of his life. Again Marsh performed his diplomatic duties well, establishing a personal friendship with King Victor Emmanuel and arranging for regular shipments of Italian war materials to the Union Army during the Civil War. He traveled in the Italian Alps, studying glaciers, and continued to write scholarly articles on philology.

Not long after arriving in Rome, Marsh sat down to write the book that reflected his growing interest in the environment and conservation. *Man and Nature*, published in 1864, challenged the contemporary American enthusiasm for unhindered development. "Man is everywhere a disturbing agent," Marsh wrote, and then went on to detail ancient civilizations that had fallen into ruin as a consequence of human destruc-

tiveness. Nineteenth-century industrialization, he warned, was destroying our forests, our deserts, our lakes and streams, and the animal populations that lived in these environments. An early voice for ecology, Marsh argued that conservation and environmental protection were issues that extended to all parts of the natural world: no segment could be considered independent of another. In *Man and Nature* Marsh expressed views a century ahead of his time, warning of overpopulation, food shortages, and chemical pollutants, and championing solar power, land-use planning, wilderness areas, and game preserves.

Man and Nature was read widely in both Europe and America, and revised editions were published in 1874 and 1885. One of Marsh's avid readers was young John Muir, who had come across the book shortly after it first appeared and who was inspired by Marsh's words to become an active conservationist. By the early 20th century, however, *Man and Nature* had been largely forgotten. With the birth of the new environmental movement in the early 1960s the book was rediscovered and a new edition was printed by Harvard University Press in 1965.

George Perkins Marsh died quietly in Italy—on holiday at a forestry school in the mountains near Florence—in the summer of 1882. Appropriately, students from the school carried his coffin down the mountainside. His extensive publications in philology have long since been forgotten, but *Man and Nature*, called "the fountainhead of the conservation movement," is again read and applauded.

"It is time for some abatement in the restless love of change which characterizes us. . . . We have felled forest enough everywhere, . . . far too much. . . . The ravages committed by man subvert the relations and destroy the balance which nature had established . . . and she avenges herself upon the intruder by letting loose her destructive energies."

—from *Man and Nature* (1864)

FURTHER READING

Curtis, Jane. *The World of George Perkins Marsh, America's First Conservationist.* Woodstock, Vt.: Woodstock Foundation, 1982.

Lowenthal, David. *George Perkins Marsh: Versatile Vermonter.* New York: Columbia University Press, 1958.

Marsh, George Perkins. *Man and Nature.* 1864. Reprint. Edited by David Lowenthal. Cambridge: Harvard University Press, 1965.

Wild, Peter. "George Perkins Marsh: The Prophet from Vermont." In *Pioneering Conservationists of Eastern America.* Missoula, Mont.: Mountain Press, 1986.

Louis Agassiz

TEACHER

Contemporary accounts of Louis Agassiz, the Swiss-born naturalist and legendary professor of zoology at Harvard University, portray a remarkable man who combined great intelligence with the charm and persuasive skills of a showman like his contemporary, the American impresario P. T. Barnum. Throughout his life, Agassiz used those personal skills to his advantage—first to find the means to establish himself as a natural historian, and then to further the career that he ultimately chose for himself and believed was his most important work: teaching.

Agassiz knew even as a young boy that he wanted to study science, and he wrote in his notebook that he hoped to become "a scientific man of letters." His parents, a country parson and his wife, had other plans for Louis: after several years of secondary education, he was to earn his livelihood as a businessman. But at 16, Agassiz, with the backing of his

Zoology professor Louis Agassiz was photographed during a lecture at Harvard University in the 1860s.

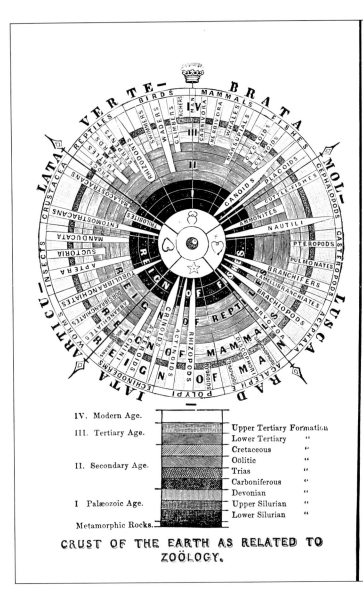

PRINCIPLES OF ZOÖLOGY:

TOUCHING

THE STRUCTURE, DEVELOPMENT, DISTRIBUTION,
AND NATURAL ARRANGEMENT

OF THE

RACES OF ANIMALS, LIVING AND EXTINCT

WITH NUMEROUS ILLUSTRATIONS.

PART I.
COMPARATIVE PHYSIOLOGY.

FOR THE USE OF SCHOOLS AND COLLEGES.

BY

LOUIS AGASSIZ AND A. A. GOULD.

REVISED EDITION.

BOSTON:
GOULD AND LINCOLN,
59 WASHINGTON STREET.
NEW YORK: SHELDON AND COMPANY.
CINCINNATI: GEO. S. BLANCHARD.
1860.

IV. Modern Age.

III. Tertiary Age. — Upper Tertiary Formation
— Lower Tertiary "
— Cretaceous "
II. Secondary Age. — Oolitic "
— Trias "
— Carboniferous "
— Devonian "
I. Palæozoic Age. — Upper Silurian "
— Lower Silurian "

Metamorphic Rocks.

CRUST OF THE EARTH AS RELATED TO ZOÖLOGY.

A diagram of the Earth's crust from Agassiz's *Principles of Zoology,* one of the most popular college textbooks in the 19th century. Along the outer ring are the four divisions of the animal kingdom advanced earlier in the century by Georges Cuvier: *vertebrata* (vertebrates), *mollusca* (mollusks), *radiata* (radiates), and *articulata* (articulates).

teachers and a physician uncle, got them to agree to send him to the University of Lausanne to study zoology. After one year there, the enthusiastic Agassiz talked his parents into letting him attend medical school at the University of Zurich.

Agassiz had no intention of being a physician, but as a medical student he could ground himself in the sciences of zoology, anatomy, and physiology. Continuing to let his parents think that he was pursuing a medical career and needed more prestigious schooling, he transferred to the University of Heidelberg in 1826 and to the University of Munich a year later. His parents, who were paying for his schooling from their meager funds, reluctantly supported him.

In addition to his charm and powers of persuasion, Agassiz had a gift for seizing every opportunity for advancement. Trying to find a field in which he could readily distinguish himself, he quickly determined that no one in Munich specialized in ichthyology, the study of fish. He had enjoyed fishing as a young boy; why not become an ichthyologist? Off he went to the market to gather specimens, which he brought home to dissect and examine; in a short time he had established himself as the university's expert on fish. A year after his arrival he had published his first book, a descriptive catalog of fish that a professor had collected in Brazil. Seeing still another way to gain recognition, he dedicated it to Baron Cuvier and sent a copy to the elderly but still influential scientist at the Jardin des Plantes. Cuvier responded with thanks and promised to use some of the material in his studies.

By 1830 Agassiz had earned both a doctorate in the natural sciences and a medical degree at the University of Munich. Pursuing his dream of becoming a scientific man of letters, he decided to write a major work on fish fossils. He did research while he lived at his parents' home in Switzerland for a year, then talked his father and other family members into paying for further study in Paris. At the Jardin des Plantes he met Cuvier, who was so impressed with Agassiz that he gave the young man his own fish collections, including fossil specimens, notes, and drawings.

Agassiz's arrival in Paris coincided with the dispute between Cuvier and Geoffroy Saint-Hilaire over Lamarck's theories about the interrelatedness of animal species. Agassiz revered Cuvier and sided with him; for the rest of his life he stubbornly refused to recognize any relationship between fossil specimens from different periods.

The sudden death of Cuvier in May 1832 was a great loss for Agassiz—but he had already ensured his further financial support and professional advancement by calling on Alexander von Humboldt. The baron, as he had done with so many needy students, gave Agassiz money and also arranged for a teaching appointment at a new secondary school in the Alpine region of Neuchâtel, then under Prussian rule.

Agassiz proved to be a popular teacher and was also able to continue work on his book, *Recherches sur les poissons fossiles* (*Investigations of Fish Fossils*), which he published over a 10-year period beginning in 1833. The book described, classified, and illustrated all known fossil fish from collections throughout Europe, and introduced readers to 1,700 different species that swam in ancient seas. Humboldt enthusiastically promoted the book—on his

recommendation subscriptions were sold that paid for its publication—and its author became known to the scientific community throughout Europe and England. *Recherches sur les poissons fossiles* expressed the conservative point of view that would characterize all of his later writing: no relationship existed between species; each had been a separate creation.

As new folios of *Recherches sur les poissons fossiles* were issued, Agassiz turned his attention to another area of natural history: the study of glaciers. Observations of the Aar and other glaciers and their continuing movements led him to develop his theory of the Ice Age: Europe had once been covered by an enormous glacier, a giant sheet of moving ice that swept along everything in its path, creating geological formations and phenomena that could still be observed—moraines, gravel ridges, scattered boulders. Agassiz presented his theory in what many consider his most important work, *Études sur les glaciers* (*Studies of Glaciers*, 1840), and it received wide acceptance among geologists, most notably Charles Lyell.

Besides his work on fossil fish and glaciers, Agassiz also published books and monographs on other subjects, including freshwater fish and mollusks. In Neuchâtel he had set up his own publishing house and staffed it with scientists and illustrators; he devoted much of his attention to this enterprise, neglecting his family. He had married in 1833, the year he settled in Neuchâtel, and fathered three children. Tensions increased between Agassiz and his wife as his professional life consumed his time, energy, and money. Most of what he earned was spent on more specimens, more assistants; little was left for Mrs. Agassiz to manage her household while her husband enjoyed his role as a leading citizen and famous scientist. In 1845, exhausted and ill, she left him, taking their children to live with her family.

Agassiz knew how to raise money,

Louis Agassiz

BORN

May 28, 1807
Motier, Switzerland

DIED

December 14, 1873
Cambridge, Massachusetts

EDUCATION

Attended universities of Lausanne, Zurich, and Heidelberg; Ph.D., M.D., University of Munich

MAJOR INTERESTS

Zoology; geology

ACCOMPLISHMENTS

Made extraordinary contributions to the study of extinct fish and glaciers; revolutionized the teaching of natural history in the United States; professor of zoology, Harvard University, 1847–73; established Museum of Comparative Zoology at Harvard; cofounder, American Association for the Advancement of Science and National Academy of Sciences; published works include *Recherches sur les poissons fossiles* (1833–43), *Études sur les glaciers* (1840), and *Contributions to the Natural History of the United States* (4 volumes, 1857–62)

HONORS

Elected to Royal Society of Edinburgh, Royal Society of London, American Academy of Arts and Sciences, and Philadelphia Academy of Natural Sciences; received Copley Medal from Royal Society of London; received Prix Cuvier and Monthyon Prize from French Academy of Sciences

Agassiz's reputation as a zoologist was established by his book *Recherches sur les poissons fossiles (Investigations of Fish Fossils),* published in several volumes between 1833 and 1843. These hand colored engravings of fossilized fish were included in the first edition.

but he was not skilled at managing it. The publishing house headed toward collapse, and Agassiz looked for more opportunities—this time in America. He announced that he would travel to the United States "for a visit." To pay for the trip he appealed to Humboldt, who got him a grant from the king of Prussia; Agassiz himself secured an invitation from the Lowell Institute in Boston to give a series of lectures. In the fall of 1846 he said good-bye to friends and family and sailed to America; he never returned to Europe.

Agassiz discovered his true calling as a lecturer: he had been born to teach. His talks in Boston were greeted enthusiastically and his reputation quickly spread; he was invited to speak in Charleston, South Carolina, and during his first months in America gave public lectures on natural history in other cities along the east coast. Everywhere Agassiz was warmly greeted: he was poised and charming, and his central message—that all life had been specifi-

cally created for a purpose by God, and that man was God's highest creation—was embraced by his audience.

Settling outside of Boston in Cambridge, Massachusetts, the home of Harvard University, Agassiz established a "research center" and brought over many of his old assistants and illustrators from Neuchâtel. By September 1847, less than a year after his arrival in America, he had skillfully managed his appointment to a newly created professorship in zoology at Harvard. Agassiz became a popular teacher who emphasized direct observation of nature rather than the use of textbooks, and he inspired many of his students to become teachers themselves. The joy and security that he found at Harvard remained with him for the rest of his life.

In 1848 Agassiz published his first book in America, *Principles of Zoology,* which soon became a popular text; 16 editions were printed during Agassiz's lifetime. In 1850 he remarried—his first wife had died of tuberculosis in

"The study of nature has one great object . . . : to trace the connection between all created beings, to discover, if possible, the plan according to which they have been created, and to search out their relation to the great Author."

—from *Methods of Study in Natural History* (1863)

Switzerland—and eventually his three children came to America to live with him. The new Mrs. Agassiz, Elizabeth Cabot Cary, 15 years younger than her husband, was also interested in science; she helped him organize his work and founded a secondary school for young women that gave the Agassiz family an additional source of support.

Agassiz continued his research on fish, exploring the eastern coastal waters and leading an expedition to the Great Lakes. Under his direction and through his talent for fund-raising, the Museum of Comparative Zoology was established at Harvard. Agassiz also found time to write a number of papers and books, most notably *Contributions to the Natural History of the United States* (four volumes, 1857-62), which was well-received by the general public but disappointed the scientific community for its defense of the increasingly outmoded idea that all species had been specially created.

The publication of Charles Darwin's *Origin of Species* in England in 1859 had quickly set off a debate on evolution throughout the Western world. Many faculty members at Harvard supported Darwin; Agassiz predictably denounced him. As his opposition grew, his scientific reputation declined—but his popularity outside of academic circles was greater than ever before. During the early 1860s, he traveled along the Eastern Seaboard, giving a series of lectures to large, appreciative audiences on his opposition to Darwin. The lectures were later published in the magazine *Atlantic Monthly*, and then issued as a book, *Methods of Study in Natural History* (1863), which became a best-seller.

Agassiz's later years were marred by quarrels with many of his colleagues, often over petty matters. He devoted most of his energies to "his" museum, raising funds and enlarging its collections. In 1865-66 he traveled with his wife to Brazil, bringing back more than 80,000 specimens; he and Elizabeth Agassiz later coauthored a book about their journey, which included further refutations of Darwinism. In 1871 Agassiz embarked on a yearlong trip to California, sailing around South America and stopping at Darwin's own "laboratory," the Galapagos Islands, where, once again, he claimed to find no evidence to support the theory of evolution.

Agassiz spent the last year of his life establishing a natural history institute for schoolteachers on an island off the Massachusetts coast and preparing more lectures opposing Darwinism. At his death in December 1873 he was widely mourned. Boston newspapers reported the news in editions edged in black; Agassiz had been one of the city's favorite citizens for more than a quarter of a century. Harvard suspended classes on the day of his funeral. Even faculty members with whom he had quarreled acknowledged that this Swiss émigré had done more than anyone to encourage the teaching of natural history in America.

For his gravestone, Agassiz's friends and family had a large boulder brought from the Aar glacier on which they carved his epitaph, a single word: "Teacher."

FURTHER READING

Adams, Alexander B. "The Teacher from Switzerland." In *Eternal Quest: The Story of the Great Naturalists*. New York: G. P. Putnam, 1969.

Agassiz, Elizabeth Cary, ed. *Louis Agassiz: His Life and Correspondence*. 2 vols. Boston: Houghton Mifflin, 1886.

Agassiz, Louis. *Essay on Classification*. 1857. Reprint. Edited by Edward Lurie. Cambridge: Harvard University Press, 1962.

———.*The Intelligence of Louis Agassiz: A Specimen Book of Scientific Writings.* Selected by Guy Davenport. 1963. Reprint. Westport, Conn.: Greenwood Press, 1983.

———. *Lake Superior: Its Physical Character*. 1850. Reprint. Salem, N.H.: Ayer, 1970.

———. *Methods of Study in Natural History*. 1863. Reprint. Salem, N.H.: Ayer, 1970.

"Agassiz, Louis." In *Dictionary of American Biography*. Vol. 1. New York: Scribners, 1964.

Lurie, Edward. *Louis Agassiz: A Life in Science*. Chicago: University of Chicago Press, 1960; abridged ed., 1967.

———. *Nature and the American Mind: Louis Agassiz and the Culture of Science*. Canton, Mass.: Watson Publishing/Science History Publications, 1974.

Tharp, Louise. *Adventurous Alliance: The Story of the Agassiz Family of Boston*. Boston: Little, Brown, 1959.

Charles Darwin

THE QUIET
REVOLUTIONARY

Charles Darwin shares his birth date—February 12, 1809—with another famous man in history, Abraham Lincoln. However, unlike Lincoln, who was born into poverty on the American frontier, Charles Darwin had parents who were wealthy and well-educated, and expected great achievements from this son of a distinguished family.

His grandfather Erasmus Darwin had been a prominent 18th-century scientist and poet; his mother was a daughter of Josiah Wedgwood, a famous English potter; his father was an energetic physician, writer, and amateur naturalist. By Charles's teenage years, however, his family had concluded that he was destined only for a mediocre future. His father thought he was stupid and lazy, and he was constantly criticized by his older sister, Caroline, who tried to teach him at home in place of their mother, who was ill for many years. After Mrs. Darwin's death, when Charles was eight, he was sent to several local schools, where, to no one's surprise, he was an indifferent student.

In 1825, Darwin's father, desperate for his son to have a profession, sent Charles to the University of Edinburgh to study medicine with his older brother. But Darwin was bored by his medical studies, too; he was more interested in collecting fish and plant specimens along the coast with several friends who were marine biologists. He also liked to hunt birds, and began to keep careful records of every species he had shot down—the first hint of his future activity as a collector. After two years, he gave up medical school; having learned that he would probably inherit enough money to live comfortably, he decided to do nothing more than become a sportsman. His father, however, insisted that he train for another profession. Becoming a clergyman seemed the only remaining choice.

Because ministers in the Church of England needed a college degree, Charles had to get university training. With the help of a tutor Dr. Darwin had hired for his son, Charles was able to pass the entrance examinations to Cambridge and enrolled there as a student in 1828. Again, he was an undistinguished student, but his interest in natural history began to expand. At Cambridge he became a beetle collector, and was befriended by several science professors, including the geologist Adam Sedgwick, who took him along on several field trips and introduced him to Charles Lyell's *Principles of Geology*. He discovered Humboldt's *Voyage* and was fascinated by the German baron's travels in Latin America.

After graduating from Cambridge in 1831 Darwin made plans to visit the sites of Humboldt's explorations in Tenerife, but then some friends recommended him for the position of naturalist on a government surveying ship, the H.M.S. *Beagle*, sailing around the world. The job hardly seemed worth pursuing: the voyage was only routine, the boat was uncomfortable and run down, and Darwin would receive no salary. In fact, other naturalists had turned down the offer. Understandably, Darwin's father was opposed: "Find me one intelligent man who approves of your going on this venture, and I'll give my consent," he said. Charles turned to his grandfather Josiah Wedgwood—who convinced the older Darwin that his son would be missing a great opportunity.

The *Beagle* left England on December 31, 1831, with the inexperienced Charles Darwin aboard, beginning a five-year voyage that would become one of the most famous in history. Stopping first at the Cape Verde Islands, the ship continued across the Atlantic to South America, making several stops along the eastern coast, then passing through the Strait of Magellan into the Pacific and up the western coast. Darwin was fascinated by what he saw: strange geological formations, unusual animals and fossil specimens, native peoples who seemed far different from Englishmen.

Often Darwin was able to remain on land for days at a time while the *Beagle* sailed to survey the offshore waters; this was especially welcomed by him, because he suffered acutely from seasickness. He spent considerable time studying the geology of each region he visited, and collected hundreds of crates of rocks, plants, and animals that he shipped back to England.

Throughout the voyage Darwin kept a journal of his experiences; he also recorded thousands of observations in a series of notebooks. He was increasingly fascinated by the variety of plant and animal life that he saw and slowly came to realize that living things could not have all been created at once but had instead developed over millions of years. How had this evolution come about? When the *Beagle* arrived in the Galapagos Islands in September 1835,

Darwin was presented with a living laboratory to develop his theory.

The Galapagos are a cluster of volcanic islands lying 600 miles west of the South American coast, along the equator. Their inhabitants were nearly all birds and reptiles; many, such as iguanas and giant tortoises, were found nowhere else in the world yet resembled species found on the South American continent. Had these animals once crossed over from the mainland by a land bridge that no longer existed? Darwin rejected that idea because other, different animals would have also used it.

Charles Darwin's family thought he was slow-witted and destined for a life of mediocrity. Largely self-trained as a naturalist, Darwin proved them wrong when he published *On the Origin of Species,* the most influential book of the 19th century.

During his visit to the Galapagos Islands, Darwin counted 13 different species of finch, including this large ground finch. He wondered why there were so many—and finally concluded that each "had been taken and modified for different ends." This notion of adaptation and survival formed the basis for Darwin's theory of evolution.

He was also puzzled by the fact that different species existed on different islands: "I never dreamed," he later wrote, "that islands about fifty to sixty miles apart, placed under a quite similar climate, would have been differently tenanted."

The *Beagle* continued its journey westward in October 1835. Throughout the remainder of the trip, Darwin concentrated primarily on geology, particularly on the formation of ocean reefs. Arriving back in England a year later, he began sorting his notes and specimens and preparing for publication the journal he had kept of his trip; it eventually appeared in 1839 as *Voyage of the Beagle*. Darwin also became an active participant in meetings of the Geological Society and a close friend of Charles Lyell.

As Darwin prepared his geological observations for publication, he still thought about the varied animal and plant life that he had seen, particularly in the Galapagos Islands, and wondered what caused some species to develop while others became extinct. In the fall of 1838 he took time from his writing to read an important and controversial new book, *An Essay on the Principle of Population as It Affects the Future Improvement of Society*, by the British economist Thomas Malthus. Malthus argued that the expansion of human population was restricted by such forces as disease, crime, and war. Perhaps, Darwin thought, a similar kind of selection process occurred in nature: as different species struggled to survive, "favourable variations would tend to be preserved, and unfavourable ones to be destroyed. The result of this would be the formation of new species. Here, then, I had . . . a theory by which to work." As he prepared and published books on coral reefs, barnacles, volcanoes, and other topics suggested by his long voyage, he also made notes on how new species developed, a process of research and thought that would continue for the rest of his life.

Darwin was greatly assisted by the woman he married in January 1839, his cousin Emma Wedgwood. After returning to England in 1836, he was ill for most of his life, and it was Emma who nursed him and maintained a quiet, comfortable household, where he could pursue his work without interruption. (Darwin's symptoms—headaches, nausea, insomnia, heart problems—have led modern researchers to believe that during the voyage of the *Beagle* he contracted Chagas' disease, transmitted by the bites of tropical insects.) In 1842 they moved from London and settled for the remainder of their lives in the rural village of Down, on the coast of Kent, eventually raising a family of 10 children.

At Down House, Darwin led a calm,

> *"There is grandeur in this view of life. . . . Whilst this planet has gone cycling on according to the fixed law of gravity, from so simple a beginning endless forms most beautiful and most wonderful have been, and are, being evolved."*

—from *Origin of Species* (1859)

Charles Darwin

BORN

February 12, 1809
Shrewsbury, England

DIED

April 19, 1882
Down, England

EDUCATION

Edinburgh University; B.A., Cambridge University

MAJOR INTEREST

Natural history

ACCOMPLISHMENTS

Founder of modern theory of evolution, set forth in his most famous book, *On the Origin of Species by Means of Natural Selection* (1859), and explained further in its sequel, *The Descent of Man* (1871); author of numerous other works, including *Voyage of the Beagle* (1839), the journal of his famous trip around the world aboard the H.M.S. *Beagle* (1831–36), and *The Structure and Distribution of Coral Reefs* (1842), the first modern explanation of reef formation

HONORS

Numerous awards from British and European scientific societies, including the Copley Medal of the Royal Society of London (1864); honorary doctoral degree from Cambridge University (1877)

scholarly life, alternating work with rest and exchanging letters on his developing theory with leading scientists of the day, including Charles Lyell and botanists Asa Gray and Joseph Hooker. As the years went by and Darwin still struggled to shape his notes and thoughts into the great book on evolution that he wanted to write, Lyell and others worried that another scientist might step forth at any time to present a similar theory.

Darwin was, after all, not the first person to propose that new species had evolved over time. He was familiar with Lamarck's theory, which was still being examined by contemporary scientists; even his grandfather Erasmus Darwin had written a book, *Zoonomia*, that advanced a theory of evolution. Nevertheless, Darwin was unprepared for a letter he received one day in June 1858 from a young naturalist named Alfred Russel Wallace who was living in the Molucca Islands of the Far East. Wallace had corresponded with Darwin a few times in the past; this time he enclosed a paper he had written. Would Darwin please read it and tell him his reaction?

Darwin was stunned to find that Wallace had described his own theory of evolution: animal and plant life had not all been created at once, or at separate times in history; instead, species had evolved—and continued to evolve—by an apparently random process of natural selection rather than through the external intervention or design of a divine force.

What should he do? Try to suppress Wallace's paper? Or let him publish it, and receive credit for a discovery that Darwin had made independently? An honorable man, Darwin knew that he could not deny Wallace's work. He turned to Lyell and Hooker for advice. Their solution was to make a joint presentation to the Linnean Society that included not only Wallace's work but documentation of Darwin's earlier independent investigations and conclusions. The historic paper, "On the Tendency of Species to Form Varieties; and on the Perpetuation of Varieties and Species by Natural Means of Selection," was read to the society on July 1, 1858, and published in the annual *Journal of the Linnean Society*. Amazingly, there was virtually no response to the first public proclamation of a theory that would be debated throughout the world.

With Lyell's and Hooker's encouragement, Darwin set to work on what he called an "abstract" of his theory, and Lyell talked a publisher into printing the resulting 500-page book. *On the Origin of Species by Means of Natural Selection, or the Preservation of Favoured Races in the Struggle for Life* was published on November 24, 1859. All 1,250 copies sold out on the first day, but the initial response was subdued. Favorable comments came from several scientists, including the biologist Thomas Huxley, who reviewed the book for the *Times* of London, but others, including Lyell himself, were cautious in voicing their opinions.

Two months later, when a second edition of *Origin of Species* was published, sales were equally brisk, but controversy quickly erupted. Attacking Darwin and his ideas were clergymen, as well as scientists—including his former mentor, geologist Adam Sedgwick— who still believed that divine will and not "natural selection" was responsible for the creation of life. Darwinism was argued at scientific meetings, challenged in church sermons, reported sensationally in newspapers and magazines, and soon oversimplified into a belief that man was directly descended from apes.

Darwin, however, had eminent defenders, most notably Huxley, Hooker, Gray, and eventually Lyell, who gave full support to Darwin's theory in the 10th edition of his *Principles of Geology* (1865). Indeed, a majority of eminent scientists, in England and Europe as well as in America, had become Darwin's supporters by the end of the decade that followed the publication of *Origin of Species*. As early as 1864 he achieved the formal recognition of the Royal Society, which awarded him its highest honor, the Copley Medal.

However, the popular debate over natural selection continued, particularly among supporters of orthodox religious views; even in the late 20th century, Darwin's ideas—often misinterpretations of them—have been criticized and rejected by new generations of creationists, those who believe that God directly intervened in the creation of every living species.

Despite continuing illness, Darwin published further, related writings, including *The Variation of Animals and Plants Under Domestication* (1868), an examination of plant and animal breeding, and *The Descent of Man* (1871), a sequel to the *Origin of Species* that traced the relationship of man to other animals. Among his numerous other works were a study of emotional expression in man and animals and five books on plant fertilization and growth.

Darwin published his last book, a study of vegetable mold, not long before his death in April 1882. He was honored with burial in Westminster Abbey and received tributes from around the world. The son who had been such a disappointment to his family as a young man had grown up to become one of the most distinguished figures in the history of science.

FURTHER READING

Adams, Alexander B. "The Great Discovery" and "Champions of the Cause." In *Eternal Quest: The Story of the Great Naturalists*. New York: G. P. Putnam, 1969.

Bowlby, John. *Charles Darwin: A New Life*. New York: W. W. Norton, 1991.

Darwin, Charles. *The Autobiography of Charles Darwin*. Edited by Nora Barlow [Darwin's granddaughter]. New York: Harcourt, Brace, 1958.

———. *The Collected Papers of Charles Darwin*. Edited by Paul H. Barrett. Chicago: University of Chicago Press, 1980.

———. *The Essential Darwin: Selections and Commentary*. Edited by Kenneth Korey. Boston: Little, Brown, 1984.

———. *On the Origin of Species by Natural Selection*. 1859. Reprint. Cambridge: Harvard University Press, 1964.

———. *On the Origin of Species by Natural Selection*. 1859. Abridged ed. Edited by Philip Appleman. New York: W. W. Norton, 1975.

de Camp, L. Sprague, and Catherine Crook de Camp. *Darwin and His Great Discovery*. New York: Macmillan, 1972.

Desmond, Adrian, and James Moore. *Darwin*. New York: Warner, 1992.

Farrington, Benjamin. *What Darwin Really Said*. Rev. ed. New York: Schocken Books, 1982.

Huxley, Julian, and H. B. D. Kettlewell. *Charles Darwin and His World*. New York: Viking, 1965.

Irvine, William. *Apes, Angels, and Victorians: The Story of Darwin, Huxley, and Evolution*. New York: McGraw-Hill, 1955.

Miller, Jonathan, and Borin Van Loon. *Darwin for Beginners*. New York: McKay, 1989.

Moorehead, Alan. *Darwin and the Beagle*. 1969. Revised and reprinted. New York: Penguin, 1979.

Stone, Irving. *The Origin: A Biographical Novel of Charles Darwin*. Garden City, N.Y.: Doubleday, 1980.

Von Hagen, Victor Wolfgang. "Charles Darwin." In *South America Called Them: Explorations of the Great Naturalists*. New York: Knopf, 1945.

Darwin's critics frequently accused him— incorrectly—of claiming that human beings had descended from apes. This cartoon from an 1871 British magazine depicts Darwin as an orangutan.

Asa Gray

DARWIN'S VOICE IN AMERICA

On a September morning in 1857, Charles Darwin sat in his study in Down, England, and wrote a letter to an American botanist at Harvard University named Asa Gray. Darwin had met Gray nearly two decades earlier, during the American's first visit to England, and had corresponded with him about North American and Asian plants. Darwin respected Gray, who had become the most eminent botanist in the United States, and wanted his opinion of a theory he had been trying to clarify for years.

The theory that Darwin outlined in his letter to Gray was, of course, the evolution of species by means of natural selection. The following year, when Darwin received a letter from another botanist, Alfred Russel Wallace, asking him to consider an identical theory, Darwin used a copy of his letter to Gray to prove that he had, independently, made the same discovery. And in 1859, when Darwin finally published his *Origin of Species*, Gray—who had replied two years earlier that he thought Darwin's theory had merit—was the first American to receive an advance copy. Gray became Darwin's staunch defender throughout the United States, giving speeches and writing

Asa Gray working in his study at Harvard University, where he founded the botany department in 1842. He taught for the rest of his life at Harvard, which became the seat of American botanical studies during the 19th century.

Gray was fascinated throughout his life by a flowering plant that he named *Shortia galacifolia*. As a young man, Gray had identified a dried specimen of the plant as a separate species; when he was in his early 70s *Shortia* was rediscovered in the Carolina mountains and he traveled there to see it bloom.

articles in support of Darwinism for the rest of his life.

Asa Gray's interest in plants began at an early age, a natural consequence of his rural upbringing. The eldest of eight children, Gray was born in 1810 to a prosperous farmer in Oneida County, New York. He attended area schools until the age of 15, when he was sent to Fairfield Academy in nearby Herkimer County. Here he had his first formal instruction in natural science and became especially interested in botany. He read everything the school library had on the subject, then bought a copy of Amos Eaton's best-selling *Manual of Botany for the Northern States* (1817) and used it to identify area plant species.

Gray continued his interest in botany during his four years at the academy and two additional years at its medical school, from which he graduated in January 1831 at the age of 20. But he had no intention of practicing medicine. Instead, he supported himself for five years as a high school teacher and spent vacations on botanical collecting expeditions in the eastern states, joining fellow botanist John Torrey of New York City. In 1834 Gray issued his first book, a handmade list of plants illustrated with actual dried specimens. Two years later Gray was appointed curator of the Lyceum of Natural History in New York and published his first textbook, *Elements of Botany;* the *Elements* was the first American botanical guide to use the natural, not the Linnean, system of classification and thus became a competitor of Amos Eaton's manual.

Gray's reputation was spreading, and in 1838 he was invited to become the first professor of botany at the University of Michigan. Before accepting the post he went on a yearlong trip to England and Europe, buying books for the university and also examining American plant specimens in herbariums abroad as part of his work with Torrey on their book, *Flora of North America* (two volumes, 1838–43). During his first visit abroad Gray also became acquainted with many leading scientists and naturalists, including Darwin.

Upon his return to America, Gray decided not to go to Michigan; instead he remained in New York to continue his work with Torrey on the *Flora,* the first volume of which had been well-received. He also made an extensive collecting trip to Virginia and North Carolina and worked on his *Botanical Text-Book* (later renamed *Structural Botany*), which was published in 1842; its accurate identifications and clear illustrations soon led to its acceptance as a standard work, and in later years it was reissued in a number of editions.

By now Asa Gray was a widely known and respected naturalist. In 1842, not yet 32 years old, he accepted an invitation from Harvard to become the Fisher Professor of Natural History and to establish the university's first botany department. Gray remained on the Harvard faculty until his death 46 years later, living with his wife in a house in the Botanical Garden formerly occupied by Thomas Nuttall. He corresponded with scientists throughout the world and traveled frequently, making five extended visits to Europe as well as several collecting trips to California, Mexico, and Florida.

Gray's professional accomplishments were astonishing and were made possible not only by his enormous intelligence and friendly nature but also by the perfect health he enjoyed throughout his life. He was a member of 66 scientific organizations, ranging from the Royal Society of London to the Polk County, Iowa, Agricultural Society. A founder of the National Academy of Sciences, he served as president of the American Association for the Advancement of Science, and for a decade (1863–73) as president of the American Academy of Arts and Sciences; he was also a regent of the Smithsonian Institution for many years. As the

Asa Gray

BORN

November 18, 1810
Sauquoit, New York

DIED

January 30, 1888
Cambridge, Massachusetts

EDUCATION

M.D., Fairfield Medical School
(Herkimer County, New York)

MAJOR INTEREST

Botany

ACCOMPLISHMENTS

Made extensive studies of the plants of North America; author of more than 350 books, monographs, and articles on botany, including *Manual of the Botany of the Northern United States, from New England to Wisconsin and South to Ohio and Pennsylvania Inclusive* (1848), commonly known as *Gray's Manual,* the standard work on the subject; professor of natural history at Harvard, where he established the university's botany department

HONORS

Honorary degrees from Oxford, Cambridge, and Edinburgh universities; elected president of the American Association for the Advancement of Science; fellow, Royal Society of London; elected member and president of American Academy of Arts and Sciences longtime editor of the *American Journal of Science*, he contributed numerous reviews, biographies, and news articles that together represent a history of botany in the second half of the 19th century. He was also a frequent contributor to the *Nation*, a leading journal of opinion, and to other periodicals for both scientific and general audiences.

Gray's publications during his lifetime included more than 350 books, monographs, and long articles, nearly all of them about the flora of North America. His most famous book was the *Manual of the Botany of the Northern United States*, first published in 1848. *Gray's Manual*, as it was called, was a considerably more comprehensive work than his earlier *Elements of Botany*. It quickly became a popular guide to American plants and is still recognized as the standard work on the subject; it has been reprinted in numerous editions.

In addition to his work on North American plants, Gray was also the first modern Western scientist to study the flora of Japan. At Gray's request, a naturalist named Charles Wright traveled with a U.S. Navy expedition to the Far East in the mid-1850s and brought back a collection of Japanese plants that matched specimens found only in the eastern part of North America. Gray concluded that the plants had once grown across the entire northern part of the continent but had been cut off from the West by glaciers. His monograph on the subject, published in 1859, established his reputation as a world-renowned botanist. Charles Darwin was particularly interested in Gray's findings, which illustrated his own theory of variation and adaptation in plant and animal life.

Gray spent his later years working on an enlargement of the *Flora of North America*, entitled *Synoptical Flora of North America*, which was published during the last decade of his life. He was also, of course, actively engaged in the debate over evolution. Darwin especially valued Gray's strong defense and support of his theory of natural selection because of Gray's own reputation as a religious man. Gray himself often publicly stated that he saw no conflict in accepting Darwinism while professing firm Christian beliefs, and even lectured at the Yale Divinity School on the theme of natural science and religion. His many articles in support of Darwin's theory were collected in a book called *Darwinia*, published in 1876, which was widely read.

On Gray's 75th birthday, in 1885, he was honored by 180 American botanists who presented him with a silver vase embossed with 13 plants that he had either named or studied closely. One of them was *Shortia galacifolia*, a plant he had identified and named nearly 50 years earlier, during his first trip to Europe.

Gray had found the dried specimen of the rare perennial at the Jardin des Plantes in Paris; it had been brought there by André Michaux from the Carolina mountains in the late 18th century. Gray, pronouncing the plant a unique species, named it in honor of a Kentucky botanist named Charles Wilkins Short. Back in America, Gray tried in vain to find other specimens of *Shortia*. For many years other botanists were unsuccessful in their search, and many concluded that Gray had misidentified another plant.

Then one day when Gray was in his early 70s, he learned that *Shortia galacifolia* had been found again in the Carolina mountains. Feeling vindicated at last, he journeyed to the spot to look for the first time upon living specimens of the plant he had named so many years before. It was one of the happiest moments of his long life.

"The harmony of Nature and its admirable perfection need not be regarded as inflexible and changeless. Nor need Nature be likened to a statue, or a cast in rigid bronze, but rather to an organism, with play and adaptability of parts, and life and even soul informing the whole."

—from "Sequoia and Its History," *Darwinia* (1876)

FURTHER READING

Dupree, A. Hunter. *Asa Gray*. Cambridge: Harvard University Press, 1959.

Gray, Asa. *Darwinia*. 1876. Reprint. Edited by A. Hunter Dupree. Cambridge: Harvard University Press, 1963.

————. *Manual of the Botany of the Northern United States* [*Gray's Manual*]. 1848. Reprint. Irvine, Calif.: Reprint Services Corporation, 1992.

"Gray, Asa." In *Dictionary of American Biography*. Vol. 4. New York: Scribners, 1964.

Henry David Thoreau

THE SAGE OF WALDEN POND

"I went to the woods because I wished to live deliberately, to front only the essential facts of life," wrote Henry David Thoreau in his classic work, *Walden*. For 26 months, from July 1845 to September 1847, Thoreau lived in a small house he had built himself on the shores of Walden Pond, a glacial lake a few miles south of Concord, Massachusetts. He ate local fruit and vegetables, planted beans, swam, read, wrote a book, and kept a journal in which he recorded observations of flora and fauna. The journal became the basis for *Walden; or, Life in the Woods* (1854), a collection of 18 essays that describe his experience.

Thoreau was not a trained naturalist; in fact, he was suspicious and even contemptuous of science, which he believed had complicated human lives more than it had enriched them. The Walden experiment was his attempt to prove that anyone could live simply, "free and uncommitted," for it was Thoreau's philosophy that "a man is rich in proportion to the number of things which he can afford to let alone." In the woods, far from people and "things," with only animals for company, Thoreau was comfortable and content.

Most of Thoreau's relatively short life—he died at the age of 44—was spent in the simple but beautiful surroundings of

Henry David Thoreau's essays about natural history earned him the title "father of American nature writing."

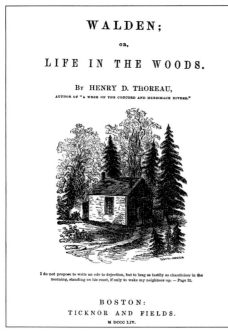

For the title page of the first edition of *Walden*, Thoreau chose a sentence from the text: "I do not propose to write an ode to dejection, but to brag as lustily as chanticleer in the morning, standing on his roost, if only to wake my neighbors up."

Concord, a village near Boston where he was born in 1817. The family had a small business—making pencils in a shed attached to their house—but were not especially prosperous. As a small boy, Thoreau enjoyed playing in the countryside with his mother's relatives and developed the attachment to Concord that kept him a resident there for most of his life.

Thoreau was sent to school at the local Concord Academy, where he did well enough to prepare for college. At Harvard University, which he entered at 16, he was a good student but went his own way, reading what he wished in the library rather than fulfilling class requirements. A famous line from *Walden* explains the path that Thoreau had already chosen for his life: "If a man does not keep pace with his companions, perhaps it is because he hears a different drummer."

When Thoreau graduated from Harvard in 1837 he had no particular career in mind. He tried teaching at the local grammar school but lasted only a few weeks. He made pencils with his father for a year, then started a school in Concord with his brother, John; its curriculum included field trips in the nearby countryside to study nature directly, apparently the first time such an approach had been used in American education. During vacations the two brothers traveled in the area observing plants and animals.

Their most memorable journey was a trip in September 1839 by canoe to Concord, New Hampshire, which Thoreau later wrote about during his stay at Walden Pond; the book was published two years later as *A Week on the Concord and Merrimack Rivers* (1849). John's worsening health led to the school's closing in 1841, and again Thoreau was out of a regular job. But this situation did not seem to trouble him: he had decided to become a "nature poet." In 1837 he had met the poet and essayist Ralph Waldo Emerson, who had moved to Concord two years earlier. Emerson suggested that he keep a journal, and also encouraged Thoreau to write about his observations of nature. Their friendship grew, and after the Thoreaus' school closed Emerson invited Henry to stay with his family.

For two years Thoreau lived in the Emerson household and was welcomed as a member of the poet's literary circle, which included Bronson Alcott (the father of Louisa May Alcott, author of the children's classic *Little Women*) and other eminent writers. The group sponsored a magazine called *The Dial*, which published Thoreau's poems as well as his first essay on nature, "The Natural History of Massachusetts" (July 1842). Despite this success he suffered a severe loss with the sudden death of his brother, John, from lockjaw in 1842.

Mourning his brother and seeking a wider audience for his writing, Thoreau moved to Staten Island, New York, in the spring of 1843 to be a tutor to the children of Emerson's brother William while he tried to sell articles and essays. He met leading literary figures but his efforts to publish his work were unsuccessful, and he missed being back home: as he wrote in a letter to his mother, "Methinks I should be content to sit at the back door in Concord, under the poplar tree, henceforth forever." By early 1844 he was home again, making pencils.

The idea for building a house at Walden Pond had occurred to Thoreau as early as December 1841, according to an entry in his journal. It may have been suggested by his visit to a Harvard classmate who had lived in a hut during the winter of 1841-42 at nearby Sandy Pond. By this time Thoreau had apparently given up any thought of marrying and having a family; he had been devastated in 1840 when a young woman to whom he had proposed marriage rejected him. In the spring of 1845, weary of pencil-making, Thoreau was ready to retreat into nature, where he could meditate, read, and write—and put into practice his belief in the value and possibility of living "free and uncommitted," as he later wrote.

Thoreau's sojourn at Walden Pond was interrupted only once: in July 1846, when he spent a night in the Concord jail for refusing to pay a poll tax (a tax, now outlawed, that citizens had to pay in order to vote). Although—to his annoyance—an aunt paid the tax for him and he was released the next morning, he wrote an essay, "Civil Disobedience," in which he defended the right of the individual conscience against the power of the majority: he had refused to pay the tax because of his opposition to slavery and the Mexican War. The essay was largely ignored when it was first published, in 1849; it was rediscovered in the late 19th century and today is celebrated as a classic.

"We need the tonic of wildness,—to wade sometimes in marshes where the bittern and the meadow-hen lurk, and hear the booming of the snipe; to smell the whispering sedge where only some wilder and more solitary fowl builds her nest, and the mink crawls with its belly close to the ground. . . . We can never have enough of nature."

—from "Spring," *Walden* (1854)

When he left Walden Pond in September 1847, Thoreau moved back to his father's house, then lived with the Emersons for a while. He continued to write essays and poems, and supported himself by making pencils, surveying, and collecting reptiles for Harvard's natural history department; after his father's death in 1859 the pencil business became his full-time occupation. His continual residence in Concord was interrupted only by excursions to Cape Cod, Maine, and eastern Canada; he was able to sell long essays about these trips to several magazines, and after his death they were collected and published in several books (*The Maine Woods*, 1864; *Cape Cod*, 1865; and *A Yankee in Canada*, 1866).

During his lifetime, Thoreau received little public recognition. *A Week on the Concord and Merrimack Rivers* sold only 220 of the 1,000 copies that were printed; the remainder were dumped unceremoniously on his doorstep by the printer. *Walden* was somewhat more successful, although it took five years to sell 2,000 copies.

Thoreau's fellow villagers—outside of Emerson's circle—considered him an eccentric failure. In his later years his passionate opposition to slavery and his service as a "conductor" on the Underground Railroad, helping slaves flee north into Canada, were looked upon with suspicion, as was his reverence for abolitionist John Brown and his public display of grief over Brown's hanging in 1859.

After Thoreau's death from tuberculosis in 1862, Emerson's efforts led to publication of many of his collected poems and essays and his increasing recognition by the end of the century. Today Thoreau is revered as a major American literary figure, as a symbol of conscience—and as the father of American nature writing. This fact was recognized by the Wilderness Society, a conservation organization founded in 1935, when it chose Thoreau's words as its motto: "In wildness is the preservation of the world."

FURTHER READING

Derleth, August William. *Concord Rebel: A Life of Henry David Thoreau*. Philadelphia: Chilton, 1962.

Krutch, Joseph Wood. *Henry David Thoreau*. New York: Sloane, 1948.

Lebeaux, Richard. *Young Man Thoreau*. Amherst: University of Massachusetts Press, 1977.

Thoreau, Henry David. *Cape Cod*. 1865. Reprint. New York: Penguin, 1987.

———. *H. D. Thoreau: A Writer's Journal*. 1906. Reprint. Edited by Laurence Stapleton. New York: Dover, 1960.

———. *The Maine Woods*. 1864. Reprint. New York: Penguin, 1988.

———. *Walden*. 1854. Reprint. New York: Random House, 1991.

———. *A Week on the Concord and Merrimack Rivers*. 1849. Reprint. East Orleans, Mass.: Parnassus Imprints, 1987.

EARTHKEEPERS

Henry David Thoreau

BORN
July 12, 1817
Concord, Massachusetts

DIED
May 6, 1862
Concord, Massachusetts

EDUCATION
A.B., Harvard University

MAJOR INTEREST
Nature writing

ACCOMPLISHMENTS
A leading American literary figure, considered the father of American nature writing; author of several classic works, including *A Week on the Concord and Merrimack Rivers* (1849), and *Walden; or, Life in the Woods* (1854), an account of his two years at Walden Pond, near Concord, Massachusetts

Alfred Russel Wallace

IN THE SHADOW
OF DARWIN

As one of eight children born to a poor librarian in a small English village, Alfred Russel Wallace knew from the time he was a small boy that he would not receive much formal education. The most that any of the Wallace children could expect was a few years at a local grammar school. The elder Wallace, however, filled his house with books and instructed the children himself when his funds were low. When Alfred was 14, he was sent from the family home to earn his own living as a surveyor, apprenticed to an older brother.

Out in the countryside day after day, Wallace became more and more interested in the natural world. He collected fossils and wildflowers, and taught himself simple astronomy. When he lost his job as a surveyor in 1844, he was able—despite his lack of schooling—to get a teaching job in Leicester. By day he taught mathematics, reading, and writing; at night and on holidays he read extensively from books in the town library, encouraged by the headmaster of the school who recommended titles to him. Humboldt's *Voyage* and Darwin's *Voyage of the Beagle* particularly excited him, and he vowed that someday he, too, would travel to remote parts of the world.

Alfred Russel Wallace in his later years. As a young naturalist traveling in the Far East, Wallace independently discovered the principle of natural selection that was also the basis for Charles Darwin's theory of evolution.

"It must strike everyone that the numbers of birds and insects of different groups, having scarcely any resemblance to each other, which yet feed on the same food and inhabit the same localities, cannot have been so differently constructed and adorned for that purpose alone."

—from *A Narrative of Travels on the Amazon and Rio Negro* (1853)

Another book he read during his years in Leicester was Thomas Malthus's *Essay on the Principle of Population*, but a decade would pass before Wallace seriously considered the implications of Malthus's theory.

In Leicester Wallace's interest in natural history was encouraged by a new friend, Henry Walter Bates, the son of a prosperous hosiery manufacturer in the town. Bates liked to collect insects and instructed Wallace in entomology; Wallace, in turn, taught Bates all the botany he knew. During a short visit to Paris in 1847, Wallace visited the Jardin des Plantes and was fascinated by the enormous collections of specimens. Back home, he went to the British Museum to look at the insects, and an idea began forming in his mind: given his interest in natural history, why not pursue a career as a naturalist? If institutions paid for specimens, then perhaps he and his friend Bates could finance a trip to South America by collecting for the British Museum. The museum approved their proposal, and they also found a private collector who agreed to purchase duplicate specimens. With their support assured, Wallace and Bates sailed to Brazil in April 1848.

Making their headquarters the port city of Belém, the two naturalists spent the next 16 months exploring the region of the Pará and Orinoco rivers and collecting butterflies and other flora and fauna that they shipped back to England. In August 1849 they decided to go on separate collecting trips in order to gather more specimens. For the next three years Wallace made a series of journeys along the Amazon, Negro, and Uaupés rivers, before returning to England in the late summer of 1852. Bates, meanwhile, remained in Brazil until 1859 and made extensive explorations of the Amazon valley.

Although he had sent many specimens back to England, Wallace took most of what he had collected, including many live birds and monkeys, aboard the *Helen* when it sailed from Belém in August 1852. En route home, the ship caught fire and to Wallace's great regret all of his specimens were destroyed. In London a small settlement from the insurance company provided immediate living expenses and allowed him to write a book about his journey; many years later, *A Narrative of Travels on the Amazon and Rio Negro* became a popular travel book, but when it was published in 1853 it attracted virtually no interest.

Still Wallace was determined to be a professional naturalist. His years in Brazil had matured him and led him to think more and more about the origins of the great variety of species he had seen and collected. There had to be some principle, he reasoned, that determined their forms. To further increase his knowledge, he attended meetings of entomological and zoological societies and became a frequent visitor to the natural history collections of the British Museum while he dreamed of exploring another remote area of the world.

Alfred Russel Wallace

BORN

January 8, 1823
Usk, England

DIED

November 7, 1913
Broadstone, England

EDUCATION

Self-educated

MAJOR INTEREST

Natural history

ACCOMPLISHMENTS

Codiscoverer, with Charles Darwin, of the principle of natural selection as the basis for evolution; made extensive explorations of South America and the South Pacific; author of numerous works, including *Contributions to the Theory of Natural Selection* (1870)

HONORS

Awarded the Darwin Medal by the Royal Society of London (1890); Darwin-Wallace Medal of the Linnean Society (1908); the Order of Merit by King Edward VII (1910)

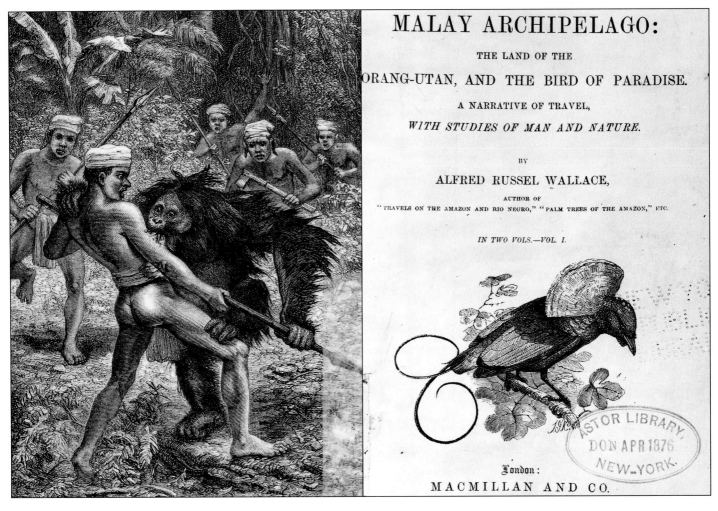

Wallace discussed evolution in a number of books and articles, including his most popular work, a travel narrative called *The Malay Archipelago,* first published in 1869.

Wallace had proved to himself during his years in Brazil that he could sell specimens he collected, but he needed to find a region that had not yet been thoroughly covered by naturalists. One such area was the Malay Archipelago of Southeast Asia. In early 1854 Wallace sailed to Singapore, arriving in April. Within two months he had amassed thousands of insects in the interior, including 700 different kinds of beetles, an amazing feat considering the constant danger he faced from tigers. "It was rather nervous work," he wrote later, "hunting for insects among the fallen trunks and old sawpits, when one of these savage animals might be lurking close by, waiting an opportunity to spring."

By the fall of 1854 Wallace had arrived in Sarawak, on the island of Borneo. When heavy rains prevented him from collecting, he began to assemble notes he had been making on the origin of species and submitted the resulting paper, "On the Law Which Has Regulated the Introduction of New Species," to the *Annals and Magazine of Natural History* in England, which accepted it for publication in 1855. Wallace's "law" was his belief that every species had come into existence coexisting with a related species that had been its predecessor—that is, no form of life had "appeared," or been created, spontaneously and independently. Henceforth, as he later wrote, "the question of *how* changes of species could have been brought about was rarely out of my mind."

Wallace thought about this question as he continued his collecting journey eastward through the archipelago. The lack of any response to his article had disappointed him; in 1857 he wrote directly to Darwin, who replied that in fact he had read it approvingly and discussed it with geologist Charles Lyell, who also agreed with Wallace. In February 1858, lying in bed recovering from an attack of tropical fever on Ternate, in the Molucca Islands, Wallace was suddenly reminded of the book he had read by Thomas Malthus many years earlier. Malthus had argued that the human population was constantly being reduced by crime, disease, and war; only those who were most fit survived. Could it be that the same principle of "the struggle for existence" and "the survival of the fittest" applied to all forms of life?

Rising from his bed, Wallace began to write a paper explaining his new theory; two days later he had finished "On the Tendency of Varieties to Depart Indefinitely from the Original Type." Quickly he wrote a covering letter and placed it with the paper into an envelope addressed to Charles Darwin in England. Four months later Darwin opened the envelope and discovered that Wallace had devised a theory similar to the one he had been trying to write about for years.

Charles Lyell and botanist Joseph Hooker advised Darwin that the fairest solution to the dilemma was to make both his and Wallace's findings public as soon as possible. Accordingly, Lyell and Hooker presented Wallace's paper and a summary of Darwin's own views at a meeting of the Linnean Society in London on July 1, 1858. Meanwhile, Wallace pursued his collecting as far east as New Guinea through "continual rain, continual sickness, and little wholesome food" while he nervously awaited word from Darwin.

Weeks later, the letter finally arrived; in it, Darwin explained the situation and the way it had been handled, and enclosed a similar note from Hooker. Instead of being upset and angry at the news of Darwin's own discovery, Wallace was pleased, even flattered, to hear that he, a virtually unknown naturalist, had come up with the same idea as a far more eminent man. A decade after Darwin published his *Origin of Species*, Wallace published his two essays together as *Contributions to the Theory of Natural Selection* (1870).

Wallace returned from the Far East in 1862 a fairly prosperous man, thanks to the sale of his collections. He had had enough of the discomforts of travel and exploration in primitive areas. He married and settled for the remainder of his life in rural Broadstone, in the south of England, where he gardened and wrote several books about the implications of evolution, including *Geographical Distribution of Animals* (1876). In *The Malay Archipelago,* published in 1869, he made an important distinction between the eastern and western islands of the archipelago, drawing what came to be known as Wallace's Line between them. Those animals west of the line were Oriental, those east of it Australian; neither group in any way resembled the other.

By the 1870s, Wallace had lost a great deal of money by investing in friends' businesses that ultimately failed, and was having a difficult time supporting his family, which now included two children. Darwin, hearing of his difficulties, organized a group of leading scientists to secure a government pension for Wallace. To make more money, Wallace accepted an invitation to lecture at the Lowell Institute in Boston in 1886 on "The Darwinian Theory." The lectures were very well received and contributed to the acceptance of evolution in the United States. After the lectures, Wallace traveled to California, where he met the conservationist John Muir and deplored the destruction of the giant redwoods.

In his later years Wallace wrote often about social issues, including a book in support of state ownership of land. His last work, *Social Environment and Moral Progress,* was completed when he was 90, not long before his death. Although many wanted him to be buried in Westminster Abbey, next to Darwin, his family made his grave on a hill near his home and marked the spot with a stump from a petrified tree.

FURTHER READING

Adams, Alexander B. "A Coincidental Discovery" and "Champions of the Cause." In *Eternal Quest: The Story of the Great Naturalists.* New York: G. P. Putnam, 1969.

Beddall, Barbara G., ed. *Wallace and Bates in the Tropics: An Introduction to the Theory of Natural Selection.* New York: Macmillan, 1969.

George, Wilma. *Biologist Philosopher: A Study of the Life and Writings of Alfred Russel Wallace.* New York: Abelard-Schuman, 1964.

Wallace, Alfred Russel. *The Malay Archipelago.* 1869. Reprint. New York: Oxford University Press, 1987.

———. *My Life.* New York: Dodd, Mead, 1905.

———. *Narrative of Travels on the Amazon and Rio Negro.* 1889. Reprint. Brooklyn, N.Y.: Haskell, 1969.

———. *Tropical Nature and Other Essays.* 1878. Reprint. New York: AMS Press, 1972.

More Earthkeepers to Remember

George Ord (1781-1866), American naturalist and philologist (an authority on languages), assisted Alexander Wilson with the preparation of *American Ornithology* and completed the final volumes after Wilson's death; he later published a revised edition of the work that included a large amount of additional material (1824-25). Ord also accompanied Thomas Say on a collecting expedition to Georgia and Florida in 1818 and was responsible for the acquisition of a number of rare specimens. As a philologist, Ord made major contributions to a revised edition of Samuel Johnson's *Dictionary*.

Charles Waterton (1782-1865), an English naturalist, explored the northern regions of South America—now Colombia, Venezuela, Brazil, and Guyana—during a 20-year period (1804-24). During this time he also traveled through Canada as far west as present-day Alberta, where the Waterton Lakes were later named after him. In 1825 he published *Wanderings in South America,* an enormously popular account of the animals he had seen there. The book has been reprinted many times, and as recently as 1984 in the United States. Waterton's *Essays on Natural History* (1871) was published after his death. Encouraged by Sir Joseph Banks, Waterton stuffed many of the specimens he collected and is considered the father of modern taxidermy.

Turkish-born **Constantine Rafinesque** (1783-1840) traveled in the United States from 1802 to 1805, then settled in Sicily, where he studied plants and fish for a decade. He returned to the United States in 1815 and three years later became a professor of botany at Transylvania University in Kentucky, where he founded a botanical garden. In 1826 he resettled in Philadelphia and taught at the Franklin Institute but made frequent collecting trips in the eastern states. Rafinesque strongly advocated the natural system of plant classification developed by Antoine Laurent de Jussieu, and his ideas about the creation of new species of plants and animals foreshadowed Darwin's theory of evolution. Rafinesque's autobiography, *A Life of Travels and Researches in North America and South Europe*, was published in 1836.

English naturalist **William Swainson** (1789-1855) was the author of the 11-volume *Cabinet Cyclopaedia of Natural History*, published during the 1830s by Dionysius Lardner, and three volumes in the *Naturalist's Library* (1833-45), published by the Scottish naturalist **Sir William Jardine** (1800-74). In his writing Swainson introduced the quinary system of species classification, an esoteric approach to the subject based on the number five, but it was never widely adapted. In 1840 Swainson emigrated to New Zealand, where he became the country's attorney general.

Naturalist and Lutheran clergyman **John Bachman** (1790-1874) was born in New York State but moved to eastern Pennsylvania as an adult. He taught school near Philadelphia and became acquainted with Alexander Wilson and other naturalists in the city. In 1815 Bachman became the pastor of a Lutheran church in Charleston, South Carolina, and soon emerged as a leading religious figure in the state. He met John James Audubon for the first time in the fall of 1831, when Audubon stayed at Bachman's house during a trip through the South, and soon became a trusted associate. Bachman is best known for his collaboration with Audubon on *The Viviparous Quadrupeds of North America* (1845-48)—he edited the work and wrote a major portion of the text. Bachman was a founder of the South Carolina State Horticultural Society and wrote numerous scientific papers on animals and plants, including a catalog of ferns.

American botanist **Almira Hart Lincoln Phelps** (1793-1884), a native of Connecticut, taught science in women's schools along the Eastern Seaboard and wrote several textbooks. Her *Familiar Lectures on Botany*, first published in 1829, went through several editions and by 1872 had sold more than 375,000 copies. Phelps was aided in the writing and editing of her book by the botanist **Amos Eaton** (1776-1842), author of the best-selling guide *Manual of Botany for the Northern States*, first published in 1817. In 1859 Phelps became the second woman to be elected to membership in the American Association for the Advancement of Science (the first was the astronomer Maria Mitchell). Phelps's older sister Emma Hart Willard (1787-1870) was a noted teacher and pioneer in women's education.

John Torrey (1796-1873), an American botanist and chemist, founded the Lyceum of Natural History (later the New York Academy of Sciences) in 1817 and in 1836 became

Quaker naturalist Graceanna Lewis made many illustrations of birds and plants, including this watercolor of leaves and fruit of the swamp black tupelo tree, painted in fall 1892.

New York State's botanist. From 1838 to 1843 he collaborated with Asa Gray, his pupil, on the *Flora of North America.* In 1843 Torrey published his *Flora of the State of New York.*

English ornithologist **John Gould** (1803-81) published more than 40 lavishly illustrated books about birds during his lifetime, writing texts to

Botanist Almira Hart Lincoln Phelps wrote one of the most popular textbooks of the 19th century, *Familiar Lectures on Botany*. First published in 1829, it eventually sold nearly half a million copies.

accompany drawings and paintings by his wife and other artists. A professional acquaintance of Charles Darwin, he identified the various finches Darwin found on the Galapagos Islands as a single species.

Painter **John Cassin** (1813-69), a native of Philadelphia, was one of America's leading ornithologists in the 19th century. His best-known work, *Illustrations of the Birds of California, Texas, Oregon, British and Russian America*, was published in 1856. He was also the author of *Catalogue of North American Birds* (1858), considered the first modern work of American ornithology.

English botanist **Joseph Dalton Hooker** (1817-1911), a close associate of Charles Darwin, published three studies of plant life in Antarctica, New Zealand, and Tasmania upon his return from an expedition to these regions (1839-43). He also explored the northern frontier of India and cataloged species there. In 1865 Hooker succeeded his father, Sir William Jackson Hooker, as director of Kew Gardens. He served as president of the Royal Society of London from 1873 to 1878. Hooker's other published works include a guide to plants of the British Isles and the lengthy *Genera plantarum* (1862-83), coauthored with fellow botanist **George Bentham** (1800-84).

Scottish botanist **Richard Spruce** (1817-93) spent 15 years (1849-64) gathering specimens in South America. His journals were edited by Alfred Russel Wallace and published after Spruce's death as *Notes of a Botanist on the Amazon and the Andes* (1908).

Encouraged by John Cassin, Quaker naturalist and Philadelphia native **Graceanna Lewis** (1821-1912) published Part 1 of her *Natural History of Birds* in 1868. Cassin's death the following year left her without a mentor and she was unable to continue the project. However, Lewis continued to be active in the field of natural history, popularizing the subject through lectures as well as articles for leading periodicals. Lewis was a leading figure in the back-to-nature movement of the late 19th century, which saw the formation of clubs called Agassiz Associations throughout the United States.

The Austrian monk **Gregor Mendel** (1822-84) experimented for many years with plant seeds in his monastery garden and concluded that characteristics are passed on to subsequent generations. Mendel, who believed that heredity was the basis for evolutionary change, is considered the founder of the science of genetics.

French entomologist **Jean Henri Fabre** (1823-1915) was celebrated for his essays about insects. His books include *Annales des sciences naturelles* (*Annals of the Natural Sciences*; 1855-58) and *Souvenirs entomologiques* (*Entomological Remembrances*; 10 volumes, 1879-1907).

American zoologist **Spencer Fullerton Baird** (1823-87) was the author of more than 1,000 publications in the field of natural history, including the *Catalogue of North American Mammals* (1857) and the *Catalogue of North American Birds* (1858). Baird was associated for most of his professional life with the Smithsonian Institution, first as assistant secretary (1850-78) and then as head of the organization (1878-87). He also served as the first director of the U.S. Commission of Fish and Fisheries (1871-87).

Henry Walter Bates (1825-92), an English naturalist, accompanied Alfred Russel Wallace on his 11-year collecting expedition in Brazil (1848-59). Bates returned to England with 14,712 different species of insects, 8,000 of which had never been identified before. In 1861 Bates delivered a paper to the Linnean Society of London that described a form of mimicry in nature. Batesian mimicry, as it is now called, is a type of biological resemblance in which the appearance of a dangerous organism is mimicked by a harmless organism. The mimic gains protection because potential predators mistake it for the original, harmful model and therefore leave it alone. In addition to numerous papers on entomology, Bates published a two-volume account of his travels in South America as *The Naturalist on the River Amazonas* (1863).

Thomas Huxley (1825-95) was among the most prominent of English biologists in the 19th century. An authority on fossil fishes and reptiles as well as comparative anatomy, he was a strong supporter of Charles Darwin and his theory of evolution. Huxley's books include *Man's Place in Nature* (1863), *Lessons in Elementary Physiology* (1866), *Anatomy of Vertebrated Animals* (1871), and *Collected Essays* (nine volumes; 1898). Huxley's eldest son, Leonard Huxley (1860-1933), became a well-known classical scholar and was the father of biologist Julian Huxley (1887-1975) and novelist Aldous Huxley (1894-1963), the author of *Brave New World* (1932).

English ornithologist **Henry Seebohm** (1832-95) is best known for his bird-collecting trips in 1875 and 1877 to Siberia, a region then largely unknown to Western naturalists. Seebohm's *The Birds of Siberia: A Record of a Naturalist's Visits to the Valleys of the Petchora and Yenesei* was published in 1901, six years after his death. Seebohm also traveled throughout Europe and in Turkey gathering birds, and acquired Far Eastern species from other collectors. His other books include a multivolume history of British birds, a study of the birds of Japan, and a posthumously published study of the thrush family.

Howard Saunders (1835-1907), an English naturalist and collector, traveled through the Andes Mountains and along the Amazon River of South America in 1861-62. He later traveled extensively in Spain and other parts of Europe in search of bird specimens. Saunders's numerous publications include *An Illustrated Manual of British Birds*, first published in 1889. Many articles on his South American and Spanish trips appeared in the periodicals *Ibis* and *The Field: The Country Gentleman's Newspaper*.

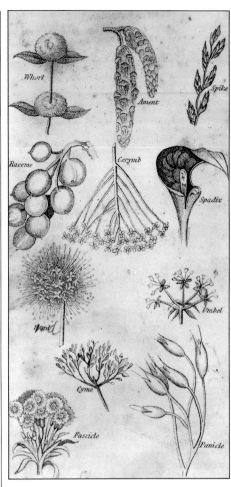

An illustration from the chapter "Inflorescence" in Phelps's *Familiar Lectures* shows various types of plant flowers. (*Inflorescence* means "the flowering part of a plant.")

Grand Canyon of the Yellowstone by Thomas Moran, whose illustrations helped convince Congress of the area's natural beauty. In 1872 Congress established Yellowstone National Park, the nation's—and the world's—first public nature preserve.

3 The Birth of Conservation

In the years following the U.S. Civil War, which ended in 1865, American naturalists began to express concern as wilderness areas grew significantly smaller. For the first time in its history, the country seemed in danger of losing natural resources that had long been taken for granted. The encroachment of civilization was a major factor: settlement now extended across the entire continent; by 1870 the U.S. population had grown nearly tenfold since the first official census 80 years earlier, when less than 4 million people lived in the entire United States. The growth of commerce and industry in the final decades of the 19th century depended upon often ruthless plundering of water resources, timber, and coal and other minerals in the vast public lands of the West, and buffalo and other animal species were hunted down to the verge of extinction.

In the prophetic *Man and Nature*, written at the U.S. Embassy in Rome as Confederate and Union troops clashed on Southern battlefields back in America, George Perkins Marsh had warned against human destruction of the environment, not only in his own country but throughout the industrialized Western world. Inspired by Marsh, first a few and then many voices began calling for conservation in the final decades of the 19th century and the early years of the 20th.

Part 3 begins with the story of a one-armed Civil War veteran turned geologist who made the watersheds of the American West a lifelong cause. The event that inspired his crusade was a historic trip down the Colorado River that occurred just five years after the first publication of *Man and Nature*. The geologist—who was also an expert on Native Americans and a staunch defender of their rights—was named John Wesley Powell.

John Wesley Powell

GEOLOGICAL PIONEER

Early on the morning of May 24, 1869, a one-armed Civil War veteran who taught geology at a small Illinois college stepped into a rowboat in Green River, Wyoming, to begin a historic journey. Exactly two weeks earlier another historic event had taken place in Promontory, Utah, some 120 miles to the west: the completion of the first transcontinental railroad across North America. There was a connection, not yet realized, between these two events: John Wesley Powell, the geologist and explorer of the Colorado River, would soon be a severe critic of the rapid development of the American West that accompanied the building of the railroad.

Powell's later career as a conservationist would have been difficult to imagine in his childhood. In fact, the need for conservation of natural resources was hardly considered in the early 19th century. The vast American continent appeared to offer a never-ending abundance of wildlife, pasture, timber, minerals, and water to those hardy enough to overcome the adversity of hostile Indians, powerful storms, and primitive living conditions. Powell's parents, originally from England, had migrated to New York State in 1830; after John's birth four years later they moved westward, settling briefly in Ohio and Wisconsin before making their permanent home in Wheaton, Illinois. The elder Powell farmed; he was also a Methodist preacher, and when it became clear that young John had inherited his gift for public speaking, the ministry was thought to be his likely career.

John Wesley Powell's formal education, however, was sporadic. By his early 20s he had attended Illinois, Oberlin, and Wheaton colleges; he returned home to work on the family farm rather than remaining long enough to get a degree. Powell's early interest in botany grew during these years, and he began making collecting trips down the Mississippi and Ohio rivers. He also joined the Illinois Society of Natural History and was elected its secretary.

When the Civil War began, Powell was commissioned a second lieutenant in the Union Army. In 1862 he was severely wounded at the Battle of Shiloh, in Tennessee, and his right arm was amputated at the elbow. Despite this handicap he continued to serve with the army, rising to the rank of major of artillery. When he was discharged, in early 1865, Powell briefly taught geology at Illinois Wesleyan College, then became museum curator and lecturer at Illinois Normal University. Here he organized summer trips of students and amateur naturalists to the Rocky Mountains; General Ulysses S. Grant, the Union commander under whom Powell had served, provided troops to accompany the travelers and protect them from Indian attacks.

Geologist and ethnologist John Wesley Powell pauses to chat with a Paiute Indian during a survey of northern Arizona Territory in 1869, the same year that he became the first person known to have navigated the Colorado River.

During the summer of 1868 Powell saw for the first time the gorges of the Green and Colorado rivers, and made up his mind to undertake a risky and first-time adventure: exploring them by boat. Both the Smithsonian Institution and Congress responded to his appeal for financial sponsorship, and the following May Powell and nine assistants pushed off in four boats from the Green River shore, headed south. Their ultimate destination was the Grand Canyon of the Colorado River, more than 500 miles away. Ahead of them lay a difficult journey navigating treacherous currents, rocks, and waterfalls.

As the days and weeks passed, no further word was heard from the party, whose trip had attracted national attention. Then suddenly, in late June, a man appeared in Illinois claiming to be the sole survivor of the Powell expedition and telling a tearful story of Powell's heroism as his boats plunged helplessly into a whirlpool. Newspapers across the country printed the story, and Powell and his men were presumed lost. Residents of the area below the Grand Canyon became especially watchful for any signs of debris from the destroyed boats.

More weeks passed. Then, on August 29, 100 days after Powell had left Green River, several men fishing near the mouth of the Grand Canyon saw a strange sight: a group of ragged, cheering

Sitting in a chair strapped to his boat, the *Emma Dean,* Powell thoroughly explored the Colorado River as part of a study of western natural resources for the U.S. government. His report urged support for water conservation and led to the establishment of the U.S. Geological Survey.

In 1878 Powell presented to Congress a written account of his decade's work in the West, entitled *Report on the Lands of the Arid Region.* In it he warned that the systematic plundering of the area's riches by greedy speculators would soon destroy it. The region was especially vulnerable because it lacked an abundant, renewable supply of fresh water; therefore, whoever controlled the water that did exist had control of the whole region. Yet the government, through its various land-grant policies, was making no attempt to see that water rights were fairly distributed.

Powell proposed many reforms, including the widespread adoption of cooperative farming in the West, a system that had already been put into use by the Mormons in Utah. However, these were largely ignored; powerful mining, railroad, and ranching interests were not ready to hear that their schemes were devastating the land. Only in the late 20th century have many of Powell's ideas been recognized as valuable; had they been adopted a hundred years earlier, much of the severe environmental damage suffered in the West might have been avoided.

Powell did have some success in another area: getting Congress to establish the U.S. Geological Survey (1879), which brought together all the separate government surveying agencies that had been in existence for many years. Its first head was a friend of Powell's, a young geologist named Clarence King. Powell himself was named to head the newly established Bureau of Ethnology, within the Smithsonian Institution. When King resigned from the USGS in 1880, Powell was named as its new director; for the next 14 years he ran both agencies.

Powell proved to be a highly skilled administrator, and under his leadership the Geological Survey became the most powerful organization of its kind in the world; it was especially active in mapping water resources and encouraging

men—what turned out to be Powell and five of his assistants—rowing toward them. The "sole survivor" had lied; in fact, he had had nothing to do with the Powell expedition and had made up the story to get attention.

Overnight John Wesley Powell became a hero as the story of his navigation of the tortuous Colorado River spread across the country. But his real work had just begun. Powell spent the next 10 years surveying the Rocky Mountains, making 30 separate trips interrupted by periodic visits to Washington, D.C., to ensure continued government support. He made maps; gathered information on natural resources, particularly water and minerals; made careful studies of the various Native American cultures; and collected thousands of plant and animal specimens and Indian artifacts for the Smithsonian.

"You are piling up a heritage of conflict and litigation over water rights, for there is not sufficient water to supply the land."

—from an address to the International Irrigation Congress, Los Angeles, October 1893

irrigation projects. To make the public aware of the USGS's accomplishments, Powell began a publishing program, issuing a series of bulletins, monographs, topographical and geological maps, and atlases. Geological Survey publications continue to be a valuable part of the agency's work.

Powell's work at the Bureau of Ethnology was equally impressive. As early as 1877 he had established his reputation as an ethnologist with the publication of *Introduction to the Study of Indian Languages*. At the bureau he promoted the study of Indian cultures and prepared a map of the distribution of 58 Native American languages in the United States and Canada; first published in 1891, the map is still considered accurate.

Many honors came to Powell in his later years, including honorary doctorates from Harvard University and the University of Heidelberg—despite the fact that he had never earned a college degree. As he grew older his injured arm became increasingly painful, and every summer he retreated with his wife and daughter from the heat and humidity of Washington, D.C., to a house in Maine. He was still there, on an extended vacation, in September 1902 when he died suddenly of a cerebral hemorrhage.

FURTHER READING

The Colorado River Region and John Wesley Powell: A Collection of Papers Honoring Powell on the 100th Anniversary of His Exploration of the Colorado River, 1869–1969. Washington, D.C.: Government Printing Office, 1969.

Darrah, William Culp. *Powell of the Colorado*. Princeton, N.J.: Princeton University Press, 1951.

Place, M. T. *John Wesley Powell: Canyon's Conqueror*. Boston: Houghton Mifflin, 1963.

Powell, John Wesley. *Selected Prose of John Wesley Powell*. Edited by George Crossette. Boston: David R. Godine, 1970.

"Powell, John Wesley." In *Dictionary of American Biography*. Vol. 8. New York: Scribners, 1964.

Stegner, Wallace. *Beyond the Hundredth Meridian: John Wesley Powell and the Second Opening of the West*. Boston: Houghton Mifflin, 1954.

Terrell, John Upton. *The Man Who Rediscovered America: A Biography of John Wesley Powell*. New York: Weybright & Talley, 1969.

Wild, Peter. "John Wesley Powell and the Rediscovery of the West." In *Pioneer Conservationists of Western America.* Missoula, Mont.: Mountain Press, 1979.

John Wesley Powell

BORN

Mount Morris, New York
March 24, 1834

DIED

Haven, Maine
September 23, 1902

EDUCATION

Attended Illinois, Oberlin, and Wheaton (Illinois) colleges

MAJOR INTERESTS

Geology; ethnology; conservation

ACCOMPLISHMENTS

Explored and surveyed the Rocky Mountains and the Grand Canyon of the Colorado River for the U.S. government; author of *Exploration of the Colorado River of the West and Its Tributaries* (1875); also wrote *Report on the Lands of the Arid Region of the United States* (1878), regarded as a milestone in conservation literature; head of both the U.S. Geological Survey (1880–94) and the Bureau of Ethnology (1879–1902)

HONORS

Honorary degrees from Columbia, Harvard, and Heidelberg universities

John Burroughs

THE SAGE OF SLABSIDES

One day in October 1863 in Washington, D.C., as the Civil War raged only a few miles away, two men who would one day become famous writers met each other for the first time. One was an itinerant poet named Walt Whitman, who kept revising a collection of poems, *Leaves of Grass*, which he had first published eight years earlier. The other man was a 26-year-old government clerk, John Burroughs, who had published several essays about nature back in his home state of New York. The meeting was an important one in Burroughs's life, for it was Whitman's encouragement and practical assistance that enabled Burroughs to become one of the most popular nature writers of all time.

John Burroughs was born in 1837 on a farm near Roxbury, New York, as the seventh of ten children. His birthplace was in the foothills of the Catskill Mountains, a region he loved and where he would spend most of his life. He attended local schools, and at 17 began earning his living as a teacher, first in nearby Ulster County and then for brief periods in Illinois and New Jersey before returning to New York State. Burroughs had

John Burroughs writes one of his nature essays at Slabsides, his cabin near the Hudson River in New York State.

"Let not care and humdrum deaden us to the wonders and the mysteries amid which we live, nor to the splendors and the glories."

—from *Leaf and Tendril* (1908)

John Burroughs

BORN

April 3, 1837
Delaware County, New York

DIED

March 29, 1921
En route from California to New York

EDUCATION

Ashland Collegiate Institute and Cooperstown Seminary (New York State)

MAJOR INTEREST

Nature writing

ACCOMPLISHMENTS

Wrote popular essays celebrating nature that encouraged public sympathy for conservation; author of more than 30 books, including *Wake-Robin* (1871), *Locusts and Wild Honey* (1879), *Signs and Seasons* (1886), *Ways of Nature* (1905), *Leaf and Tendril* (1908), *Time and Change* (1912), *The Summit of the Years* (1913), and *Under the Apple-Trees* (1916)

HONORS

Elected to the American Academy of Arts and Letters; received honorary degrees from Yale and Colgate universities

always loved being outdoors, tramping in nearby woods and fields, and as a young man he began spending many of his leisure hours teaching himself botany.

In the mid-1850s Burroughs took several leaves from teaching to attend two college-level institutions in New York State, Ashland Collegiate Institute and Cooperstown Seminary. Here he learned to write essays and discovered with pleasure the works of the English poet William Wordsworth and the American essayist and poet Ralph Waldo Emerson. At the age of 20, the newly married schoolteacher declared solemnly to his bride that he intended someday to become an author, too.

For six more years Burroughs taught full time while he tried to write, using nature as his subject and *Leaves of Grass* as a source of inspiration. By 1863 he had published a poem and several nature essays in local New York newspapers, and he had discovered a new passion: birdwatching. Early that year, browsing in the library of the U.S. Military Academy at West Point, he had seen for the first time a copy of Audubon's *Birds of America*. The experience, he wrote, was like "bringing together fire and powder." Impatient with his progress as a writer, he impulsively decided to resettle his family in Washington, where he could find a higher-paying job and also, he hoped, cultivate a friendship with Whitman, who was working there as a nurse tending wounded Union soldiers.

From the moment of their first meeting, the aspiring nature writer and the older poet were close friends. On days off from his tedious job in the U.S.

Treasury Department, Burroughs would accompany Whitman on his hospital rounds, and the poet became a frequent guest for breakfasts and dinners at the Burroughs' modest house on Capitol Hill. The two friends often went for long hikes together in the surrounding woods, sharing their reflections on art and nature, and Burroughs's first published book was a study of his new mentor (*Notes on Walt Whitman as Poet and Person*, 1867).

It was Whitman who helped Burroughs to overcome his doubts that he could become a successful nature writer and who suggested that he focus on the subject he particularly loved: birds. In spare moments, on and off the job, Burroughs began composing a series of essays that first appeared in the *Atlantic Monthly* in 1865 and were published together seven years later as his first nature book, with a title suggested by Whitman: *Wake-Robin*.

The popularity of *Wake-Robin* encouraged Burroughs to write additional nature essays, and by 1873 he felt secure enough as a writer to leave his job at the Treasury Department and return to New York State. He settled with his family on a farm near the Hudson River, 80 miles north of New York City, where he maintained a small vineyard and grew celery. His second essay collection, *Winter Sunshine*, was published in 1875, and a third, *Birds and Poets*, in 1877. Both were reviewed favorably—the American novelist Henry James praised Burroughs as a "more sociable Thoreau"—and established his importance as a leading nature writer in America. Henceforth, he published an

Burroughs stands outside Slabsides with family members. Encouraged as a young man by the poet Walt Whitman, Burroughs became America's most widely read nature writer.

FURTHER READING

Barrus, Clara. *John Burroughs, Boy and Man*. Garden City, N.Y.: Doubleday, 1920.

Burroughs, John. *Birch Browsings: A John Burroughs Reader*. Edited by Bill McKibben. New York: Penguin, 1992.

————. *Camping and Tramping with Roosevelt*. 1906. Reprint. Salem, N.H.: Ayer, 1970

————. *The Heart of John Burroughs's Journals*. Edited by Clara Barrus. 1928. Reprint. Irvine, Calif.: Reprint Services Corporation, 1989.

————. *A Sharp Lookout: Selected Nature Essays of John Burroughs*. Edited by Frank Bergon. Washington, D.C.: Smithsonian Institution Press, 1987.

"Burroughs, John." In *Dictionary of American Biography*. Vol. 2. New York: Scribners, 1964.

Kelley, Elizabeth Burroughs. *John Burroughs: Naturalist*. New York: Exposition Press, 1959.

Renehan, Edward J., Jr. *John Burroughs: An American Naturalist*. Post Mills, Vt.: Chelsea Green, 1992.

Shatraw, Harriet Barrus. "The Magic of John Burroughs." *Conservationist*, June-July 1974, 20-21.

Wild, Peter. "John Burroughs: The Harvest of a Quiet Eye." In *Pioneer Conservationists of Eastern America*. Missoula, Mont.: Mountain Press, 1986.

average of a book every other year, to increasing acclaim.

In 1895 Burroughs built a small cabin, a retreat that he called Slabsides, about a mile from his home. Here, close to the nature he loved, he wrote books and entertained visitors from all over the world who had come to meet him. Burroughs also traveled extensively throughout the United States (including Alaska) and in Europe, Canada, and the Caribbean, often accompanying wealthy businessmen as a nature guide. His friends included the naturalist John Muir and President Theodore Roosevelt, as well as tycoons Thomas Edison, Henry Ford, Harvey Firestone, and E. H. Harriman.

Although Burroughs did not involve himself directly in political issues, he began as he grew older to speak out against the "riotous, wasteful, and destructive spirit" of progress that was devastating a "fertile and bountiful"

continent, and he became a significant voice in the new conservation movement. Thousands of ordinary people, untrained in the sciences, who had learned to appreciate flowers, birds, and other wildlife through the essays of Burroughs, joined the movement. Moreover, his friendship with leading industrialists softened their initial opposition to conservation, and even encouraged some of them to give it financial help. The conservation-minded President Roosevelt quickly saw the value of having the "Sage of Slabsides" as an ally and liked to be seen as often as possible with him.

Active to the end of his life, Burroughs died in late March of 1921, a few days before his 84th birthday, on a train bringing him back to his beloved New York retreat from a winter stay in California. His last words were "How far are we from home?"

John Muir

JOHN-O'-THE-MOUNTAINS

I n a room of the Wisconsin Historical Society in Madison a curious device is displayed. A spindly assemblage more than six feet high, made from a pendulum, large gears, and compasses as long as human legs, it supports a stack of yellowed, crumbling books. This so-called studying machine, a combination desk and clock, was the invention of a young student named John Muir at the University of Wisconsin in the early 1860s. The device helped the resourceful Muir to use his time efficiently: at predetermined intervals it would thrust a new book into his hands, replacing the one he had been reading.

Inventions were John Muir's early passion, as exciting an interest to him in his youth as the giant redwoods of northern California would become when he was middle-aged. They were a natural consequence of his skill in whittling, a pastime that his strict and religious father disapproved of. The Muir family had emigrated to Wisconsin from their native Scotland in 1849,

John Muir leans against one of northern California's giant redwood trees, preserved through his successful efforts to create Yosemite and Sequoia National Parks.

Muir (right) posed with President Theodore Roosevelt during a camping trip to Yosemite in 1903. As an adviser to Roosevelt, Muir persuaded him to create more national parks and national forests and to establish national monuments in endangered natural areas.

His father, however, objected to any of his children staying up at night, but, as John recalled years later, Daniel Muir relented somewhat when he saw his son with a book of religious history: "If you *will* read, do it in the morning. You may get up as early as you like." The excited John woke up on the following morning at one o'clock, but it was too cold to read and much too early to start a fire. He decided to use these precious hours of freedom to create his first invention, a small sawmill. Other gadgets followed, many of which had clocks as their centerpiece. One of them, what John dubbed "an early-rising machine," connected a clock to a crossbeam supporting his bed; at a preset hour the device tilted the bed, dumping its occupant on the floor.

Despite his new mechanical interests, John Muir did not neglect his studies. By early 1861 he was able to enter the University of Wisconsin, where he took courses in chemistry and geology and impressed science professor Ezra Carr. In Carr's classes Muir learned about Louis Agassiz's theory of an ancient Ice Age, during which much of the Northern Hemisphere's topography had been created. Years later, in California, Muir would apply this knowledge to his study of the Sierra Mountains. Dr. Carr and his wife welcomed Muir into their home and became his mentors and lifelong friends.

In the summer of 1863, pursuing a new interest in botany, Muir began a series of walking tours through the Midwest and into Canada. He eventually settled near Indianapolis, where his mechanical ability got him a job in a carriage factory. Here an accident occurred that changed the direction of his life. One day in 1867, as he adjusted a machine belt, a file pierced his right eye and he became totally blind. Despondent and in terrible pain, he lay for weeks in bed, wondering what he would do for the rest of his life. He decided that if his sight were restored, he would "bid adieu to

when John was 11 years old. Establishing a homestead in the wilderness was hard work, and John and his seven young brothers and sisters were expected to labor like grown-ups to build and maintain a large farm. John's elementary education had ended when the family left Scotland, but he loved to learn and was always looking for new books. During a long day that might include splitting wood, plowing, making fences, hoeing, mowing, and cutting grain, he looked forward to evening, when at last he would be free to read.

"Any fool can destroy trees. They cannot run away; and if they could, they would still be destroyed, chased and hunted down as long as fun or a dollar could be got out of their bark hides. . . . God has cared for these trees, saved them from drought, disease, avalanches, and a thousand straining, leveling tempests and floods; but he cannot save them from fools. Only Uncle Sam can do that."

—from an article in *Atlantic Monthly*, August 1897

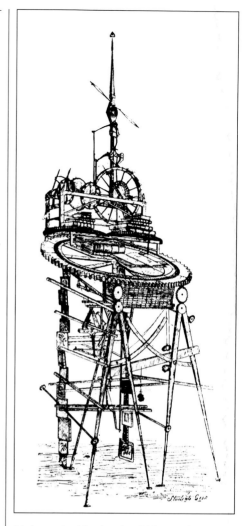

Muir made this sketch of his "student's desk," which included a bookshelf and a clock. Built by Muir while he was attending the University of Wisconsin, the mechanical device periodically selected a new book for him to read.

mechanical inventions" and devote himself to the study of nature, "the inventions of God." In fact, his vision slowly returned to normal, and as soon as he was well Muir set out on foot for Florida, intending to travel on to South America.

During his extensive trip Muir kept a detailed journal, recording the weather, topographical features, and plants and animals he encountered, as well as personal reflections; it was published nearly 50 years later, after his death, as *A Thousand-Mile Walk to the Gulf* (1916). Muir reached as far south as Havana, but a severe attack of malaria curtailed his plans to continue on to the Amazon. Instead he sailed for San Francisco, intending to cure his illness in the chill of the Sierras.

Arriving in California in the spring of 1868, Muir headed for Yosemite Valley, where he remained for six years. He worked for a while on sheep ranches, then got a part-time job at a sawmill that left him plenty of time to explore the nearby mountains. Soon Muir was serving as a guide for the tourists who were beginning to visit the area, and he developed a reputation as a colorful local "character" who could regale his listeners with mountain lore. A number of visitors, including many scientists, were sent by his old friends the Carrs, who now lived in Berkeley, where Dr. Carr taught at the University of California.

Muir frequently talked with visiting scientists about his theory that Yosemite had been formed from the action of glaciers over many thousands of years—and not, as popularly believed, from an enormous single earthquake. Encouraged to express this view in writing, he sent the resulting article to the New York *Tribune*, which published it in December 1871. A month later, it was reprinted in a leading science periodical, *Silliman's Journal*. Through influential friends of the Carrs he was soon launched on a writing career that would continue for the rest of his life.

Muir began selling articles on the scenic wonders of the West to national magazines, including *Harper's Weekly*, *National Geographic*, and *Century*, and traveled to Utah, Nevada, the Northwest, and Alaska, observing glaciers and growing increasingly interested in trees. By 1880 he felt financially secure enough to start a family of his own. His bride, who had been introduced to him by the Carrs, was Louie Stretzel, the daughter of an expatriate Polish doctor who had become a leading horticulturist in California. Acquiring part of the doctor's ranch in Martinez, across the bay from San Francisco, Muir spent the 1880s establishing a successful vineyard.

The final and most important chapter of Muir's career opened in 1889, when Robert U. Johnson, the editor of *Century* magazine, accompanied Muir on

Muir Woods in Marin County, California, was established in honor of John Muir in 1908.

afterward the third national park, Sequoia, also in California, was created.

The momentum created by Muir, with the continued encouragement of Johnson, led to further conservation legislation. In 1891 Congress passed the Enabling Act, which allowed the President to protect timberlands from cutting. As a consequence, President Benjamin Harrison set aside 13 million acres as forest reserves, the first of what later became the national forests. Back in 1876 Muir had called for the creation of a national commission to investigate the state of the nation's forests and devise a plan for their conservation. The Forestry Commission was finally created in 1896 by President Grover Cleveland, and Muir acted as its adviser. On the basis of the commission's 1897 report, the President created 13 new forest reserves, totaling 21 million acres.

The conservation movement that Muir had been instrumental in founding had opponents, however: commercial interests did not like having their sources of livelihood taken away from them, and they succeeded in getting Congress to restore the former status of Cleveland's newly created reserves until March 1898. Muir responded by writing two impassioned pleas during the spring and early summer of 1897: one, in *Harper's Weekly*, was entitled "Forest Reservations and National Parks"; the other, "The American Forests," was published in the *Atlantic Monthly*. Public opinion was aroused once again, and the additional forest reserves were restored.

Muir continued his conservation campaign during the administration of President Theodore Roosevelt. In 1903 he invited the President along on a camping trip to Yosemite and used the opportunity to persuade Roosevelt that more national parks and forest reserves were needed. During the remaining six years of his presidency, Roosevelt set aside 148 million more acres as national forests and approved the establishment of six new national parks. At his urging,

a camping trip to familiar territory, the Yosemite Valley. Dismayed at the damage sheep ranching and lumbering had done to the area, both men decided to launch a campaign to save Yosemite. Articles by Muir extolling the region's wonders were printed in *Century* and other national periodicals, together with a plea that they be saved from further destruction. Thousands of citizens responded, bombarding Congress with appeals, and in 1890 Yosemite, the second national park, was created. Soon in 1906 Congress also passed the Lacey Antiquities Act (1906), which provided for the designation by the President of national monuments; Roosevelt established 16 such monuments, including Muir Woods in Marin County, California.

In 1892 Muir had founded the Sierra Club, an organization of conservationists; he served as its president for the remainder of his life. He also continued writing, creating books from the extensive journals he had kept over the years. His first volume was *The Mountains of California*, published in 1894; another five appeared during his lifetime, including a volume of memoirs, *The Story of My Boyhood and Youth* (1913), and four more were published after his death in 1914.

At the age of 74, during the winter of 1911–12, Muir fulfilled a lifelong dream by touring the Amazon, and he also visited Africa. Everywhere he went, at home and abroad, he was welcomed as a beloved figure, nicknamed "John-o'-the-Mountains." However, his final years were marred by his failure to prevent a dam from being built at beautiful Hetch-Hetchy Valley in Yosemite National Park. Supporters of the project argued that it was needed to provide power and water for the city of San Francisco, although evidence from the government's own Board of Army Engineers suggested that another site was preferable. Despite nationwide protests, Congress voted to dam the valley in 1913, and the bill was signed into law by President Woodrow Wilson.

The conversion of Hetch-Hetchy proved to be the environmental disaster that Muir had predicted, but he did not live to see its consequences. In death, however, he received a measure of vindication: three years after approving construction of the Hetch-Hetchy dam, an embarrassed Congress passed a comprehensive protection bill that prevented further "tampering" with national park lands.

FURTHER READING

Clarke, James Mitchell. *The Life and Adventures of John Muir*. San Francisco: Sierra Club Books, 1980.

Fox, Stephen R. *John Muir and His Legacy: The American Conservation Movement*. Boston: Little, Brown, 1981.

Jones, Holway R. *John Muir and the Sierra Club: The Battle for Yosemite*. San Francisco: Sierra Club Books, 1965.

Muir, John. *John of the Mountains: The Unpublished Journals of John Muir*. Edited by Linnie Marsh Wolfe. Boston: Houghton Mifflin, 1938.

———. *The Story of My Boyhood and Youth*. 1913. Reprint. San Francisco: Sierra Club Books, 1989.

———. *A Thousand-Mile Walk to the Gulf*. 1916. Reprint. Boston: Houghton Mifflin, 1981.

———. *Travels in Alaska*. 1915. Reprint. San Francisco: Sierra Club Books, 1988.

———. *Wilderness Essays*. Layton, Utah: Gibbs Smith, 1989.

———. *The Wilderness World of John Muir*. Edited by Edwin Way Teale. Boston: Houghton Mifflin, 1976.

———. *The Yosemite*. 1912. Reprint. San Francisco: Sierra Club Books, 1992.

"Muir, John." In *Dictionary of American Biography*. Vol. 7. New York: Scribners, 1964.

Sanborn, Margaret. *Yosemite: Its Discovery, Its Wonders, and Its People*. New York: Random House, 1981.

Turner, Frederick. *Rediscovering America: John Muir in His Time and Ours*. New York: Viking, 1985.

Watkins, T. H. *John Muir's America*. New York: Crown, 1976.

Wild, Peter. "The Mysteries of the Mountains and Practical Politics." In *Pioneer Conservationists of Western America*. Missoula, Mont.: Mountain Press, 1979.

Wolfe, Linnie Marsh. *Son of the Wilderness: The Life of John Muir*. New York: Knopf, 1945.

EARTHKEEPERS

John Muir

BORN
April 21, 1838
Dunbar, Scotland

DIED
December 24, 1914
Los Angeles, California

EDUCATION
Attended University of Wisconsin

MAJOR INTEREST
Forest conservation

ACCOMPLISHMENTS
Considered the father of America's national parks; Sequoia and Yosemite National Parks in California established largely through his efforts (1890); founder of the Sierra Club (1892); author of numerous articles and 10 books, including *Our National Parks* (1901), *The Yosemite* (1912), *The Story of My Boyhood and Youth* (1913), and *A Thousand-Mile Walk to the Gulf* (1916)

HONORS
Muir Woods National Monument in Marin County, California, created in his honor (1908); Muir Glacier, in Alaska, and the John Muir Trail, Muir Pass, and Mount Muir, all in California, named after him; elected a fellow of the American Association for the Advancement of Science and a member of the American Academy of Arts and Sciences; received honorary degrees from Harvard and Yale universities, and from the universities of California and Wisconsin

George Bird Grinnell

A CRUSADER FOR BUFFALO AND INDIANS

Whearn he was eight years old, George Bird Grinnell received his earliest lessons in natural history from his first school-teacher: Lucy Audubon, the widow of John James Audubon, the famous painter of birds. Grinnell's father, a wealthy New York stockbroker, had moved his family in 1857 from Brooklyn to a house on the grounds of Audubon Park, the Audubon family estate on the then-rural northern tip of Manhattan. Mme. Audubon ran a small primary school for local children in her home, and young George, who called her "Grandma," became one of her most devoted pupils. Years later, when he founded the first Audubon Society, Grinnell named it in tribute to Lucy as well as her husband.

After receiving his secondary education at a military boarding school, Grinnell followed his family's wishes and entered Yale University, but during his undergraduate years he was an indifferent student. In the summer of 1870, following his graduation, he joined 11 other Yale students on a fossil-hunting expedition to the Far West led by Professor Othniel Marsh, a prominent paleontologist at the university's Peabody

Ill health forced George Bird Grinnell to trade a promising career as a paleontologist for the editorship of *Forest and Stream*. He made the magazine a leading voice for wildlife conservation.

> "We see already the dawning of a day, when in suitable situations, the forests, the birds and the animals so ruthlessly swept away in the past may be in a measure reestablished and, within proper limits, may be preserved for the benefit of future generations."

—from *Hunting and Conservation* (1925)

George Bird Grinnell

BORN

September 20, 1849
Brooklyn, New York

DIED

April 11, 1938
New York City

EDUCATION

B.A., Ph.D., Yale University

MAJOR INTERESTS

Conservation; ethnology

ACCOMPLISHMENTS

Leader of America's first wildlife conservation movement; led effort to establish Glacier National Park; founder of the first Audubon Society; supporter of Native American rights; editor of *Forest and Stream* (1876–1911); author or editor of numerous books on conservation and ethnology, including *Hunting and Conservation* (1925) and *The Cheyenne Indians* (1923)

HONORS

Mount Grinnell, Grinnell Lake, and Grinnell Glacier in Glacier National Park, Montana, named after him

Museum. The students saw the trip as an opportunity for adventure, despite the intense heat, poor food, and constant threat of Indian attacks; digging up dinosaur bones and meeting legendary figures such as frontier scout "Buffalo Bill" Cody provided brief moments of excitement before they settled down to pursue careers, like their fathers', in banking and commerce. For young Grinnell, however, the trip was a life-changing experience. Though he, too, came home to work in his father's office, he vowed to return to the West as soon as possible.

The first opportunity came in the summer of 1872, and Grinnell used his vacation to hunt buffalo with friendly Pawnee Indians. A second came two years later, when he volunteered as a naturalist on General George Custer's first expedition to the Black Hills of South Dakota. Tired of working as a stockbroker, he decided to pursue a career in paleontology, which would allow him to make frequent Western visits. In the fall of 1874 he enrolled as a graduate student at Yale, where he worked as an assistant at the Peabody. The following summer he went west again on an expedition led by Colonel William Ludlow to Yellowstone National Park, and wrote valuable reports on the mammals and birds of the region; included in one of them was a protest against the widespread slaughter of buffalo—the first hint of Grinnell's future career as an ardent conservationist.

Grinnell's love of natural history, his training in paleontology, and his growing interest in the Plains Indians led him to return to the West nearly every summer for the next 40 years. He became an authority on the Pawnee, Cheyenne, and Blackfoot tribes, and throughout his life championed the welfare of Native Americans. While pursuing concurrent careers as a naturalist, editor, and conservation advocate, Grinnell maintained his interest in Native American ethnology. He published several books about Indian life and lore, including the classic two-volume study *The Cheyenne Indians* (1923).

After Grinnell received his Ph.D. in paleontology in 1880, his doctor advised him to leave the Peabody Museum, where long, intense hours classifying dusty fossils were damaging his health. Since 1876 Grinnell had also been serving as natural history editor of the sportsmen's magazine *Forest and Stream*; when the editor-in-chief's job became available he took it and remained there for 35 years.

Under its founder and previous editor, Charles Hallock, the magazine had begun calling for restrictions on hunting and fishing as a way of stopping the rapid depletion of game. Now Grinnell launched a campaign to establish a new system of regulations, proposing that states place restrictions on the number of animals that could be killed ("bag limits"), charge hunting fees that could be used to finance conservation programs, and appoint game wardens to see that the regulations were enforced. Grinnell's crusade spread from *Forest and Stream* to other magazines across the nation, rousing public protest that led to the widespread passage of game-protection laws by the beginning of the 20th century.

Grinnell's interest in wildlife conservation had arisen during his first visit to Yellowstone with the Ludlow expedition, when he observed with horror the random slaughter of buffalo. Yellowstone, a wilderness area in northwest Wyoming, had been declared the first national park in 1872. Although its remoteness discouraged all but a handful of tourists from visiting the area, hunters came in droves, drawn by the abundant game—unbelievable as it may seem today, no laws protected the park's animals for more than two decades. During this period Yellowstone's wildlife population dwindled. Hardest hit were the buffalo: by the 1880s only a single small herd remained.

As editor of *Forest and Stream*, Grinnell launched a movement to protect the animals of Yellowstone and to establish a system of national parks as conservation centers, using the nearly extinct buffalo as a symbol around which supporters could rally. Victory came with the passage in 1894 of the Yellowstone Act, which protected all birds and animals in the park, and with the creation of the National Park Service in 1916 to oversee the increasing numbers of parks in the system. One of these was Montana's Glacier National Park, established in 1910 largely through Grinnell's efforts.

Grinnell founded and became active in several prominent organizations allied with the nation's first conservation movement. In 1886, again using *Forest*

A view of Glacier National Park, established in Montana in 1910 after years of campaigning by Grinnell. Indian paintbrush blooms in the foreground; the distant peak is Mt. Clements.

and Stream to recruit support, he started the first Audubon Society. He joined Theodore Roosevelt in the founding of the Boone and Crockett Club in 1887 to enlist sportsmen in the cause for wildlife conservation, and served as its president for nine years (1918-27). Grinnell was one of the founders of the New York Zoological Society (1895) and helped to draw up plans for the New York Zoological Park (the Bronx Zoo), which opened in 1899. In 1911 he helped set up another animal protection group, the American Game Association, and in 1925, at the age of 76, was elected president of the National Parks Association.

During the 1930s, the Depression, not conservation, was the nation's major concern, and Grinnell's increasingly poor health forced him to reduce his activities. In retirement he lived quietly with his wife in New York City, and by the time of his death, in April 1938, he was a largely forgotten figure. Only in the late 20th century, with the rebirth of

the conservation movement, are Grinnell's achievements fully appreciated.

FURTHER READING

Diettert, Gerald A. *Grinnell's Glacier: George Bird Grinnell and Glacier National Park*. Missoula, Mont.: Mountain Press, 1992.

Grinnell, George Bird. *The Passing of the Great West: Selected Papers of George Bird Grinnell*. Edited by John F. Reiger. Norman: University of Oklahoma Press, 1985.

Grinnell, George Bird, and Charles Sheldon, eds. *Hunting and Conservation*. New Haven: Yale University Press, 1925.

"Grinnell, George Bird." In *Dictionary of American Biography*. Supplement 2. New York: Scribners, 1958.

Wild, Peter. "George Bird Grinnell: Western Frontiersman, Eastern Editor." In *Pioneer Conservationists of Eastern America*. Missoula, Mont.: Mountain Press, 1986.

William Temple Hornaday

MOUNTING A
WILDLIFE CRUSADE

en percent of the human race," wrote conservationist William Temple Hornaday at the height of his campaign to preserve animal life, " . . . will lie, steal, throw rubbish in parks, and destroy wildlife whenever and wherever they can do so without being stopped by a policeman and a club." Although the zealous and temperamental Hornaday might not have hesitated to bludgeon anyone he saw defiling nature, he was wise enough to know that the best "club" in defense of nature was a series of strict laws that protected it against desecration. Hornaday—taxidermist, zoo director, and conservation leader—devoted much of his professional life to the passage of such laws.

Born in 1854 on an Indiana farm, Hornaday moved with his family several years later to a new homestead in Wapello County, Iowa. The birds of the midwestern prairies were the first animals to capture his imagination. Many years later he still remembered abundant flocks of prairie chickens, turkey vultures, and passenger pigeons in the nearby fields during his childhood. Orphaned at 15, he lived for a few months with various family members. During a stay with relatives back in his home state of Indiana, Hornaday saw a display case of stuffed birds and made up his mind to one day study taxidermy.

At 16, Hornaday entered a small Iowa college, Oskaloosa, for a brief period; two years later he transferred to the Iowa State Agricultural College (now Iowa State University). In the school library he was especially drawn to books on natural history, including Audubon's *Birds of America,* Audubon and Bachman's *Quadrupeds of North America,* and several accounts of explorers in Africa. Determined more than ever to become a taxidermist, the 19-year-old Hornaday left Iowa State at the end of his sophomore year, without a degree, and moved to Rochester, New York.

Rochester was the site of Ward's Museum, a center for training in taxidermy. Its proprietor, Henry Augustus Ward, took on the enthusiastic Hornaday as an assistant. Impressed with the young man's talents, Ward sent Hornaday on a series of worldwide collecting trips, beginning in 1874 with an expedition to Florida, Cuba, and the Bahamas. During the next eight years Hornaday traveled for Ward to South America, India, Ceylon, the Malay Peninsula, and Borneo, bringing home hundreds of what he called "zoological riches," crated specimens that he had shot. Hornaday's romantic, adventure-filled account of his travels in the Far East and his battles with disease, ferocious animals, and headhunters was published in 1885 as *Two Years in the Jungle.* The book was an enormous success and sold out 10 separate editions.

Hornaday's accomplishments at Ward's Museum led to his appointment in 1882 as chief taxidermist at the U.S. National

Against a backdrop of animal heads, William Temple Hornaday works at his desk at the Bronx Zoo. As the designer and first director of the zoo, he created a model institution and became an influential spokesman for worldwide wildlife conservation.

> "Here is an inexorable law of Nature, to which there are no exceptions: No wild species of bird, mammal, reptile, or fish can withstand exploitation for commercial purposes."

—from *Our Vanishing Wildlife* (1913)

William Temple Hornaday

BORN

December 1, 1854
Hendricks County, Indiana

DIED

March 6, 1937
Stamford, Connecticut

EDUCATION

Attended Oskaloosa College (Iowa) and Iowa State Agricultural College

MAJOR INTEREST

Wildlife conservation

ACCOMPLISHMENTS

Created the first natural habitat wildlife exhibits in American museums; created the first natural habitat zoo; conservation crusader; chief taxidermist, U.S. National Museum (1882–90); first director of the New York Zoological Park (the Bronx Zoo; 1896–1926); president, the American Bison Society (1907–10); author of numerous papers and 15 books on zoology and conservation, including *The Extermination of the American Bison* (1889), *Our Vanishing Wildlife* (1913), and *Wild Life Conservation in Theory and Practice* (1914)

HONORS

Honorary degrees from the University of Pittsburgh, Yale University, and Iowa State College

Museum, part of the Smithsonian Institution in Washington, D.C. Here he created the first natural habitat exhibit in a museum, a grouping of American bison, and went on to set up other three-dimensional exhibits of animals mounted in natural settings. Today we are used to seeing such installations in science museums around the world, but before Hornaday's time the relatively few animal specimens displayed to the public were mounted in small glass cases; the majority of specimens in museum collections were stored and used only for study by scientists. Live animals in early zoos were also displayed unimaginatively, usually confined to small cages. During his years at the National Museum, Hornaday began a crusade for lifelike exhibits of both stuffed and living animals, and began a collection of live specimens.

Impressed with his efforts, officials of the Smithsonian obtained an appropriation from Congress of nearly $300,000 to build a national zoological park, and they put Hornaday in charge. He soon grew impatient, however, with bureaucratic delays and in 1890 resigned angrily when changes in his plans for the project were made without his consent. At the same time he left his position at the National Museum and moved back to New York State, this time to Buffalo, where he wrote one of the first textbooks in his field, *Taxidermy and Zoological Collecting* (1891), and sold real estate for six years.

In 1896 a new chapter in Hornaday's professional life opened when he accepted an offer from the New York Zoological Society to become the first director of the New York Zoological Park (the Bronx Zoo, now called the International Wildlife Conservation Park), in New York City. Here he was given a free hand in designing a zoo according to his own specifications, with an emphasis on the creation of natural surroundings for the exhibition of a wide variety of wildlife. The result was an outstanding institution that served as a model for later zoos around the world.

With the support of the Zoological Society, Hornaday decided that his job included not only the promotion of scientific study and collecting but also wildlife protection. As early as 1889, in his book *The Extermination of the American Bison,* Hornaday had expressed his concern over declining numbers of wildlife, a consequence of unlimited hunting and the takeover of formerly public lands for private use. Capitalizing on his prestige as director of a world-famous zoo and as a popular author, Hornaday became a leader of the contemporary movement for wildlife conservation, speaking out in support of laws to protect wild animals.

One of Hornaday's major accomplishments was the establishment in 1910 of the Zoological Society's Permanent Wildlife Protection Fund as an "army of defense" to promote conservation. During his years as zoo director Hornaday raised hundreds of thousands of dollars to fund his conservation crusade, which took the form of more books—*Our Vanishing Wildlife*, published in 1913, was especially popular—numerous pamphlets and other publications, speeches, and intensive lobbying efforts in Congress. Among his wealthy contributors were many leading industrialists, including Andrew Carnegie and Henry Ford, whose support for conservation laws undoubtedly hastened their adoption.

Although Hornaday was a hunter throughout his life, he believed that hunting had to be regulated to protect animals from greedy slaughter by that "ten percent of the human race" that could not regulate itself. Hornaday's efforts led to the federal government's program early in the 20th century to save the bison by establishing a number of wildlife preserves in the West. Thanks in large part to Hornaday's unrelenting pressure, Congress passed important wildlife protection legislation, including the Bayne Law, prohibiting the sale of native game; the Federal Tariff Act of 1913, which included a provision banning the importation of wild-bird plumage to make hats; and the McLain Bird Protection Bill, which prohibited the hunting of migratory birds.

Despite these successes, Hornaday was not a universally well-liked man. His zealous, single-minded devotion to the cause of conservation alienated many people, and he was often rude, opinionated, and overbearing. Even mild-mannered George Bird Grinnell found him difficult to work with. Nor was Hornaday a defender of the right of all forms of wildlife to survival. In his later years he became a foe of what he called "bad animals": those who killed other animals or people. Hornaday believed that owls, coyotes, hawks, eagles, and wolves should always be exterminated. Today that view seems stupid and cruel as conservationists battle to save many

Hornaday persuaded the U.S. government to set up bison preserves. Here Hornaday (holding pole) and zoo staff members prepare to send a bison to the Wichita Wildlife Refuge in Oklahoma.

predators from extinction—but surprisingly, Hornaday's opinion was shared by many contemporary naturalists.

Hornaday retired as director of the New York Zoological Park in 1926 and lived at his home in Stamford, Connecticut, with his wife and daughter. He continued to write about conservation issues, however, and published his 15th and last book, *Thirty Years War for Wild Life: Gains and Losses in the Thankless Task*, in 1931, when he was 76 years old.

Hornaday died six years later, reviled by some but celebrated by many more, including, as one writer put it, "the mute inhabitants of our forests and uplands, who found in him a stout-hearted and able defender."

FURTHER READING

Hornaday, William Temple. *Our Vanishing Wildlife: Its Extermination and Preservation.* New York: New York Zoological Society, 1913.

———. *Wild Life Conservation in Theory and Practice.* New Haven: Yale University Press, 1914.

"Hornaday, William Temple." In *Dictionary of American Biography.* Supplement 2. New York: Scribners, 1958.

Wild, Peter. "William T. Hornaday: Warrior for Wildlife." In *Pioneer Conservationists of Eastern America.* Missoula, Mont.: Mountain Press, 1986.

Anna Botsford Comstock

TEACHING A LOVE OF NATURE

Young Anna Botsford never intended to make a career out of nature study. In fact, like most women in the 19th century, she did not plan on having a career at all. Born in a log cabin in rural New York State, she grew up on a farm and learned from her mother the housekeeping skills that were an essential part of a female upbringing. However, Mrs. Botsford, as Anna later recalled, also passed on to her only child her passionate love of nature, and she taught her daughter the names of constellations and wildflowers.

Anna Botsford enjoyed reading, and a wealthy neighbor, who had a large library, often invited the young woman over to borrow books and to talk about literature, art, and music. Both parents also encouraged her intellectual interests. They believed in the value of a formal education for women as well

Anna Botsford Comstock combined a lifelong interest in natural history with artistic and writing talents to create the *Handbook of Nature Study,* the first comprehensive nature guide published in America.

Comstock initially learned the art of wood engraving so that she could illustrate her husband's books on entomology. Later, she made engravings for her own books—and sometimes for pleasure, such as *Moths on a Moonlight Night,* shown above.

as men, and Anna was sent to a girls' secondary school not far from her home to prepare her for admission to college.

In 1874 Anna Botsford entered Cornell University—one of only a few coeducational institutions of higher learning—to study modern languages and literature. She was required to take science courses as well, and became friends with her zoology instructor, a man not much older than she named John Henry Comstock. Comstock's specialty was entomology; he had collected thousands of insects and

planned to make their study his life's work. Anna returned home after a year at Cornell, but she and Comstock wrote often to each other, became engaged, and married in 1877.

At Cornell Anna set up housekeeping while Comstock taught his classes and did research, but she also acted as her husband's assistant, writing letters, preparing diagrams and illustrations for his lectures, and managing his laboratory. In 1878 Comstock took a leave of absence from Cornell to become chief entomologist for the U.S. Department of

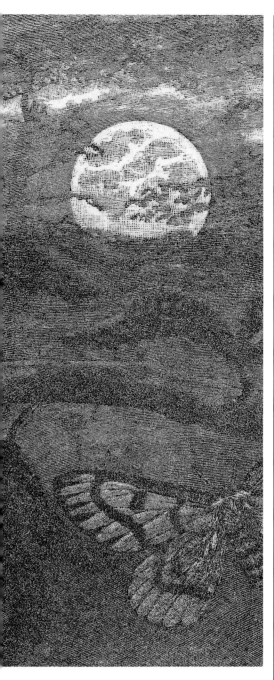

Anna Botsford Comstock

BORN

September 1, 1854
Cattaraugus County, New York

DIED

August 24, 1930
Ithaca, New York

EDUCATION

B.S., Cornell University

MAJOR INTERESTS

Entomology; nature study; wood engraving

ACCOMPLISHMENTS

Author of the best-selling *Handbook of Nature Study* (1911; revised 1939, 1970, 1986) and other books; professor of nature study, Cornell University

HONORS

One of the first women elected to Sigma Xi, the national science honor society; received honorary doctorate from Hobart College; named one of the 12 most outstanding women in the United States by the League of Women Voters, 1923

"Too many men who seek the out-of-doors for rest at the present time can only find it with a gun in hand. . . . Far better will it be when, through properly training the child, the man shall be enabled to enjoy nature through seeing how creatures live rather than watching them die."

—from the *Handbook of Nature Study* (1911)

tions for her husband's work as well as other drawings of insects.

Anna Botsford Comstock's enthusiasm and aptitude for the study of natural history were so obvious that her husband urged her to reenroll at Cornell in the fall of 1881, this time as a science student. While she completed coursework for a bachelor's degree, she also began the illustrations for Henry's book *An Introduction to Entomology* and learned the art of wood engraving, first by correspondence lessons and then by attending classes at Cooper Union in New York City.

When the book was published in the fall of 1888, Anna's engravings earned her election to Sigma Xi, making her one of the first four women to be inducted into that national science honor society. She was also the third woman to be elected a member of the American Society of Wood Engravers. That winter the Comstocks traveled to Germany, and during a visit to an art museum in Berlin Anna was happily surprised to see her engravings of moths and butterflies on display; they had been borrowed without her knowledge from the Society of Wood Engravers.

Agriculture, and the couple moved to Washington, D.C.

Anna continued to assist her husband with both office and laboratory work, but now she was given a formal position and paid for her efforts. During Henry's three years at the USDA, the Comstocks traveled together to California, where Henry studied scale insects infesting citrus fruit trees while Anna made detailed drawings of specimens. When they returned to Cornell in 1881, Anna was allowed her own workshop, where she continued producing illustra-

Anna's next project was the illustration of Henry's new book, *Manual for the Study of Insects*, which was published in 1895. On the title page she was listed as the "junior author," and Henry acknowledged in the preface that she had contributed substantial parts of text as well as all the engravings. Anna was now 41 years old. The Comstocks had been unable to have their own children, but Anna liked young people and as a faculty wife had made the Comstock home a favorite gathering place for her husband's students. Now a new nature study movement involving children was gaining momentum in rural New York State, and Anna seized the opportunity to participate.

In the late 19th century the rural population of New York was beginning to dwindle as large numbers of young people left the farms for cities. To try to counteract this trend, the state government began a program at Cornell's College of Agriculture to encourage nature study in the schools, headed by Professor Liberty Hyde Bailey, Jr., chairman of the Department of Horticulture at Cornell. Anna was one of several people asked to do a survey of the public school curriculum and to write a series of instructional pamphlets about nature for teachers.

In 1898, impressed with her work, Cornell named her an assistant professor of nature study, but the board of trustees objected to the title of "professor" for a woman and changed her status to "lecturer." Anna's duties, however, were extensive. Dividing her time between class- and fieldwork, she taught during the school year and conducted classes at special summer institutes established to train teachers. Soon she was in demand all over the state, lecturing at teachers' colleges and at Chautauqua, the celebrated educational center near Buffalo; as her fame spread, she also gave talks at seminars in Virginia and Washington, D.C.

Despite her busy schedule, Anna found time to continue collaborating with her husband. In the early 1900s they wrote books together about spiders and butterflies that included Anna's drawings and engravings. Anna also began writing and publishing books of her own, including a novel and a collection of essays about insects entitled *Ways of the Six-Footed* (1903).

Secure in her position at Cornell—she now had her own one-woman nature study department, an assistant, and office and lab space— Anna turned to a project that had been growing in her mind for some time: writing a lengthy guide for teachers that would cover the entire field of natural history. No one encouraged her; she was told that there was no audience for such a book. But Anna persisted, working steadily for several years to complete it. Finally, in 1911, the *Handbook of Nature Study* was published…nearly a thousand pages arranged into 232 illustrated lessons about North American plants, animals, rocks and minerals, astronomy, and weather. It was an instant best-seller and soon became known as "the Nature Bible" throughout the country, used not only by teachers but also by ordinary people curious to learn more about natural history. Anna was now widely celebrated as "the dean of American nature study," and her lectures were in even greater demand.

The success of the *Handbook* led Cornell's board of trustees to approve Anna's promotion to assistant professor in 1913; six years later she was named a full professor of nature study. She officially retired from the faculty in 1921— Henry had done so seven years earlier— but continued teaching classes and giving lectures as well as editing the *Nature Study Review*, the magazine of the American Nature Study Society, and writing articles about natural history for *Compton's Young People's Encyclopedia*.

One morning in 1923 Anna Botsford Comstock opened the *New York Times* and read that the League of Women Voters had voted her one of the 12 greatest women in America. She also received other awards, including membership in the honorary society Phi Kappa Phi and an honorary doctorate from Hobart College. Her last four years were divided between teaching and nursing her husband, who had suffered a stroke in 1926. She taught her final class in August 1930 and died two weeks later of cancer; her husband survived her by seven months.

Back in 1909, when Anna Botsford Comstock began working on her *Handbook of Nature Study*, Henry Comstock had tried to discourage her, predicting that the book would be a failure. He was wrong, of course. The *Handbook* is still in print, more than 80 years after its first publication. It has been revised several times and translated into many languages, and is the all-time best-selling book published by Cornell University Press.

FURTHER READING

Bonta, Marcia Myers. "Anna B. Comstock." In *Women in the Field: America's Pioneering Naturalists*. College Station: Texas A&M University Press, 1991.

Comstock, Anna Botsford. *The Comstocks of Cornell*. No date. Reprint. Ithaca, N.Y.: Cornell University Press, 1953.

———. *Handbook of Nature Study*. Ithaca, N.Y.: Cornell University Press, 1911; revised 1939, 1970, 1986.

———. *How to Know the Butterflies*. New York: Appleton, 1904.

———. *Ways of the Six-Footed*. 1903. Reprint. Ithaca, N.Y.: Cornell University Press, 1977.

"Comstock, John Henry." In *Dictionary of American Biography*. Supplement 1. New York: Scribners, 1944.

Theodore Roosevelt

CARRYING A BIG STICK
FOR CONSERVATION

he list of specimens presented to the American Museum of Natural History in New York City during the year 1871 includes a bat, a turtle, a squirrel skull, 12 mice, and 4 birds' eggs—all donated by "Mr. Theodore Roosevelt, Jr." The boy who would grow up to become President of the United States—the most conservation-minded in history—had collected the specimens during the Roosevelt family's summer vacation in the Adirondack and White mountains. That trip—his first encounter with the wilderness—remained with him as a wonderful memory for the rest of his life.

By the time Theodore Roosevelt, Jr., turned 13 in the fall of 1871, he knew that he wanted to pursue a career as a naturalist. For years he had been reading books for children about natural history and exploration. Now he began collecting and studying small animals and birds and even established his own "Roosevelt Museum of Natural History" on the fourth floor of the family home in New York City. His reading

Theodore Roosevelt, U.S. President, outdoorsman, and protector of nature, posed for a photographer at Glacier Point in the Yosemite Valley.

Roosevelt's love of natural history was evident from an early age. As a teenager he drew this bird portrait from a specimen he collected for his personal "museum."

material also grew more sophisticated as he tackled books by John James Audubon and by the American naturalist Spencer Fullerton Baird.

Roosevelt's parents encouraged his growing interest, believing that outdoor activity relieved his chronic asthma, and even arranged for him to have lessons in taxidermy with John G. Bell, who had stuffed specimens for Audubon many years earlier. The senior Roosevelt, a wealthy businessman and philanthropist, had a further reason to sympathize with his son's new passion: his own similar interests had led him to found the American Museum of Natural History in 1869.

The Roosevelt children—Theodore had a brother and two sisters—received their formal education from private tutors, a common practice among wealthy families in the 19th century. Foreign travel was also viewed as educational, and the family took several extended trips abroad. During the winter of 1872-73 they remained in Egypt, living on a large houseboat on the Nile. The delighted Roosevelt spent most of his time shooting birds along the riverbank,

then returned to the boat to dissect and stuff them.

Theodore Roosevelt entered Harvard in 1876; he had chosen the university because of its outstanding reputation in the natural sciences, achieved in part through the efforts of the late Professor Louis Agassiz, whose son was now curator of Harvard's Museum of Comparative Zoology. At college Roosevelt transformed his living quarters into a smaller version of his home "museum," collecting, dissecting, preserving, and sometimes mounting specimens. He was not especially popular at Harvard: some students thought his behavior was odd; others refused to come to his rooms, complaining of the smell.

His social life may have been less than satisfactory, but Theodore Roosevelt—he dropped the "Jr." after the death of his father in 1878—excelled in class. Although he took science courses throughout his four years, he became increasingly interested in American history, and by the time of his graduation, with honors, in 1880, he no longer planned a career as a naturalist. Many years later, he complained that the university's science classes placed too much emphasis on training him as "a microscopist and section-cutter" rather than giving him opportunities for fieldwork in natural history. He did not, however, give up his interest in the outdoors: as an adult he became an avid sportsman, an enthusiastic hunter and fisherman.

Having given up the idea of becoming a naturalist, Roosevelt could not decide on another career to pursue. There was little pressure to earn a living, however, because of the inheritance he had received from his father. He studied law briefly at Columbia University, then turned to writing about history, publishing his first book, *The Naval War of 1812*, in 1882. Republican party politics soon beckoned, and he was elected to the New York State Assembly for three terms (1882-84). Here he established a reputation as a crusader for reform that would remain with him throughout his life, but he did not seem especially interested in making politics a career.

Roosevelt had married soon after graduating from Harvard. After the sudden death of his wife four years later, in 1884, he retreated to ranch lands he had bought in the Dakota Territory. His experiences with cowhands and cattle led to two more books, *Hunting Trips of a Ranchman* (1885) and *Ranch Life and the Hunting Trail* (1888). In the late 1880s he also published several studies of American history and began what became a four-volume work, *The Winning of the West* (1889-96).

Roosevelt's support of Benjamin Harrison in the 1888 Presidential election led to his appointment as a U.S. Civil Service commissioner following Harrison's victory, and in early 1889 Roosevelt moved with his second wife to Washington. During his six years in the national capital, Roosevelt enhanced his reputation for reform while he continued to publish books about politics, history, and outdoor life, including *The Wilderness Hunter* (1893).

Back in New York City, Roosevelt served for two years as president of the Board of Police Commissioners under a new reform mayor, then moved back to Washington in 1897 as Assistant Secretary of the Navy under President William McKinley. His sudden emergence as a nationally known figure came a year later, when he resigned from the Navy Department to take an active role in the Spanish-American War in Cuba. Leading a volunteer cavalry regiment known as the Rough Riders, he took San Juan Hill—and came home a national hero. That fall, on the basis of his newfound popularity, he was elected governor of New York State.

Two years later, in the summer of 1900, Roosevelt was picked by William McKinley's backers to be the Vice Presidential candidate in McKinley's try for a second term. The Republican ticket won in November, and the Roosevelt family—which now included six children—moved to Washington. But Roosevelt served only six months as Vice President: on September 14, 1901, William McKinley was assassinated in Buffalo, and 42-year-old Theodore Roosevelt was sworn in as President of the United States, the youngest man ever to hold the office.

Roosevelt's accomplishments during his seven and one-half years as President—he was elected to a second term in 1904—were considerable. Abroad they included the building of the Panama Canal, as well as negotiating an end to the Russo-Japanese War, which earned him the Nobel Peace Prize in 1906. At home he was a zealous reformer who championed individual economic freedom against industrial monopolies, earning the nickname "trust-buster." (A trust is a combination of businesses that restricts competition.) Again on behalf of the public, he oversaw the passage of the first federal laws regulating the manufacture and sale of food and drugs.

Roosevelt's style was vigorous, like the cowhands he had come to admire in the West. His ideal was what he called "the strenuous life": "I'd rather wear out than rust out," he often said. He was also fond of saying that to accomplish something it was necessary only to "speak softly, and carry a big stick," but his own voice was loud and blunt: if he believed strongly in something—and he had a strong opinion about nearly everything—he defended it with passion.

One of Roosevelt's strongest interests was conservation, a consequence of his early interest in natural history and his later activities as a sportsman. During his extended visits to the Dakota Territory in the mid-1880s, he had noted the consequences of unwise land use. In 1887 he had joined with conservationist George Bird Grinnell in founding the Boone and Crockett Club, an organization of sportsmen dedicated

Theodore Roosevelt

BORN

October 27, 1858
New York City

DIED

January 6, 1919
Oyster Bay, New York

EDUCATION

A.B., Harvard University

MAJOR INTERESTS

Politics; American history; natural history; conservation

ACCOMPLISHMENTS

Vice President (1897-1901) and President (1901-09) of the United States; first U.S. President to lead a campaign for conservation; created the U.S. Forest Service; set aside 148 million acres for national forests and created six national parks; established the first federal wildlife refuge in the United States; encouraged passage of the Reclamation Act of 1902, which provided financing for irrigation projects in the West; supported passage of the Antiquities Act of 1906, which created 16 national monuments totaling 1.4 million acres; established National Conservation Commission; author of numerous books on American history, politics, and outdoor life, including *The Winning of the West* (4 volumes, 1889-96), *African Game Trails* (1910), and *Through the Brazilian Wilderness* (1914)

HONORS

Elected to Phi Beta Kappa at Harvard; winner of the Nobel Peace Prize (1906) for mediating the end of the Russo-Japanese War; awarded numerous honorary degrees

In 1903 Roosevelt, John Muir (fourth from right), and other members of the Sierra Club visited Yosemite.

to conserving game. As governor of New York, he had turned to Grinnell for advice on natural resource management. As President, he now had a new adviser on conservation: Gifford Pinchot, a young Yale-educated forester who was head of the Department of Agriculture's Forestry Division.

Pinchot was a crusader himself, devoted to scientific management of the nation's forests, and wholeheartedly opposed to the waste of any of the nation's natural resources. Pinchot's belief that the federal government had to play a major role in conservation overturned long-standing policy: throughout much of the 19th century the U.S. government had either given away public land or sold it for only a token amount of money; this encouraged rapid development of the land's natural resources and was a major factor in the nation's economic growth. But by the 1880s, as citizens became concerned about the long-term consequences of

unregulated development, a movement for conservation was born and received growing support throughout the country.

Thanks to the written appeals and intense lobbying of leaders such as John Muir and George Bird Grinnell, Congress began passing legislation to protect land and wildlife. The Enabling Act of 1891 allowed the President to set aside timberlands to protect them from lumbering companies. The first national forests were established during the 1890s, but by Roosevelt's administration they totaled only 40 million acres.

With Pinchot's encouragement and support, Roosevelt decided to make the federal government an active promoter of conservation. He began by expanding the forest reserve system and transforming the Forestry Division into the more powerful U.S. Forest Service, with a mandate to manage government-owned forests scientifically so that they would continue to yield timber for future generations. During Roosevelt's years as

President, 21 new national forests were created totaling 148 million acres.

Roosevelt's efforts on behalf of conservation were greater than those of any other President in history. He supported the Reclamation Act of 1902, which set aside receipts from public land sales to pay for irrigation of dry regions in the West. Roosevelt also supported passage of the Antiquities Act of 1906, which authorized the creation of 16 national monuments—land tracts that included archeological or other historic sites—totaling 1.4 million acres.

In 1908 Roosevelt held a White House conference on conservation and then established the National Conservation Commission to make a study of the nation's resources. Roosevelt established the first U.S. Wildlife Refuge on Pelican Island, Florida, in 1903; during his years in office he proclaimed 50 additional refuges across the country. Roosevelt also approved the establishment of six national parks—Crater Lake (Oregon), Grand Canyon (Arizona), Lassen Volcanic (California), Mesa Verde (Colorado), Petrified Forest (Arizona), and Wind Cave (South Dakota).

After leaving office in 1909, Roosevelt went on a yearlong trip abroad that included a hunting expedition in Africa. He returned to write a book, *African Game Trails: An Account of the Wanderings of an American Hunter-Naturalist* (1910), and to assume leadership of the growing Progressive movement. In 1912, breaking with the Republican party, he ran for President as the Progressive party's candidate against William Howard Taft, the Republican incumbent, and Democrat Woodrow Wilson, the ultimate victor. During the campaign he was the victim of an assassination attempt by a fanatic during a speech in Milwaukee; he survived because the impact of the bullet was offset by his glasses case and a folded copy of his speech in his breast pocket.

Taking a break from political life, Roosevelt served as president of the American Historical Association and wrote his autobiography, published in 1913. In 1914 he embarked on an expedition to the South American wilderness, exploring the La Plata River and writing about his adventures in *Through the Brazilian Wilderness*, published the same year. The trip was not entirely successful, however: he contracted several tropical infections from which he never fully recovered, and his health declined steadily.

Despite illness and the loss of sight in one eye—he had been blinded while President during a boxing match in the White House but did not allow his handicap to be revealed to the public—Roosevelt became a passionate advocate of the Allied cause before America's entry into World War I. He was acutely disappointed when the President refused his offer to lead a volunteer brigade into the conflict. All four of his sons later served in the war, and one was killed in action. Active to the end, Roosevelt published four more books on politics and history before dying in his sleep in January 1919 at the age of 60.

Monuments throughout the country pay tribute to the 26th President, including 70,000-acre Theodore Roosevelt National Park, in North Dakota. His most enduring symbol, however, is a toy stuffed animal known to millions of children as the teddy bear. In November 1902 a New York newspaper ran a cartoon showing President "Teddy" Roosevelt, dressed in his Rough Riders uniform, protecting a frightened bear cub. The wife of a Brooklyn candy store owner saw the cartoon and decided to make a few replicas of the bear, which she displayed in her store window. The "teddy bear" was born. Millions of teddy bears have been made since then for generations of children, most of whom probably do not know that their favorite stuffed animal was once a symbol of wildlife conservation.

FURTHER READING

Brooks, Chester L., and Ray H. Mattison. *Theodore Roosevelt and the Dakota Badlands*. Washington, D.C.: National Park Service, 1958.

Cutright, Paul Russell. *Theodore Roosevelt: The Making of a Conservationist*. Urbana: University of Illinois Press, 1985.

———. *Theodore Roosevelt the Naturalist*. New York: Harper, 1956.

Eliot, J. L. "T.R.'s Wilderness Legacy." *National Geographic*, September 1982, 340–63.

Hagedorn, Hermann. *The Roosevelt Family of Sagamore Hill*. New York: Macmillan, 1954.

———. *Roosevelt in the Bad Lands*. Boston: Houghton Mifflin, 1921.

McCullough, David. *Mornings on Horseback*. New York: Simon & Schuster, 1981.

Miller, Nathan. *Theodore Roosevelt: A Life*. New York: Morrow, 1992.

Morris, Edmund. *The Rise of Theodore Roosevelt*. New York: Coward, McCann, 1979.

Roosevelt, Kermit, and Theodore Roosevelt. *East of the Sun and West of the Moon*. New York: Scribners, 1926.

———. *Trailing the Giant Panda*. New York: Scribners, 1929.

Roosevelt, Theodore. *An Autobiography*. 1913. Abridged ed. New York: Scribners, 1958.

———. *Theodore Roosevelt's America: Selections from the Writings of the Oyster Bay Naturalist*. Edited by Farida Wiley. Greenwich, Conn.: Devin-Adair, 1955.

———. *Through the Brazilian Wilderness*. 1914. Reprint. Westport, Conn.: Greenwood Press, 1969.

"Roosevelt, Theodore." In *Dictionary of American Biography*. Vol. 8. New York: Scribners, 1964.

Ernest Thompson Seton

BLACK WOLF,
THE STORYTELLER

A century ago American children eagerly looked forward to each new book by one of their favorite writers, the Reverend William J. Long, of Stamford, Connecticut. Long, a minister as well as the best-selling author of such titles as *Nature Trails*, *Little Brother to the Bear*, and *Wood Folk at School*, wrote popular tales of friendly animals and their adventures in the woods.

In the last years of the 19th century and the beginning of the 20th, as the movement for wildlife and resource conservation grew in America, nature stories had become increasingly popular, among adults as well as children. Many writers like Long supplied tales that mixed fact with fiction to teach and entertain the public, often giving their animal subjects human names, traits, and personalities—and misleading readers who had no formal education in natural history.

At least one professional naturalist complained that many of these writers were doing more harm than good. In March 1903 John Burroughs published an essay, "Real and Sham Natural History," in the *Atlantic Monthly*, in which he criticized would-be naturalists who confused fact with fiction and led readers to assume that "make-believe" was truth. One of his targets was the Reverend William J. Long, but the writer who drew his harshest criticism was Ernest Thompson Seton, the author of the enormously popular *Wild Animals I Have Known* (1898).

There were several reasons why Burroughs focused his attack on Seton. Unlike Long, Seton had respectable credentials as a naturalist; he had done field research and written scientific articles and books, as well as works for a popular audience. Moreover, whereas Long wrote children's books, Seton's fictionalized nature stories were intended for adults as well as children, and thus had an even wider appeal. By writing a book "to profit by the popular love for the sensational and the improbable," Seton had, in John Burroughs's view, betrayed both himself and his readers.

A nationwide controversy erupted. Even Theodore Roosevelt, a friend of Burroughs and an acquaintance of Seton, jumped in—to defend Burroughs and to chastise what he called "nature-fakers," particularly Long. The attacks proved too much for the minister, who soon abandoned both children's books and the field of natural history and spent the rest of his life writing about English literature. Seton, however, kept on publishing his popular animal stories as well as respected nonfiction works, achieving even greater renown, and Burroughs's—and Roosevelt's—objections were eventually forgotten.

Seton, a naturalist, painter, and writer, was born in Durham, England, in 1860 to a family of Scottish descent

"No man owns the wood of the forest, or the water of the rivers, or the soil of the earth. He did not make them, they are the harvest of the land that belongs to the whole people; and only so much of them is his as he can gather with his own hands and use in his own home."

—from *The Gospel of the Redman* (1936)

In 1906 Ernest Thompson Seton, an enthusiastic outdoorsman, posed in camping clothes at his home in rural Connecticut. In scores of stories that he wrote and illustrated, Seton encouraged children to preserve wildlife and the natural environment.

A skilled illustrator of wildlife, Seton painted *Triumph of the Wolves* in 1892; it was exhibited a year later at the World's Columbian Exhibition in Chicago under a new title, *Awaited in Vain.*

named Thompson and was christened Ernest Evan. He used several surnames before legally changing his name to Ernest Thompson Seton in 1901, in recognition of an 18th-century earl and forebear, George Seton. The Thompsons immigrated to Canada in 1866 when their shipping business failed, and they settled on a farm in Ontario. Four years later they gave up rural life and moved to Toronto, but young Ernest had already made up his mind to become a naturalist.

His father, whom Ernest later remembered as a harsh disciplinarian to his 12 children, decided that the boy should become an artist because of his obvious talent for drawing. After leaving high school in 1876, Ernest was apprenticed to a portrait painter and then studied at the Ontario School of Art. In 1879 he went reluctantly to London to continue his art lessons, and the following year won a scholarship to attend the

Royal Academy of Painting and Sculpture. Having little money and in poor health, he returned to Toronto in late 1881 and a few months later set off for the Canadian province of Manitoba, his determination renewed to become a naturalist.

Seton spent most of the next five years on the prairies of rural Manitoba, leaving only for several extended stays in Toronto and New York. He helped one of his brothers build a homestead but devoted most of his time to exploring the region, studying its natural history and collecting and sketching specimens. His first publication, a monograph on the mammals of Manitoba, was followed by numerous articles on birds, which he published in *The Auk*, the journal of the American Ornithologists' Union. His growing reputation as a naturalist-illustrator led to commissions to illustrate *The Century Dictionary* (1889-91) and bird guides by the noted ornithologist Frank Chapman.

Seton now felt more secure about his future, knowing he could combine his talent for drawing with his interest in nature study. He returned to Paris in 1890 for further study in painting and anatomy, and a year later was honored with an exhibition of one of his paintings—a study of a sleeping wolf—at the Grand Salon. That same year, 1891, his first book, *The Birds of Manitoba*, was published in Canada. Seton interrupted his art studies in 1893 to return to North America briefly, where he worked as a wolf killer on a New Mexico cattle ranch; the experience inspired one of his most popular tales, "The King of Currumpaw," the story of a wolf named Lobo who is captured because of his loyalty to his mate.

Seton had begun to write and illustrate fictionalized tales of animals during his years in Manitoba. The demand for his stories increased when *St. Nicholas*, a leading U.S. children's magazine, published "Molly Cottontail" in 1889. This story of a rabbit became one of Seton's most famous and was read throughout the English-speaking world. The British poet and novelist Rudyard Kipling (1865-1936) later wrote Seton that "Molly Cottontail" had inspired him to write his famous children's work *The Jungle Book*.

During the 1890s Seton became a self-supporting writer as his animal stories were increasingly published in U.S. and Canadian magazines. He married in 1896 and several years later bought an estate in Greenwich, Connecticut, where he established a wildfowl refuge. Although this was his official residence for more than 30 years, Seton spent long periods away from home, collecting material for his books and stories, first in the western United States and then abroad. One of his most arduous field trips was a six-month-long, 2,000-mile journey by canoe through northern Canada to the Arctic Circle in 1907 to study caribou; his account of the trek was published four years later as *The Arctic Prairies*.

As his works grew in popularity, Seton also embarked on frequent lecture tours. His first collection of stories was *Wild Animals I Have Known*, which Seton himself promoted, giving talks that he illustrated with lantern slides of his own photographs and drawings. The book was an instant best-seller: within three weeks of its publication in October 1898, the entire first printing of 2,000 copies had been sold. Other successful books about nature followed during the next 40 years, including more best-selling collections of animal stories.

In 1902 Seton formally founded the League of Woodcraft Indians, an organization to promote nature study and conservation among boys. The first "tribe" had been created on Seton's estate in Connecticut in the spring of 1901; its "Indians" were local youth who had been vandalizing the grounds. At that meeting, Seton gathered 40 boys together around a campfire to teach them "Indian ways," including respect for the natural environment. The boys were invited to use his woods, provided that they did so without harming wildlife. They elected a chief and councillors, and made Seton their "medicine man," giving him the name Black Wolf. With Seton as its director, the Woodcraft movement spread throughout the United States and to other countries, and later included units for girls as well as boys. For the rest of his life, Seton was known to millions of children and their parents as "Black Wolf."

Seton's interest in teaching conservation and nature study also led him to head a committee that in 1910 established the Boy Scouts in the United States; the original group had been founded four years earlier in England by Robert Baden-Powell. Seton wrote the first *Boy Scout Manual* and served until 1915 as "chief scout" of the organization.

Ernest Thompson Seton

BORN

August 14, 1860
Durham, England

DIED

October 23, 1946
Santa Fe, New Mexico

EDUCATION

Studied art in Toronto, London, New York, and Paris

MAJOR INTERESTS

Nature study; wildlife illustration; Native American life and lore

ACCOMPLISHMENTS

Illustrator and author of 28 nature-related books, including *Wild Animals I Have Known* (1898), *Biography of a Grizzly* (1900), *Lives of Game Animals* (1927), and *Trail of an Artist-Naturalist* (1940); founder of the Woodcraft Indians (1902), an organization that introduced children to outdoor life; chief founder of the Boy Scouts of America (1910); supporter of wildlife conservation; defender of Native American rights

HONORS

Awarded the Burroughs Medal (1927) for *Lives of Game Animals*

EVEN Song.

Seton called this drawing of wolves *Evensong*.

published in four volumes between 1925 and 1928. After the death of John Burroughs in 1921, his friends had formed the Burroughs Memorial Association and established an annual award for the best nature writing of the year. In 1926 Ernest Thompson Seton—who had once been denounced as a fraud by Burroughs himself—was the recipient of the Burroughs Medal for the first two volumes of *Lives of Game Animals*.

FURTHER READING

Keller, Betty. *Black Wolf: The Life of Ernest Thompson Seton*. Vancouver: Douglas & McIntyre, 1984.

Seton, Ernest Thompson. *Biography of a Grizzly*. 1900. Reprint. Lincoln: University of Nebraska Press, 1987.

———. *Lives of Game Animals*. New York: Doubleday, Page, 1925–28.

———. *Trail of an Artist-Naturalist*. New York: Scribners, 1940.

———. *Wild Animals I Have Known*. 1898. Reprint. New York: Penguin, 1987.

"Seton, Ernest Thompson." In *Dictionary of American Biography*. Supplement 4. New York: Scribners, 1974.

From his earliest explorations of the Canadian prairies Seton was a student of Indian life and lore, which formed the basis of the Woodcraft League's philosophy and teachings and became the subject of lectures Seton gave throughout the United States, Canada, and Europe. In 1930 he separated from his wife and moved to a 2,500-acre tract near Santa Fe, New Mexico. Five years later, after a divorce, he was married a second time, to Julia Moss Buttree, who was also a writer and an authority on Indian life. Together they established the Seton Institute, an organization to promote the preservation of Native American culture, and until his death in 1946 Seton was an outspoken champion of Indian rights.

During his lifetime Seton wrote and illustrated 28 books on nature themes, including an autobiography, *Trail of an Artist-Naturalist* (1940). He claimed to be equally proud of all his publications, but he may have had a special regard for the nonfictional *Lives of Game Animals*,

George Washington Carver

THE AGRICULTURAL WIZARD

S oil conservation? Recycling? These are major concerns of the environmental movement in the late 20th century, but they are not new. Nearly one hundred years ago a former slave of the American South began showing farmers that they could make more from less—simply by taking better care of their soil and using formerly discarded materials. George Washington Carver had multiple professions in the course of his long life—botanist, chemist, inventor, educator—but the focus of all of them was wise use of the earth.

Carver's origins are so obscure that no one is even certain of his birth date. He was born on a Missouri farm owned by Moses Carver sometime during the Civil War, possibly in 1864. Slave raiders from Arkansas carried the infant George and his mother away one night when he was only a few weeks old; his mother was never found, but Moses Carver swapped a race-horse for the boy's return and he was raised by the farmer and his wife.

In his early teens George Carver—he took the surname of his master, who may have been his father—left the household to get a formal education. He worked at odd jobs for several

George Washington Carver (second from right) instructs students at Alabama's Tuskegee Institute. As director of agriculture at Tuskegee, Carver taught techniques of soil conservation to thousands of farmers throughout the South.

This rare photograph, taken in 1891, shows Carver, a self-taught artist as well as a scientist, with a painting of his favorite subject: flowers.

years while attending grade schools for African Americans in other Missouri communities and Kansas. Carver eventually completed high school in Minneapolis, Kansas, taking the middle name "Washington" to distinguish himself from another George Carver in the class.

For a while Carver homesteaded on the Kansas plains, but the work was too hard for a lone man, and in 1888 he moved to Iowa, where he eventually gained admission to Simpson College, in Indianola, supporting himself by doing laundry as well as needlework—tatting, knitting, and embroidery. At Simpson he also developed an aptitude for painting and thought for a while of becoming an artist. His teachers, however, persuaded him to study botany, knowing how much he loved plants; they may also have doubted that a black man could earn his living as an artist, since there was widespread prejudice against African Americans.

In 1891 Carver transferred to the Iowa State College of Agriculture, in Ames. His abilities were quickly recognized by the faculty; he served as an assistant to several professors and was eventually put in charge of the college greenhouse, where he conducted experiments in plant fertilization. After receiving bachelor's and master's degrees in science, Carver moved to Alabama in 1896 at the invitation of Booker T. Washington to become director of agricultural work at the Tuskegee Institute. Washington had founded Tuskegee in 1881 as a center for the education of African Americans, who had very few opportunities for learning.

Carver was a shy, hardworking man with little concern for pleasure, personal comfort, or earning money. These traits became even more pronounced as he matured. Deeply religious, he believed that he had a duty to promote human welfare—the well-being of all men and women, whether black or white—and though he often suffered from the policies of segregation, he refused to be deterred by them. Carver began his career by serving his own race, but his efforts eventually helped the entire American South.

From the moment of his arrival at Tuskegee, Carver seized every opportunity to make himself useful. He even played the piano in concerts to raise funds for the school. In addition to his regular teaching duties, he began a series of conferences at Tuskegee for African-American farmers to teach them better agricultural methods, and he also taught them about proper nutrition. He set up farm demonstration programs, including the training of extension agents—men who visited farmers and advised them on how to increase crop yields, prevent erosion, and control pests. To reach those farmers who could not come to the institute, he created a "movable school of agriculture," taking teachers and equipment in wagons to remote rural areas. Eventually the "movable school" also gave lessons in home economics, reaching the most disadvantaged settlers. Carver's idea was later adopted in rural areas throughout the world; he considered it one of his greatest achievements.

As Carver learned more about southern agriculture, he became convinced that many problems encountered by farmers were the consequence of several factors. The most important was a lack of crop diversification: farmers grew the same plant, usually cotton, year after year, depleting the soil of essential minerals. Furthermore, soil conservation was neglected, and plants did not receive adequate protection against pests. Finally, crops were not used efficiently to create farm products and by-products.

Carver mounted a systematic attack against these problems. First he

George Washington Carver

BORN

1864?
Diamond Grove, Missouri

DIED

January 5, 1943
Tuskegee, Alabama

EDUCATION

Attended Simpson College (Iowa); B.S., M.S., Iowa State College of Agriculture

MAJOR INTEREST

Agriculture

ACCOMPLISHMENTS

Improved agriculture and farm life in the American South by advocating crop diversification and composting to restore soil; introduced peanuts and sweet potatoes as major commercial crops; invented hundreds of new products from peanuts, sweet potatoes, pecans, soybeans, and other plants

HONORS

Elected a fellow of the Royal Society of London (1916); awarded the Spingarn Medal from the National Association for the Advancement of Colored People (1923); honorary degrees from Simpson College and the University of Rochester

launched a campaign to persuade farmers to plant other crops—especially peanuts, sweet potatoes, and cowpeas—in place of cotton, which had not only depleted the soil but also attracted a specific pest, the boll weevil. He also became an ardent advocate of rebuilding soil through composting, making use of all kinds of organic manner that farmers were "hauling away and burning." In his laboratory— assembled from cast-off materials he found in trash piles—Carver began a thorough study of crop diseases and ways to make plants resistant to them, and he also developed ways to preserve crops by dehydration. In fact, he pioneered such studies, which were done many years before the U.S. Department of Agriculture made similar investigations.

Carver realized that farmers would grow different crops only if a demand existed for them. Cotton had many commercial uses, but peanuts and sweet potatoes were used only by farmers themselves; they had never been grown on a large scale. Again returning to his crude laboratory, he began to develop new products from these crops. During his lifetime he invented 325 different peanut derivatives, ranging from beverages to ink to synthetic rubber, by using all parts of the plant, including the shells. He also devised a new therapy for the treatment of patients crippled by polio that included a peanut-oil massage.

In addition to his work with peanuts, Carver discovered 118 different uses for sweet potatoes and also made many new products from pecans, soybeans, cowpeas, and other crops. A minority of them were developed for commercial use, but Carver had made his point: southern agriculture could, and did, diversify, and the land was renewed in the process.

Carver never patented any of these agricultural processes, believing that their benefits should be widely shared. In fact, he obtained only one patent—for a process for extracting pigments from clay, an abundant southern resource. He never published his discoveries in scientific journals; he wrote mostly for the farmers and housewives of the South, publishing numerous agricultural bulletins on such topics as "How to Build Up Worn Out Soils," "Nature Study and Gardening for Rural Schools," and "Three Delicious Meals Every Day for the Farmer."

Widely hailed as both a scientist and a humanitarian, Carver was given many honors, including election as a fellow of the Royal Society of London. Many industrial leaders, including automobile manufacturer Henry Ford, invited Carver to join their companies and work for huge salaries, but he refused. Carver remained at Tuskegee for 47 years, working and writing until shortly before his death in 1943. Eight years later the former slave who had risen from poverty to become a world-acclaimed agricultural wizard was granted a rare honor: his birthplace at Diamond Grove was proclaimed a national monument.

"Nature study is agriculture, and agriculture is nature study—if properly taught."

—from "Nature Study and Gardening for Rural Schools"

FURTHER READING

Adair, Gene. *George Washington Carver.* New York: Chelsea House, 1989.

"Carver, George Washington." In *Dictionary of American Biography.* Supplement 3. New York: Scribners, 1973.

Elliott, Lawrence. *George Washington Carver: The Man Who Overcame.* Englewood Cliffs, N.J.: Prentice-Hall, 1966.

Holt, Rackham. *George Washington Carver: An American Biography.* Garden City, N.Y.: Doubleday, 1943; 2nd ed., 1963.

McMurry, Linda O. *George Washington Carver: Scientist and Symbol.* New York: Oxford University Press, 1981.

Gifford Pinchot

AMERICA'S FIRST NATIVE FORESTER

Silviculture—the development and care of forests—has been practiced for hundreds of years in Europe, where an unchecked demand for timber could easily use up all of the continent's limited supply of trees. In the United States, however, the scientific management of forests was begun only in the 20th century. Two men were the principal leaders of the movement to conserve America's timber resources: one was President Theodore Roosevelt; the other was his friend Gifford Pinchot.

Pinchot holds a unique distinction in U.S. history: he was the country's first native forester, a person trained to manage forests. Pinchot knew at an early age that this was what he wanted to do, but the idea was so novel that when he an-

U.S. Forest Service director Gifford Pinchot (right) accompanied President Theodore Roosevelt on a trip down the Mississippi River in October 1907.

Pinchot founded the National Conservation Association in 1909 and became a nationally known crusader for protection of the nation's forests. A contemporary newspaper cartoon depicted Pinchot as an enraged forester attacking serpents identified as "land grabbers" and "land thieves."

nounced his chosen career to school friends, they were puzzled. Why would anyone need to manage America's abundant forests? Weren't there enough trees to last forever?

In 1865, when Pinchot was born, there did seem to be an unending supply of trees and other natural resources. A year earlier, George Perkins Marsh had published *Man and Nature,* in which he warned that "we have felled forest enough everywhere, . . . far too much," but several more decades passed before conservation began to be a serious national concern. However, by the 1870s many thoughtful people were starting to question whether the country's resources

were really limitless. One of them was Gifford Pinchot's father, James, a wealthy New York merchant of French descent.

James Pinchot was a cultured man who read history for relaxation, and he knew how important France's resources, especially its forests, had been to the country's welfare. His children—Gifford, a brother, and two sisters—were taught this lesson firsthand, both at their country home in Pennsylvania and during extensive travel and residence in France. Gifford Pinchot loved being outdoors, and he listened carefully as his father talked about natural history and the need for conservation.

In 1875 a group of men concerned about the depletion of the nation's forests founded the American Forestry Association; their lobbying efforts in Congress led to the creation six years later of the Division of Forestry within the Department of Agriculture. However, the tiny division had little impact on the nation's forests; its director, a German forester named Bernhard Fernow, was a cautious man who confined his efforts to research and education.

Pinchot, who would one day succeed Fernow, was in boarding school when the Forestry Division was founded in 1881. Four years later he entered Yale University with the sole intention of becoming a forester. There were no classes yet in forestry, so Pinchot studied the sciences, including botany and meteorology. After graduation in 1889, he enrolled in the French National Forestry School in Nancy and spent a year studying forest management in France, Switzerland, and Germany. He was especially impressed by the European tradition of maintaining forests as a national resource, and vowed that he would work to establish a similar policy in his own country.

Pinchot returned to the United States in 1890 to establish himself as a forester, but at first there seemed to be no job for him. He got in touch with Dr.

Fernow at the Forestry Division, and the forester invited him on an inspection trip to Arkansas. Pinchot hoped at first that Fernow might hire him, but he found the older man so arrogant and domineering that he decided to have nothing to do with the Forestry Division while Fernow was in charge. Instead, he was hired in 1892 by the industrialist George W. Vanderbilt to set up a one-year demonstration project for the forests of Biltmore, the vast estate of the Vanderbilts in North Carolina.

Pinchot did such a good job of harvesting and planting that the forestry operation made a profit. To attract other employers he made a display of his operations for the World's Columbian Exposition, held in Chicago in 1893, and wrote an account of his activities, *Biltmore Forest,* which he mailed to newspapers throughout the country. For several years Pinchot worked from an office in New York City as a "consulting forester" for both public and private clients, and also tramped through wooded areas all over the United States to get firsthand knowledge of the country's forest resources.

In 1891 the first U.S. forest reserves, comprising 13 million acres of woods in the West, had been created by the federal government, thanks to the lobbying efforts of the American Forestry Association; the forests were placed under the jurisdiction of the General Land Office in the U.S. Department of the Interior. Five years later the National Academy of Sciences, at the direction of President Grover Cleveland, created the National Forest Commission as an advisory body to make recommendations on the forest reserves to the Interior Department, and Pinchot was named a member of the commission.

For two years, acting as a special forest agent, Pinchot traveled through the reserves, surveying them for the government. Then, in 1898, when Dr. Fernow resigned as head of the Forestry Division, Pinchot was appointed his successor. Since his days as a forestry student in France, Pinchot had wanted to work in the federal government to manage the nation's timber resources. Now he had the opportunity to influence and perhaps even make government policy.

The conservation movement of the late 19th century, led by George Bird Grinnell, John Muir, John Burroughs, Theodore Roosevelt, and others, was in full swing, working to arouse public opinion against exploitation of all the nation's natural resources—wildlife and minerals as well as trees. Already, however, lines were being drawn between *conservationists*, those who believed that careful, prudent use of natural resources would guarantee their renewal and continuation, and *preservationists*, who wanted to save most resources rather than use them.

Burroughs and Muir supported preservation, arguing that wildness should be maintained for its own sake; Grinnell and Roosevelt believed that resources should be conserved—used wisely, but protected from greedy exploiters. Gifford Pinchot was on the side of conservationists, calling for scientific management of the nation's forests that would allow them to produce timber for both present and future generations.

His first goal in his new job as head of the Forestry Division was to get the forest reserves moved out of the Interior Department and into the Agriculture Department under his jurisdiction. Pinchot wanted to expand the acreage of the reserves and at the same time put their timber under the control of the government, which would regulate its use. However, he had to convince a skeptical public that the nation's forests were better off under scientific management at the hands of the government than they would be by either outright preservation or unrestricted cutting.

Pinchot took his case to the people

Gifford Pinchot

BORN
August 11, 1865
Simsbury, Connecticut

DIED
October 4, 1946
New York City

EDUCATION
B.A., Yale University; French National Forestry School

MAJOR INTERESTS
Forestry; conservation

ACCOMPLISHMENTS
First head of the U.S. Forest Service; chief adviser on conservation issues to President Theodore Roosevelt; governor of Pennsylvania; founder of the Society of American Foresters; professor, Yale School of Forestry

HONORS
Honorary degrees from Yale, Princeton, and McGill universities

through publications and speeches, arguing for long-term interests over short-term gain. His campaign took seven years, but finally, in 1905, Congress passed a law creating the U.S. Forest Service within the Department of Agriculture. The reserves, renamed the national forests, were moved to the new service, with Pinchot as its first head.

Pinchot had support in his fight from Theodore Roosevelt, a longtime friend who had succeeded the assassinated William McKinley to the Presidency in September 1901. Pinchot became Roosevelt's chief adviser on federal regulation of natural resources and convinced the President that they should be managed "along the best modern business lines." The nation's chief forester initiated the creation in 1903 of the Public Lands Commission, which authorized the U.S. Geological Survey to make a systematic study and classification of all the nation's natural resources.

Roosevelt was able to act more assertively in support of legislation to regulate resources after his own election as President in 1904. Despite his conservationist sympathies, he pursued a dual course: he made preservationists happy by creating national parks and monuments, but listened to Pinchot's advice about timber and set aside 148 million acres as national forest land—an area equivalent to nearly five times the size of New York State.

In 1908 Pinchot and Roosevelt together organized the first White House Conference on the Conservation of Natural Resources, which was attended by the nation's governors and other leading citizens. That same year Roosevelt created the National Conservation Commission, with Pinchot as chairman. However, Pinchot did not get along well with William Howard Taft, who succeeded Roosevelt as President in

1909, and the following year he was fired as head of the Forest Service after a disagreement with Taft's Secretary of the Interior.

As a private citizen, Pinchot continued to work as an ardent spokesman for conservation. In 1909 he founded a lobbying group called the National Conservation Association and served as its head from 1910 until it disbanded in 1923. He was a major supporter of the Weeks Act of 1911, which provided for the purchase of additional forest reserves. He also taught at the Yale School of Forestry, founded by his father in 1900, and continued to serve as president of the Society of American Foresters, which he had helped establish at the turn of the century.

Dismayed by Taft's policies, which he believed were not in the best interests of conservation, he helped organize the National Progressive Republican League in 1911 and its successor, the Progressive party, in 1912, which nominated Roosevelt as its Presidential candidate. After Roosevelt's loss to Woodrow Wilson, Pinchot decided to enter politics himself and tried unsuccessfully for a seat in the U.S. Senate. In 1920 he was appointed forestry commissioner of Pennsylvania, and two years later was elected governor of the state.

Pinchot served two terms as governor of Pennsylvania, from 1923 to 1927 and from 1931 to 1935. (Pennsylvania law prevented him from serving consecutive terms.) His major accomplishments included tighter regulation of public utilities and the construction of thousands of miles of rural roads. Despite health problems, he continued to speak out on conservation and other national issues, and devised a method of extracting drinking water from fish juices that was adopted by the U.S. Navy for use during World War II. Pinchot spent his

last years working on his autobiography, *Breaking New Ground*, published after his death in 1946.

In the late 20th century, many supporters of conservation do not consider Gifford Pinchot a hero. They point to his strong support for the damming of Yosemite's Hetch-Hetchy Valley, which John Muir had strongly opposed, and claim that his policies turned the Forestry Service into an organization that served the timber industry and not the nation as a whole. At heart Pinchot may have been more a businessman than an environmentalist, but at a time when unchecked greed threatened to destroy the country's wilderness, his efforts to regulate the use of natural resources were invaluable.

FURTHER READING

Fausold, Martin L. *Gifford Pinchot: Bull Moose Progressive*. Syracuse, N.Y.: Syracuse University Press, 1961.

McGeary, Martin N. *Gifford Pinchot: Forester-Politician*. Princeton, N.J.: Princeton University Press, 1960.

Pinchot, Gifford. *Biltmore Forest*. 1893. Reprint. New York: Arno, 1970.

———. *Breaking New Ground*. New York: Harcourt, Brace, 1947.

———. *The Fight for Conservation*. 1910. Reprint. Edited by Gerald D. Nash. Seattle: University of Washington Press, 1967.

"Pinchot, Gifford." In *Dictionary of American Biography*. Supplement 4. New York: Scribners, 1974.

Wild, Peter. "Gifford Pinchot, Aristocrat." In *Pioneer Conservationists of Western America*. Missoula, Mont.: Mountain Press, 1979.

Enos Mills

PROTECTOR OF THE ROCKIES

One day in 1889 a 19-year-old boy wandered through Golden Gate Park in San Francisco. He had been working for several years at a copper mine in Butte, Montana, but the mine had shut down suddenly because of a fire, so the boy, whose name was Enos Mills, had gone to California for a brief vacation.

Young Mills had been on his own since the age of 14, working at mining or herding cattle to support himself and taking time off to climb peaks in the Rockies. He loved the wilderness and enjoyed his rather aimless roaming as a "mountain man." Strolling through the park that day, he asked a stranger about a plant and discovered that the other man shared his enthusiasm for nature. As the two walked in the park, they swapped stories of outdoor life—and Mills learned that his new friend was the naturalist John Muir.

"If it hadn't been for him, I would have been a mere gypsy," Mills later claimed, for it was Muir who told young

America's first professional nature guide, Enos Mills, tramps on snowshoes near Long's Peak Inn in Colorado.

Master of ceremonies Mills addresses a crowd at the dedication of Rocky Mountain National Park in north-central Colorado in 1915. The event capped a six-year crusade led by Mills to establish a national park in the Rockies.

"The guide sometimes takes his party to a commanding viewpoint or a beautiful spot. But views are incidental. The aim is to illuminate and reveal the alluring world outdoors. . . . A nature guide is an interpreter of geology, botany, zoology, and natural history."

—from " The Evolution of Nature Guiding," an essay by Mills now used as a training guide by the U.S. National Park Service

Mills that he should devote his life to working for the preservation of "the wild places of the West." Muir was already celebrated as the savior of Yosemite. Enos Mills decided that he would protect the Rocky Mountains.

Little is known of Mills's early life. He was born in 1870 in Kansas City, Kansas, to pioneers who had originally come from Indiana. He was apparently a sickly child and in 1884 left his family to seek a better climate in Colorado. Mills

worked on ranches and did odd jobs at a tourist hotel in Estes Park, and under the Homestead Act acquired a small piece of land at the base of Long's Peak that became his home for most of his life.

During the late 1880s Mills spent the winter months working in the copper mines of Butte. The town had a large library and he often "sat up half the night reading and writing." In the summers he returned to the cabin he had built at Long's Peak. Here he spent most days roaming through the mountains; when the weather was too bad to go outside, he taught himself arithmetic and grammar, and read biographies and history books.

With John Muir's encouragement, Mills returned to Colorado to embark on a career as a nature guide. He organized climbing trips up Long's Peak, and during rest stops entertained the travelers with talks on wildlife. He also began giving public lectures on nature topics and writing a column about Estes Park for a Denver newspaper. In 1901 he bought more property around Long's

Peak and established the Long's Peak Inn as a resort for nature lovers. The inn became widely known and provided Mills with a steady income.

Mills continued to enjoy tramping alone through the mountains, and for several winters was hired by the state of Colorado to measure the depth of snow in the Rockies. His often hair-raising adventures—he narrowly missed being the victim of avalanches and landslides—provided the basis for a series of adventure stories that he began writing for *Harper's, Atlantic Monthly, Sunset, American Boy,* and other leading periodicals. Mills's stories and lectures also emphasized the gentler side of nature—as a serene wonderland of friendly woodpeckers, amusing bears, curious skunks, and other animals that provided diversion and relaxation for people weary of civilization. He carried a camera everywhere he went and used many of his photographs to illustrate the books he later wrote.

Mills published his first book, *The Story of Estes Park and Guide Book,* in 1905. More than a dozen followed, including *Wild Life on the Rockies* (1909), *The Spell of the Rockies* (1911), *In Beaver World* (1913), and *Adventures of a Nature Guide* (1920). One of his most widely celebrated books was *The Story of a Thousand Year Pine* (1914), which was translated into several other languages and printed in braille.

Forests became one of Mills's major concerns in the early 1900s. In 1905 he toured the East Coast at his own expense and delivered a series of addresses on trees. Theodore Roosevelt heard about the talks and hired Mills as a "federal lecturer on forestry," a post he held for several years. As he traveled around the country Mills urged his audiences to support the creation of national parks, and in 1909 he formally launched a crusade to establish a park in the Rockies.

Six years—and hundreds of lectures—later, working with leading environmentalists, including Robert Marshall and Stephen Mather, Mills's long-held dream was realized: Rocky Mountain National Park was formally dedicated on September 4, 1915, with Enos Mills as master of ceremonies. A year later he helped frame the congressional act that created the National Park Service.

Mills continued to write books and articles, to operate Long's Peak Inn, and to lecture on the value of wilderness. In 1918 he married a resident of Estes Park, and they had a daughter. The instability of his childhood had been replaced by a secure middle age. And then tragedy struck. On a trip to New York City in 1922 to visit his publisher, Mills was severely hurt in a subway collision. He returned to his cabin at Long's Peak to recuperate, but the injuries, complicated by an attack of influenza, killed him a few months after the accident. He was 52 years old.

FURTHER READING

Hawthorne, Hildegarde, and Esther Burnell Mills. *Enos Mills of the Rockies.* Boston: Houghton Mifflin, 1935.

McKibben, Bill. "Hero of the Wilderness." *New York Review of Books,* November 9, 1989, 20-25.

Mills, Enos. *The Adventures of a Nature Guide.* Garden City, N.Y.: Doubleday, 1920.

———.*In Beaver World.* 1913. Reprint. Lincoln: University of Nebraska Press, 1990.

———. *The Spell of the Rockies.* 1911. Reprint. Lincoln: University of Nebraska Press, 1989.

———. *The Story of a Thousand Year Pine.* Boston: Houghton Mifflin, 1914.

"Mills, Enos." In *Dictionary of American Biography.* Supplement 1. New York: Scribners, 1944.

Wild, Peter. "Enos Mills: Propagandist of the Rocky Mountains." In *Pioneer Conservationists of Western America.* Missoula, Mont.: Mountain Press, 1979.

Enos Mills

BORN

April 22, 1870
Kansas City, Kansas

DIED

September 21, 1922
Long's Peak, Colorado

EDUCATION

Self-educated

MAJOR INTEREST

Natural history

ACCOMPLISHMENTS

America's first professional nature guide; wrote numerous accounts of his experiences in the wilds for leading periodicals; worked for establishment of Rocky Mountain National Park; his many books include *The Story of Estes Park and Guide Book* (1905), *In Beaver World* (1913), and *The Story of a Thousand Year Pine* (1914)

Ann Haven Morgan

LIFE IN A POND

To make the knowledge of the whole range of life in ponds and streams a little more easy of access is a major purpose of this book. And with that knowledge will come appreciation, and a purpose to aid in keeping the waters free from pollution. Clean waters are always charming; and nothing is more sordid or unwholesome than polluted water."

Although those sentences could easily have been written today, they appear in the foreword to a book first published in 1930: *Field Book of Ponds and Streams*, by Ann Haven Morgan. The author of the foreword was James G. Needham, a biology professor at Cornell University who had been Dr. Morgan's teacher 20 years earlier. As Morgan wrote in her preface to the book, it was Needham "who showed me how to look for things in the water." Needham also inspired Morgan's early interest in ecology.

From childhood Ann Haven Morgan—her given name was Anna; she shortened it to Ann when she was 30—seems

Zoology professor Ann Haven Morgan (left) dredges for pond creatures with Mount Holyoke College student Eileen Hines.

to have focused on a career as a biologist. She was born in 1882 in Waterford, Connecticut, to a family that was financially comfortable and believed strongly in education for both men and women. The eldest of three children, she preferred being alone, and like many who grew up to pursue a career in natural history and the biological sciences she spent as much time as possible outdoors, in the countryside surrounding her home.

Morgan's parents sent her to a private school in New London, Connecticut, for her secondary education, and enrolled her at the all-female Wellesley College, near Boston, in 1902. She was not happy at Wellesley, however; she wanted to attend a large, coeducational university where she believed the opportunities for science studies were greater. After two years she was allowed to enter Cornell, and she graduated with a bachelor's degree in zoology in 1906.

The following fall Ann Haven Morgan began teaching at Mount Holyoke, in South Hadley, Massachusetts, the first year of a lifelong association with the college. She took a leave of absence in 1909 to return to Cornell to study for a doctorate in zoology. After receiving her Ph.D. in 1912—she wrote her dissertation on mayflies—Morgan returned to Mount Holyoke and was rapidly promoted, becoming a full professor six years later.

Morgan taught a variety of classes in zoology as well as a course in water biology. She took her students on field trips to area ponds and streams to study freshwater life—the plants and animals that lived there—and gave them a firsthand introduction to ecology. A favorite site for Morgan's own research was a pond on Mount Tom, in nearby Northampton, Massachusetts. She would ride a trolley car from South Hadley to Northampton, then hike up the mountain to the pond, where she studied water bugs. In the wintertime she chopped holes through the ice to gather traps she had set to collect them. Morgan became such a familiar sight to the trolley car operators that they called her "the Water Bug Lady."

Morgan's field work in zoology and water biology took her to freshwater sites throughout the Northeast as well as to British Guiana, and she spent a number of summers on the staff of the famed Marine Biological Laboratory in Woods Hole, Massachusetts. Early in her career she had decided to write a guide to aquatic life, and for nearly two decades she collected data, photographs, and drawings for her book.

Morgan's work was published in 1930 as *Field Book of Ponds and Streams: An Introduction to the Life of Fresh Water*. The book was clearly written and easy to understand, and immediately became popular. Used by professional and amateur naturalists alike, as well as by recreational fishermen, *Field Book of Ponds and Streams* was reprinted many times and for nearly 40 years was the most widely used guidebook to freshwater life in America. Readers were so enthusiastic that many of them wrote fan letters to Morgan, telling her how much pleasure her book had provided.

Morgan now had a wide popular audience for her work, but for many years she had also been establishing a reputation among her colleagues as an outstanding biologist. In middle age and mid-career she now began receiving honors for her accomplishments—honors that were rarely, if ever, accorded women. Morgan was one of only three women to be included among the 250 entries of the 1933 *American Men of Science*. Harvard, Yale, and Cornell universities appointed her a visiting fellow. She was elected to Sigma Xi, the national science honor society, and was named a fellow of the American Association for the Advancement of Science.

In 1939 Morgan published her second book, *Field Book of Animals in*

Ann Haven Morgan

BORN

May 6, 1882
Waterford, Connecticut

DIED

June 5, 1966
South Hadley, Massachusetts

EDUCATION

B.A., Ph.D., Cornell University

MAJOR INTERESTS

Biology; ecology

ACCOMPLISHMENTS

Early advocate of ecological awareness; professor of zoology, Mount Holyoke College; author of *Field Book of Ponds and Streams* (1930), *Field Book of Animals in Winter* (1939), and *Kinships of Animals and Man* (1955)

HONORS

One of three women listed in *American Men of Science*, 5th ed. (1933); admitted to Sigma Xi, the science honor society; fellow, American Association for the Advancement of Science

An illustration from Morgan's *Field Book of Ponds and Streams* shows aquatic insects; the overlay on the left helps the reader identify each creature.

> *"Humanity created civilization out of the wilderness. Now that the wilderness is almost gone, we are beginning to be lonesome for it. We shall keep a refuge for our minds if we conserve the remnants."*
>
> —from *Kinships of Animals and Man* (1955)

Winter, an outgrowth of a course she taught in "winter biology." The guide—like her earlier book, the first of its kind—was "an introduction to the ways in which animals meet the crises and depressions of winter." Aided by drawings, diagrams, paintings, and photographs, Morgan described the cold-weather behavior of American birds, fish, mammals, reptiles, amphibians, and insects. The unique guide is still in print, more than a half century after its first publication.

Morgan retired from the Mount Holyoke faculty in 1947, but she remained active in nearly a dozen scientific organizations, including the American Society of Naturalists and the Ecological Society of America. To all of these associations she brought a concern for conservation, which had become her major interest. Not long after her retirement from Mount Holyoke she traveled extensively in the western part of the United States observing conservation projects and returned to the East to become a vigorous supporter of conservation in the Connecticut River Valley.

In retirement Morgan also wrote her third and last book, a biology text called *Kinships of Animals and Man* (1955) that focuses on ecology. Until her death in 1966, Morgan worked tirelessly to reform the science curriculum in American schools, urging that instruction in ecology be included, and during summer vacations gave conservation workshops for teachers.

FURTHER READING

Bonta, Marcia Myers. "Ann Haven Morgan." In *Women in the Field: America's Pioneering Women Naturalists.* College Station: Texas A&M University Press, 1991.

Morgan, Ann Haven. *Field Book of Animals in Winter.* New York: G. P. Putnam, 1939.

———. *Field Book of Ponds and Streams.* New York: G. P. Putnam, 1930.

———. *Kinships of Animals and Man.* New York: McGraw-Hill, 1955.

More Earthkeepers to Remember

Writer and naturalist **W. H. Hudson** (1841-1922) was born in Argentina to American parents; he moved to England in 1869 and later became a British subject. Hudson's nature books include *Argentine Ornithology* (1888), *British Birds* (1895), and several collections of essays on the English countryside. He also wrote romantic stories and novels set in the Argentine wilderness; the best-known are *The Purple Land* (1885) and *Green Mansions* (1904). Hudson's autobiography, *Far Away and Long Ago*, was published in 1918.

U.S. ornithologist **Elliott Coues** (1842-99) was the author of several 19th-century guidebooks, including *Key to North American Birds* (1872), *Birds of the Northwest* (1874), and *Birds of the Colorado Valley* (1878).

Clarence King (1842-1901) headed the decade-long geological exploration of the 40th parallel in the American West, beginning in the late 1860s, which laid the foundation for a systematic survey of the entire country. A report on the enterprise, *Systematic Geology*, was published in 1878. King was instrumental in founding the U.S. Geological Survey in 1879 and served briefly as its director. A skilled writer, King wrote numerous articles about the West as well as the book *Mountaineering in the Sierra Nevada* (1872).

Henry Fairfield Osborn's exhibits on prehistoric life, including reconstructed dinosaur skeletons, made the American Museum of Natural History world-famous.

Mary Kingsley collected flora and fauna in West Africa during the 1890s. A self-trained naturalist, she discovered new species of African fish, including those shown here in a drawing she made for the British Museum.

As a schoolboy in Lancaster, Massachusetts, **Luther Burbank** (1849-1926) read Charles Darwin's *Variation of Animals and Plants Under Domestication*, which inspired him to become a plant breeder. In 1875 he moved to Santa Rosa, California, where he established a nursery and greenhouse. Here he bred hundreds of thousands of plants and created more than 800 new varieties. Burbank wrote about his work in *Luther Burbank: His Methods and Discoveries* (12 volumes, 1914-15); *How Plants Are Trained to Work for Man* (8 volumes, 1921); and *New Creations* (1893-1901), a series of descriptive catalogs of his plants.

Henry Fairfield Osborn (1857-1935) was trained in paleontology and biology at Princeton and Columbia universities, and later taught at both institutions. As a young man he studied with biologist Thomas Huxley in London, and during his stay in England met Charles Darwin and other prominent scientists and naturalists. In 1891 Osborn began a lifelong association with the American Museum of Natural History in New York City when he was asked to organize the Department of Mammalian Paleontology (later renamed the Department of Vertebrate Paleontology). As the most eminent vertebrate paleontologist in the country, Osborn influenced subsequent generations of scientists in that field. In his role as a museum curator he popularized paleontology, and led the movement to create displays that were both educational and interesting to the nonscientific public. Osborn is credited with making "dinosaur" a household word through his world-famous exhibits at the museum. He became president of the museum in 1908 and held that post for 25 years. Osborn was also a leader in establishing the New York Zoological Society and was a strong defender of evolution. During his lifetime Osborn published nearly 1,000 articles and books on scientific topics.

U.S. botanist **Liberty Hyde Bailey, Jr.** (1858-1954), began his career as an assistant to Asa Gray at Harvard University and later served as a professor of horticulture and landscape gardening at Michigan State Agricultural College (now Michigan State University), where he created the first horticultural laboratory in the United States in 1888. As professor of botany and horticulture at Cornell University (1888-1903), he encouraged the study of plant cultivation and introduced on-site instruction to complement classroom teaching. Bailey served as dean of the New York State College of Agriculture at Cornell for a decade (1903-13), and later founded and directed (1935-51) the Bailey Hortorium, "a repository for things from the garden" that is now part of the university. Bailey wrote 700 scientific papers and 66 books, including *The Standard Cyclopedia of Horticulture* (1914; revised 1925) and the *Manual of Cultivated Plants* (1923), both of which are standard works in the field.

English explorer and naturalist **Mary Kingsley** (1862-1900) traveled throughout West Africa during the 1890s, collecting flora and fauna for the British Museum while she studied native tribes. A self-trained naturalist, Kingsley discovered eight new species of African fish, three of which were named after her. Kingsley published two books about her explorations and collection: *Travels in West Africa* (1897) and *West African Studies* (1899). After the Boer War began in 1899, she traveled to South Africa to nurse British soldiers during an outbreak of typhoid fever. Kingsley contracted the fever herself and died in June 1900, several months before her 38th birthday. In accordance with her wishes, she was buried at sea, off the coast near Simonstown. Shortly after Kingsley's death, the Royal African Society was founded in England, largely as a consequence of her pioneering studies in both anthropology and natural history on the continent.

U.S. ornithologist **Florence Merriam Bailey** (1863-1948) was the author of the *Handbook of Birds of the Western United States* (1902), illustrated by the leading bird painter of the era, Louis Agassiz Fuertes (1874-1927). Bailey's handbook was the standard guide to birds of the American West for nearly 50 years. Bailey received many awards for her writing, which included numerous articles for scientific publications as well as other books, including *Birds of New Mexico* (1921) and *Among the Birds in the Grand Canyon Country* (1939), the latter published when she was 76.

Frank M. Chapman (1864-1945) was an American ornithologist who pioneered in popularizing the study of birds. Although he never attended college, the self-taught Chapman was hired as a staff member by the American Museum of Natural History in 1887. He became curator of ornithology in 1908 and held that position until his retirement 34 years later. At the museum Chapman created the first habitat exhibits of birds; he also traveled widely in North and South America photographing and collecting specimens. His numerous publications include the popular *Handbook of Birds of Eastern North America* (1895), which served as a companion to Florence Merriam Bailey's *Handbook of Birds of the Western United States*, and *Autobiography of a Bird-Lover* (1933); he was the founder and editor (1899-1935) of *Bird-Lore* magazine. Chapman received many awards, including the 1929 John Burroughs Medal.

Children's writer, naturalist, and conservationist **Thornton W. Burgess** (1874–1965) was the author of 54 volumes of animal stories, including the popular *Old Mother West Wind* (1910) and *Mother West Wind's Children* (1911). Burgess developed a love of nature during his childhood on Cape Cod, Massachusetts; from the age of six he was forced to work outdoors at odd jobs to help support his family, but he still found time to explore the ponds, meadows, and marshes of the rural cape. For 42 years, from 1912 until 1954, Burgess wrote a daily feature called "Little Stories for Bedtime" that was syndicated in newspapers throughout the United States. Burgess believed that animal stories were the most effective way to teach moral values and a reverence for nature to children. He founded a series of conservation clubs and for many years hosted a radio program in Boston that promoted nature study. Burgess was the friend of many professional naturalists, including William T. Hornaday of the New York Zoological Society, and received a number of awards for his conservation efforts. He published an autobiography, *Now I Remember*, in 1960.

U.S. biologist, explorer, and naturalist **William Beebe** (1877-1962) was associated for many years with the New York Zoological Society. Beginning in 1899 he was curator of ornithology at the society's Bronx Zoo and in 1919 became director of tropical research for the society. He led numerous scientific expeditions to Central and South America, the Caribbean, and the Orient. In 1928 he established a tropical research center on a small island in the Atlantic Ocean near Bermuda and two years later made the first of 30 descents in a spherical diving device called the bathysphere with its inventor, Otis Barton. On these dives Beebe made detailed observations of previously unknown marine life, and in 1934 he and Barton descended to a record 3,028 feet below the surface. Beebe was a popular lecturer, and wrote many technical papers and monographs as well as books for the general public, including *Beneath Tropic Seas* (1928), *High Jungle* (1949), and *Unseen Life in New York* (1953). He collected and edited the essays that appear in *The Book of Naturalists: An Anthology of the Best Natural History* (1944), whose contributors range from Aristotle to Rachel Carson.

Plant breeder Luther Burbank (left) welcomed many prominent visitors to his California farm, including writer Jack London.

On April 22, 1970, the first Earth Day, thousands of Americans gathered in Washington, D.C., and other cities and towns across the nation to show their concern for the environment. Earth Day is now celebrated annually throughout the world.

4 A Race to Save the Earth

The American conservation movement that flourished in the early 20th century and spawned the creation of national parks and forests flagged as World War I captured both public attention and the nation's resources. In the following decade—whose frenzied excesses have been captured in its nickname, the "Roaring Twenties"—the nation seemed to have little time for serious issues. The pursuit of pleasure and consumption overrode any thoughts of what tomorrow might bring.

That inevitable tomorrow came in October 1929 with the collapse of the stock market, followed by worldwide economic depression that continued during the 1930s. In the United States, misery was compounded by widespread drought that caused crop failures throughout the Midwest and Great Plains, and by enormous wind storms that blew away millions of tons of precious topsoil in swirling, angry clouds of choking black dust. The land had been overused and abused, and it was now rebelling.

In the 18th and early 19th centuries, American pioneers pushing the frontier farther and farther west had a saying that described their enterprise: "Walk in, wear out, walk on." They would farm the plots surrounding their homesteads until the soil was no longer rich enough to produce an ample crop, and exhaust the supply of wild game in the nearby woods. And then they would move on to virgin land in the seemingly endless wilderness that stretched beyond the horizon. By the 1930s, however, Americans knew that the philosophy of their pioneer forebears was no longer practical: a new place to "walk on" to no longer existed. Slowly they set about repairing the damage done to their farmland, working fertilizers into the barren soil and employing long-known but seldom-used techniques such as crop rotation and contour plowing to produce healthier yields and prevent erosion.

In a curious twist of fate, it took World War II (1939-45) to spur an economic recovery that President Franklin D. Roosevelt had been striving for since assuming office in 1933. Technologies were developed during the war years that helped the Allied forces defeat fascism, but in peacetime their deadlier aspects gradually became known. The application of atomic energy to nonmilitary use also meant the buildup of nuclear wastes whose disposal endangered the environment. Pesticides that governments had used to protect their troops from insects bearing deadly diseases were now employed by everyone from suburban home owners trying to eliminate pesky flies to farmers seeking bigger harvests of wheat and corn—and gradually found their way into streams, rivers, and lakes across the country. Industrial growth that the war had encouraged was now manufacturing air, water, and soil pollution as an unwelcome by-product.

As a U.S. senator with a long-held interest in conservation and ecology, Gaylord Nelson was the originator of Earth Day.

By the 1960s a new movement calling for greater care of the Earth was in the offing. Its founder and heroine was a middle-aged marine biologist named Rachel Carson, who wondered why songbirds were dying in a backyard on Cape Cod. As more and more Americans learned the meaning of the word "ecology" in the ensuing decades, they discovered that the entire Earth was at risk from acid rain, global warming, deforestation, oil spills, ozone-layer depletion, overpopulation, and a host of other human-caused assaults on its fragility. Dozens of organizations in the United States and other nations launched programs to save plant and animal species from extinction, and to clean up the air and water.

Part 4 continues the story of conservation begun in Part 3 and chronicles its reemergence as environmentalism in the 1960s. It begins with the story of a man whose life bridged both movements, and who spent the 1920s in the Appalachians, far from the noisy speakeasies of the cities, creating a nature trail he had dreamed about for years. He was a forester named Benton MacKaye.

Benton MacKaye

THE TRAIL BUILDER

I n the last decades of the 1800s, as members of America's cultural and intellectual elite led the movement for conservation, increasing numbers of ordinary citizens who lived in cities and towns began seeking what Thoreau called "the tonic of wildness." Some went on camping trips in the new national parks of the Far West; others tramped in woods and fields closer to home.

By the early 20th century, hiking—or "sojourning," as it was then called—had become a popular pastime for thousands of Americans. Many joined societies formed to encourage wilderness treks, including the Appalachian Mountain Club and the Green Mountain Club in the Northeast and the Sierra Club in California. As these visitors observed the wilderness firsthand, they became enthusiastic converts to the cause of conservation and added their voices to those already calling

Benton MacKaye enjoys the view along the Appalachian Trail in western North Carolina in 1934. MacKaye created the trail as a way of preserving wilderness, which he called "the ultimate source of health."

At the first meeting of the Appalachian Trail Conference in 1925, MacKaye and his associates drew this map showing the proposed range of the trail; eventually it extended more than 2,000 miles.

MacKaye had been in love with nature as long as he could remember. His wealthy father, Steele MacKaye, was a well-known actor, playwright, inventor, and painter who had settled his family in rural Shirley Center in 1888, nine years after Benton's birth. The small hamlet, 20 miles from Thoreau's Walden Pond, became Benton MacKaye's home for most of his life. He spent many hours during his boyhood exploring the nearby woods and fields, pretending to be Alexander von Humboldt, whom he had read about in the family's extensive library. Shirley Center became fixed forever in MacKaye's mind as an ideal community, providing the minimum necessities of civilization in a rural setting.

MacKaye entered Harvard at the age of 17, but not with the intention of pursuing any of his father's interests. Five years earlier he had been taken to hear a lecture by John Wesley Powell and had been thrilled by Powell's description of his trip through the Grand Canyon. MacKaye decided then and there to have a career that would keep him outdoors as much as possible.

After graduating from Harvard in 1900, MacKaye enrolled in the new Harvard School of Forestry and received a master's degree in 1905. During the next 13 years he worked under Gifford Pinchot as a researcher for the U.S. Forest Service, then joined the U.S. Department of Labor to work on the reclamation of stump lands that had been left behind by the logging industry.

Out West the efforts of conservationists had led to the creation of national parks and monuments from vast public lands, beginning in the late 19th century, and "sojourners" and their societies lobbied the government to set aside similar tracts in the East. By the 20th century, however, there was little publicly owned land left in the eastern United States—which meant that the federal government would have to buy some of it back in order to establish loudly for government regulation of the nation's resources.

In the village of Shirley Center, Massachusetts, in the summer of 1921, a forester, regional planner, and longtime "sojourner" named Benton MacKaye (pronounced Mac-*High*) decided to write an article proposing an idea he had had for some time. Why not create a hiking trail through the wilderness of the Appalachians, the major mountain chain of the eastern United States, extending from the Northeast into the South?

> *"Our early settlers first planted civilization by inroads of population through the forest; we today, in order to restore civilization, must develop forest inroads."*

—from "An Appalachian Trail: A Project in Regional Planning" (1921)

EARTHKEEPERS

Benton MacKaye

BORN
March 6, 1879
Stamford, Connecticut

DIED
December 11, 1975
Shirley Center, Massachusetts

EDUCATION
A.B., M.A., Harvard University

MAJOR INTERESTS
Forestry; conservation

ACCOMPLISHMENTS
Proposed and created the Appalachian Trail, the world's longest man-made hiking trail (1921–1937); cofounder and president (1945–50) of the Wilderness Society; author of *The New Exploration: A Philosophy of Regional Planning* (1928) and *From Geography to Geotechnics* (1968)

preserves. Although Congress initially resisted, in 1911 it finally passed such legislation in the form of the Weeks Forest Protection Law. As written, the Weeks Law protected eastern watersheds—water drainage areas—but it paved the way for the government to acquire large expanses of countryside for preservation.

MacKaye's work, as he had hoped, kept him outdoors and made him thoroughly familiar with the wilderness of the Northeast, including many of the areas set aside for protection under the Weeks Law. He had surveyed the White Mountains of New Hampshire for Gifford Pinchot and also climbed Vermont's Green Mountains, and his assignment for the Labor Department took him into other regions of the vast Appalachian chain. In many of these wilderness areas, hikers had already established well-marked trails. It was possible, he reasoned, to make one unbroken trail running through much of the Appalachians, from Mount Washington, New Hampshire, to Mount Mitchell, North Carolina.

MacKaye's written proposal was published in the *Journal of the American Institute of Architects* in October 1921. Entitled "An Appalachian Trail: A Project in Regional Planning," it attracted wide and favorable attention. With MacKaye's continuing encouragement, various private organizations began work on sections of the trail. A year later a group of Boy Scouts had completed the first official segment, over Bear Mountain in New York.

Work continued during the next 15 years, coordinated, from 1925 on, by the Appalachian Trail Conference, newly founded by MacKaye and his followers. Although some patches of old trails were incorporated, most of the new trail had to be created "from scratch" by hardworking volunteers making their way through the forests like modern Daniel Boones. Thick undergrowth was not the trail-makers' only obstacle: because the trail crossed private as well as federal- and state-owned land, permission had to be secured from landowners before workers could continue.

Finally, however, in 1937, the Appalachian Trail, the world's longest formally laid-out hiking trail, was completed. It extended even farther than MacKaye had originally envisioned, through 14 states, from Mount Katahdin, Maine, to Mount Oglethorpe, Georgia—a distance of more than 2,000 miles.

To keep the trail in its natural state and protect it from what MacKaye called "civilizees," MacKaye and his followers negotiated an agreement between the National Park Service and the Forest Service that provided for a two-mile-wide "buffer zone" along the 875 miles of the trail that passed through federal land. Under the agreement, no "incompatible development"—roads or commercial buildings—would be allowed within this zone, although loggers were allowed to come within 200 feet of the footpath. The agreement acknowledged the government's interest in protecting the trail, and made possible the negotiation of protective arrangements with state governments. The parts of the trail passing through privately held lands remained vulnerable, however.

The successful creation of the Appalachian Trail inspired the establishment of extensive footpaths through the wilderness in other parts of the country, including major trails in Washington, Oregon, and California. In 1945 a Pennsylvania congressman named Dan Hoch proposed something new: the creation of a national system of hiking trails. The bill did not receive much support, however, and was tabled. Twenty years later, Senator Gaylord Nelson of Wisconsin, who had already established a reputation as a conservationist, revived the proposal, which was strongly supported by then-President Lyndon B. Johnson. A report by Interior Secretary Stewart Udall and lobbying by the still-active Benton MacKaye, now in his 80s, persuaded Congress to pass the National Scenic Trails Act of 1968, one of whose provisions gave the entire Appalachian Trail federal protection.

Creating the Appalachian Trail was the centerpiece of Benton MacKaye's career; he also advocated the establishment of more hiking trails in other regions, including one along the Continental Divide running through the Rocky Mountains. But trail building was not his only accomplishment. As the subtitle of his original proposal suggested, MacKaye was interested in a larger issue—a fairly new concept called "regional planning." In 1923, a year after leaving the Labor Department, he joined the Regional Planning Association, a group recently formed to study the conflict between rural life and urban industrialization and to propose environmentally sound solutions. Later, in 1935, he joined with other environmentalists to found the Wilderness Society, and he served as its president from 1945 to 1950.

For more than 50 years MacKaye was an ardent advocate of land-use policies that would ensure the preservation of rural "refuges" for city dwellers. He wrote numerous articles and several books, including the prophetic *New Exploration* (1928), which warned against the perils of unchecked industrial growth, including the creation of suburban "motor slums." Many of his ideas were later adopted as public policy, including his concept of "townless roads" to keep automobiles and their pollution as far as possible from homes—the basis for America's interstate highway system.

For most of his adult life MacKaye led a frugal, solitary existence—his wife of six years died in 1921—devoting all of his resources to the cause of regional planning. Active to the end, he died in 1975 at the age of 96. Three years later Congress declared MacKaye's proposed footpath along the Continental Divide a National Scenic Trail. It runs for 3,000 miles, from Montana to New Mexico, roughly parallel to its sister trail—and Benton MacKaye's earlier creation—in the East.

FURTHER READING

"Benton MacKaye: A Tribute." *Living Wilderness*, January-March 1976, 6-34.

Jackson, Donald Dale. "The Long Way 'Round: The National Scenic Trails System and How It Grew. And How It Didn't." *Wilderness*, Summer 1988, 17-24.

MacKaye, Benton. "An Appalachian Trail: A Project in Regional Planning." *Journal of the American Institute of Architects*, October 1921, 325-30.

———. *From Geography to Geotechnics.* Edited by Paul T. Bryant. Urbana: University of Illinois Press, 1968.

———. *The New Exploration: A Philosophy of Regional Planning.* 1928. Reprint. Urbana: University of Illinois Press, 1962.

Sutton, Ann, and Myron Sutton. *The Appalachian Trail.* Philadelphia: Lippincott, 1967.

Wild, Peter. "Benton MacKaye: The Reinvasion by Nature." In *Pioneer Conservationists of Eastern America.* Missoula, Mont.: Mountain Press, 1986.

Aldo Leopold

PIONEERING AN ETHIC OF LAND USE

O ne day in the fall of 1909 several forest rangers in Arizona Territory sat on a sunny rimrock, taking a lunch break. Suddenly they saw what they thought was a doe fording the river that ran swiftly below. As the animal climbed out of the water she was greeted by half a dozen young, who jumped at her, wagging their tails—and the rangers realized they were looking at a wolf and her cubs.

"In a second," one of the men later wrote, "we were pumping lead into the pack. . . . When our rifles were empty, the old wolf was down, and a pup was dragging a leg into impassable slide-rocks." The men scrambled down the cliff and "reached the old wolf in time to watch a fierce green fire dying in her eyes. . . . I was young then, and full of trigger-itch; I thought that because fewer wolves meant more deer, that no wolves would mean hunters' paradise. But after seeing the green fire die, I sensed that neither the wolf nor the mountain agreed with such a view."

Aldo Leopold bands quail for a wildlife study. A professional forester, Leopold was also an expert on game protection.

The cover of Leopold's *A Sand County Almanac* features Canada geese. The title refers to Sauk County, one of the so-called sand counties of southern Wisconsin and the site of Leopold's farm.

The author of those lines was Aldo Leopold, then a 23-year-old employee of the U.S. Forest Service. "In those days," he wrote, "we had never heard of passing up a chance to kill a wolf." All predators—animals who killed other animals for food—were then considered "bad," even by conservationists, and their slaughter was encouraged. The rangers that day had just been doing what was expected of them.

Leopold had joined the Forest Service earlier that year, after graduating from the Yale School of Forestry. He was born in Burlington, Iowa, in 1886, the grandson of German immigrants. The family was prosperous: both grandfathers had been successful businessmen, and Leopold's father owned a furniture factory. Young Leopold's hobby was ornithology, and he spent many hours when he was not in school birdwatching along the bluffs of the Mississippi River, near his home.

After preparing for college at Lawrenceville, a boarding school in New Jersey, Leopold entered Yale in 1905 and received a bachelor's degree three years later. He immediately enrolled in the Forestry School, completed the master's degree program in one year, and was hired by the U.S. Forest Service as an assistant at the Apache National Forest in Arizona Territory. Two years later he was appointed deputy supervisor of the Carson National Forest in New Mexico.

Leopold's interest in conservation led him to develop a game protection program throughout the Southwest that became widely recognized as a model of its kind. At the core of the program was the extermination of wolves, bears, and mountain lions, predators who killed deer, sheep, and other game. Leopold did not forget his encounter with the dying wolf, however, and he began to question the wisdom of the policy he had been upholding. His uneasiness changed to strong opposition when he discovered that instead of helping the game population to grow, the predator extermination program was hurting the herds. Without natural enemies to thin their numbers, the numbers of deer expanded enormously—but then did not have enough to eat. Weak and undernourished, they died of disease and starvation.

Leopold modified his approach to game management to take into account the importance of balance in the wild. He also became an advocate of protecting

"We abuse land because we regard it as a commodity belonging to us. When we see land as a community to which we belong, we may begin to use it with love and respect. . . . That land is a community is the basic concept of ecology, but that land is to be loved and respected is an extension of ethics."

—from *A Sand County Almanac* (1949)

sections of wilderness from commercial use. In a 1921 article in the *Journal of Forestry* he urged the Forest Service to protect wilderness areas within the national forests. By doing this, the service, which had long followed a policy of "wise use"—management for maximum economic gain—would also be acknowledging the value of wilderness for its own sake. Three years later, the service set aside 547,000 acres in New Mexico's Gila National Forest as the nation's first wilderness area.

Leopold believed that sections of protected, unspoiled wilderness had value for several reasons. First, they could be used for recreation—but recreation meant more to Leopold than distraction or amusement. Like Henry David Thoreau, John Burroughs, and Benton MacKaye, Leopold believed that wilderness offered men and women the opportunity to escape temporarily from their frenzied urban existence and experience the calming effects of nature. Wilderness also represented, in Leopold's mind, the necessary denial of unchecked progress: if we did not declare some areas off-bounds to develop-

ment, there would soon be nothing left. As he grew older, Leopold became convinced that protected wilderness offered another benefit: as an intact ecosystem—a community of organisms and their environment—it could be studied by scientists to learn more about the balance of nature.

From 1924 to 1928 Leopold worked as an administrator and consultant for the U.S. Forest Products Laboratory, a Forest Service organization in Madison, Wisconsin, then left government service to become game consultant for the Sporting Arms and Ammunition Manufacturers' Institute. He made extensive game surveys throughout the Midwest and published his findings in 1931. Leopold's work, which emphasized management as the basis for restoration, represented the first intensive study of the native American game population, and he was asked to develop a national game management policy for the American Game Protective Association.

Leopold worked for a year as a private forester. Then, in 1933, the University of Wisconsin created a department of wildlife management and named Leopold a professor. He held the position, the first of its kind in the United States, for the rest of his life. At Wisconsin, he continued to study and promote wildlife management and also worked on methods to encourage soil conservation and other environmentally sound agricultural practices. In 1935 he published a textbook, *Game Management,* which became the standard work in the field. It was based on the new science of systems ecology, which considered species and habitat as an indivisible whole.

During the 1930s Leopold developed a radically new theory of conservation, a natural outgrowth of his views on game management. He contributed articles on the subject to a number of professional journals, and during the 1940s began compiling his observations into a book, which was published as *A Sand County*

EARTHKEEPERS

Aldo Leopold

BORN

January 11, 1886
Burlington, Iowa

DIED

April 21, 1948
Sauk County, Wisconsin

EDUCATION

B.S., M.S., Yale University

MAJOR INTEREST

Ecology

ACCOMPLISHMENTS

Forester and pioneer ecologist; initiated the creation of U.S. wilderness areas under the control of the Forest Service; founded the profession of game management; cofounder of the Wilderness Society; professor of wildlife management, University of Wisconsin; author of *A Sand County Almanac* (1949), called "the bible of the modern ecology movement"

HONORS

Gold Medal, Permanent Wildlife Protection Fund; Gold Medal, *Outdoor Life* magazine

Leopold stands outside "the shack," his house in rural Wisconsin, in a photograph taken around 1940.

Almanac in 1949, after his death. In Leopold's view, man belongs to an environmental "community," all of whose members he has to learn to respect; nature does not exist as something for human beings to control.

This meant that the concept of brotherhood had to be extended beyond the human race and transformed into what Leopold called the "land ethic," which "enlarges the boundaries of the community to include soils, waters, plants, and animals, or collectively the land." The land ethic required that mankind's interests be subordinate to the interests of the environment as a whole. More than "wise use" was required: *proper* use was that which "tends to preserve the integrity, stability, and beauty of the biotic community."

Throughout his life, Leopold was active in various conservation organizations, including the Society of American Foresters, the National Audubon Society, the American Forestry Association, the Ecological Society of America, and the Wildlife Society. He was also a cofounder of the Wilderness Society, a member of President Franklin D. Roosevelt's Special Committee on Wildlife Restoration, and, from 1943 until his death, a member of the Wisconsin Conservation Commission.

Leopold and his family—he was married and had five children—lived for many years on a farm in rural Sauk County, Wisconsin. One day in April 1948 a grass fire broke out near their home. As Leopold and several of his children worked hard to put it out, he suffered a fatal heart attack. He was 62 years old.

For nearly a decade Leopold had been trying to find a publisher for *A Sand County Almanac*. Seven days before his death, Oxford University Press bought the manuscript. It was published in 1949 and for a while was a best-seller. During the 1960s *A Sand County Almanac* was rediscovered and hailed as the bible of the new environmental movement. Today it is still read throughout the world, in English and numerous translations.

FURTHER READING

Callicott, J. Baird, ed. *Companion to a Sand County Almanac: Interpretive and Critical Essays*. Madison: University of Wisconsin Press, 1987.

Flader, Susan. *The Sand Country of Aldo Leopold*. San Francisco: Sierra Club Books, 1973.

———. *Thinking Like a Mountain: Aldo Leopold and the Evolution of an Ecological Attitude Toward Deer, Wolves, and Forests*. Columbia: University of Missouri Press, 1974.

Leopold, Aldo. *Aldo Leopold's Wilderness: Selected Early Writings by the Author of "A Sand County Almanac."* Edited by David E. Brown and Neil B. Carmony. Harrisburg, Pa.: Stackpole, 1990.

———. *The River of the Mother of God and Other Essays by Aldo Leopold*. Madison: University of Wisconsin Press, 1991.

———. *A Sand County Almanac*. 1949. Reprint. New York: Oxford University Press, 1966.

Meine, Curt. *Aldo Leopold: His Life and Work*. Madison: University of Wisconsin Press, 1988.

Wild, Peter. "The Move Toward Holism: 'Thinking Like a Mountain'. . . " In *Pioneer Conservationists of Western America*. Missoula, Mont.: Mountain Press, 1979.

Grey Owl (Archibald Belaney)

THE MAN WHO
SAVED THE BEAVER

During the 1930s, one of the most renowned naturalists in the world was a man who claimed to be a half-breed Apache and called himself Grey Owl. The name, he said, had been given to him by Canada's Ojibway Indians, who had adopted him as a teenager.

Grey Owl, a longtime trapper and river guide in Ontario and Quebec, had come to public attention after a life-changing experience in 1928, when he was 40 years old: One morning when he went to one of his traps to collect the body of a beaver, two tiny orphaned beaver kittens appeared. He took them back to his cabin in the woods of Quebec, where he and his wife, an Iroquois Indian who opposed trapping, cared for them. The experience "aroused in me a distaste for killing," he later wrote. He resolved to stop trapping beaver and instead to "study them, see just what there really was to them."

In the winter of 1928-29, Grey Owl started his first colony of beavers. To support his family he began writing articles for popular periodicals about his new venture and also giving

Grey Owl, a Canadian trapper-turned-naturalist who called himself a half-breed Apache, at Prince Albert National Park in Saskatchewan during the early 1930s.

Grey Owl feeds a beaver, part of his colony of "little people" at Prince Albert National Park.

lectures in nearby communities. His work became widely known in 1930, when the national parks of Canada sponsored a film of Grey Owl with his beavers, and the following year the Canadian government sent him west to Riding Mountain National Park, in Manitoba, to found a beaver colony there.

The beaver population at Riding Mountain had been virtually exterminated by trappers nearly 200 years earlier. Grey Owl remained at the park for six months, long enough to start a small colony, but he was not happy with the area, which he described as "an island of green" surrounded by hot, dry prairie. At his request, the government sent him farther west, to Prince Albert National Park, in Saskatchewan. There, on Ajawaan Lake, he began a new beaver colony. Meanwhile, back at Riding Mountain National Park, the beavers he had reintroduced there quickly multiplied.

Grey Owl's first book, an account of Canadian woodsmen called *Men of the Last Frontier,* was published in London in the fall of 1931, shortly after he arrived in Saskatchewan. A year later it was published in New York and Toronto, and in 1935 it was followed by a second book, *Pilgrims of the Wild*, a personal account of his transformation from trapper to protector of wildlife. Grey Owl's growing fame received a further boost when the Canadian government made more films of his work with beavers.

By the mid-1930s, Grey Owl was a celebrity in both North America and England. In 1935 he made a widely publicized tour of Great Britain, giving lectures and showing movies about his beavers. Dressed in a blue serge suit and moccasins, his braided hair topped by a gray felt sombrero, the handsome Grey Owl was a romantic, entertaining figure

at a time when worldwide depression and the threat of war left little room for joy in most people's lives.

During the four-month tour, Grey Owl gave 200 lectures to more than a quarter of a million people, describing the benefits of the unspoiled wilderness and urging his listeners to work for wildlife preservation. As his biographer wrote many years later, trying to explain the reformed trapper's appeal, Grey Owl assured his audiences in "his deep and thrilling voice that somewhere there was a land where life could begin again, a place which the screams of demented dictators could not reach."

Two years later Grey Owl returned to England for a second lecture tour, the high point of which was a command performance at Buckingham Palace for King George VI and his family. The most enthusiastic guests were the king's daughters, Princess Elizabeth and

"They seemed to be almost like little folk from some other planet, whose language we could not yet quite understand. To kill such creatures seemed monstrous. I would do no more of it."

—from *Pilgrims of the Wild* (1935)

Princess Margaret. When Grey Owl, clad in full Indian regalia, finished his presentation, the 11-year-old Elizabeth—now Queen Elizabeth II—jumped up and cried out, "Oh, do go on!" Grey Owl obliged her by performing an encore.

Less than a year later, on April 13, 1938, Grey Owl died suddenly, at the age of 49, back home in Saskatchewan— and newspaper readers around the world learned for the first time who the "friend of the beaver" really was. During his lifetime Grey Owl had told the public that he had been born in Hermosillo, Mexico, to George MacNeil, a Scottish-born Indian scout in the American Southwest, and Katherine Cochise, an Apache Indian, and that his parents had once toured England with "Buffalo Bill" Cody's Wild West Show. In fact, Grey Owl's real name was Archibald Belaney, and he had been born to an English couple, George Belaney and 14-year-old Katherine Cox, in Hastings, England. George Belaney's family was wealthy and respectable, but George himself was a delinquent and an alcoholic who had run away to America in the 1870s and settled in Florida. His son, Archibald, had been born during a visit home in 1888, and the abandoned child had been raised in Hastings by his paternal grandmother and aunts.

How had Archibald Belaney changed himself into Grey Owl? As a child, he played in the woods near his home and collected mice, frogs, and snakes as pets. The imaginative Archie enjoyed reading romantic accounts of American Indians, including James Fenimore Cooper's novels and Henry Wadsworth Longfellow's poem "Hiawatha," and dreamed of immigrating to Canada. By the time he was 12, he had become a self-educated authority on Canadian Indian tribes. In 1906, when he was 18, his family paid for his passage to Ontario, believing that he would become a farmer. But Belaney had other plans: he disappeared into the Canadian wilderness and emerged several years later as an Ojibway Indian who earned his living by trapping animals and leading canoeing expeditions.

Many of his supporters were disappointed when they learned the true story of Grey Owl and his deception. But Archibald Belaney's masquerade does not change the fact that he "gave his extraordinary genius, his passionate sympathy, his bodily strength, his magnetic personal influence, even his very earnings to the service of animals," in the words of an editorial in the London *Times* after his death.

FURTHER READING

Brower, Kenneth. "Grey Owl." *Atlantic Monthly*, January 1990, 74-84.

Dickson, Lovat. *Wilderness Man: The Strange Story of Grey Owl*. New York: Atheneum, 1973.

Grey Owl. *The Adventures of Sajo and Her Beaver People*. New York: Scribners, 1935.

———. *Men of the Last Frontier*. New York: Scribners, 1932.

———. *Pilgrims of the Wild*. New York: Scribners, 1935.

Grey Owl (Archibald Belaney)

BORN
September 18, 1888
Hastings, England

DIED
April 13, 1938
Saskatchewan, Canada

EDUCATION
Grammar school

MAJOR INTEREST
Protecting wildlife

ACCOMPLISHMENTS
Saved the beaver from near-extinction in western Canada; advocated wildlife protection in lectures, articles, and books; author of six books, including *Men of the Last Frontier* (1931) and *Pilgrims of the Wild* (1935)

Olaus Murie

Margaret Murie

AT HOME IN
THE WILDERNESS

I n the summer of 1924, when a field biologist named Olaus Murie and a young woman named Margaret Thomas announced their plans to marry, there seemed nothing unusual about the union, apart from the fact that the groom was somewhat older than the bride. The 35-year-old Murie was working for the U.S. Biological Survey in Alaska; Thomas had recently become the first woman to graduate from the University of Alaska.

From the start, however, theirs was not a conventional marriage. The ceremony was scheduled for the afternoon of August 18 (the bride's birthday) in the village of Anvik, on the Yukon River, but Murie arrived late—he had been banding waterfowl near the mouth of the Yukon—and the vows were not exchanged until 2:30 A.M. on August 19. At 5:00 A.M. the newly married couple boarded a steamer and headed upriver to the village of Bettles, above the Arctic Circle, to begin a wilderness adventure together that would last for 39 years.

Margaret Thomas Murie was no stranger to the hardships of wilderness life. She had been born in Seattle in 1902, but nine years later moved with her mother and stepfather to Fairbanks, Alaska, then an isolated frontier village with only 10 streets and log cabins for houses. She adapted quickly to her new home, despite harsh living conditions and isolation, and loved to explore the countryside.

As a teenager, Margaret, nicknamed "Mardy," cheerfully traveled to school in Chitina, a hazardous nine-day trip by horse-drawn sleigh. At the age of 17, she entered Reed College in Portland, Oregon, to become a teacher, but two years later changed her mind and returned home to Fairbanks. One evening at a friend's house she met a biologist from Minnesota named Olaus Murie, who was on his way north to study Alaskan caribou. A few days later, they took a boat trip together up the Chena River. Mardy was impressed with his ease and lack of self-consciousness—in the evening, after dark, he exchanged calls with a great horned owl—but shortly afterward Murie set off on his expedition and Mardy remained at home, helping her mother.

In the fall of 1921 she moved to Boston, to attend Simmons College, but the following summer she was back in Fairbanks. Again she encountered Murie, and this time their friendship had time to develop into a serious relationship. Murie was doing research at a camp near Mt. McKinley, and Mardy enrolled at the University of Alaska to study business administration. They married soon after Mardy's graduation.

Like his bride, Olaus Johan Murie had grown up in harsh surroundings. Born on a small farm near Moorhead, Minnesota, in 1889, Murie was the son of Norwegian immigrants. His

father died when Olaus and his two brothers were small children, and the boys worked hard, helping their mother with chores and earning extra money by plowing for area farmers. For recreation, Olaus and his brother Adolph built a canoe and paddled it up and down the Red River, near their home, looking for bird nests. Like his brother, Adolph would also grow up to become a distinguished biologist and nature writer.

After graduating from high school, Olaus Murie spent several years at nearby Fargo College, in North Dakota, studying biology. When his professor moved to Pacific University, in Oregon, Olaus transferred there, too, and

graduated in 1912. He immediately went to work for the Oregon state game warden, collecting specimens and taking photographs of wildlife.

In 1914 Murie joined an expedition in sub-Arctic Canada sponsored by the Carnegie Museum of Pittsburgh. Murie, an ornithologist, and two Ojibway Indian guides traveled north by canoe to remote, unmapped islands in Hudson Bay, collecting and preserving bird specimens. The trip was arduous and the adventurers nearly lost their lives in the frigid waters. When the expedition ended, Murie stayed on in the North, traveling through snow and ice and 40-below-zero temperatures with Eskimos

Margaret Murie

BORN

August 18, 1902
Seattle, Washington

EDUCATION

B.S., University of Alaska

MAJOR INTEREST

Conservation

ACCOMPLISHMENTS

Leading advocate of conservation; longtime officer of the Wilderness Society; author of *Two in the Far North* (1962), *Island Between* (1978), and, with Olaus Murie, *Wapiti Wilderness* (1966)

HONORS

Numerous awards, including honorary doctorate, University of Alaska (1976), National Audubon Society Medal (1980), John Muir Award (Sierra Club, 1983)

and Cree Indians and reveling in the harsh landscape that he later described as a "wonderland."

In 1917 Murie went on a second Canadian expedition for the Carnegie Museum, this time north through Labrador to a trading post on Baffin Island, near the Arctic Circle. Again Murie was oblivious to the dangers, recording in his diary how delighted he was to encounter birds and other wildlife. After serving briefly overseas as an observer with the U.S. Army's balloon service during World War I,

Murie returned to the North, this time to Alaska as an employee of the U.S. Biological Survey (now called the U.S. Fish and Wildlife Service).

Traveling by dog team, canoe, river steamer, and on snowshoes, Murie spent eight years in Alaska, primarily studying the caribou but also becoming an expert on other native wildlife, including waterfowl and brown bears. It was in the midst of this assignment that Murie married Mardy Thomas. They lived for two months in a one-room log cabin in Bettles, then journeyed north to a camp

Margaret Murie pauses for lunch during a visit to a wilderness area near Twin Lakes, Colorado.

Olaus Murie

BORN

March 1, 1889
Moorehead, Minnesota

DIED

October 21, 1963
Jackson, Wyoming

EDUCATION

B.S., Pacific University; M.S., University of Michigan

MAJOR INTERESTS

Biology; conservation

ACCOMPLISHMENTS

Leading advocate of conservation; led efforts to establish Arctic National Wildlife Range; campaigned for passage of the Wilderness Act (1964); cofounder, director, and president of the Wilderness Society; author and illustrator of numerous articles and books, including *The Elk of North America* (1951) and *Field Guide to Animal Tracks* (1954)

HONORS

Numerous awards, including honorary doctorate from Pacific University (1949); Aldo Leopold Memorial Award, Wildlife Society (1952); Pugsley Medal, American Scenic and Historic Preservation Society (1954); Conservation Award, American Forestry Association (1954); National Audubon Society Medal (1959)

in the Endicott Mountains. In the spring of 1925, Mardy moved to Washington State to give birth to their first child, then rejoined her husband a year later, bringing the baby along. The three Muries immediately set out on an expedition to study bird migration patterns near Alaska's Old Crow River, in the Arctic. Many years later Mardy recounted her wilderness "housekeeping" experiences in *Two for the North* (1962), which Olaus illustrated.

In 1926–27 Olaus Murie earned a master's degree in biology at the Univer-sity of Michigan, and following his graduation resettled his family near Jackson Hole, Wyoming, which became their home for 37 years. The Biological Survey had assigned Olaus to study the life history of an elk herd that lived in the area. Many years later he published the results of his research in the book *The Elk of North America* (1951). Olaus and Mardy had two more children, a girl and a boy, and all five Muries went along on Olaus's research expeditions throughout the state.

As the years passed, the Muries became active in town affairs in Jackson Hole. Their log cabin residence in nearby Moose became a gathering place for area residents to discuss political issues, particularly those relating to conservation, while Olaus continued his wildlife research, including a study of black bears in Yellowstone Park. Olaus's attitudes toward the environment had always been somewhat at odds with the government's "wise-use" policy, and in his work with the Biological Survey he nearly always advocated species preser-vation. His studies of the dwindling Wyoming elk herd, for example, led to the adoption of policies that brought a healthy increase in their population. By the time of his retirement from govern-ment service, in 1945, he had become convinced that preservation of wilder-ness areas was essential, a belief fully shared by his wife and children.

In 1935 Olaus Murie had joined with Benton MacKaye, Robert Marshall, and others to found the Wilderness Society. In 1946 he was invited by the governing board to become director of

"The wonder of the world, the beauty and the power, the shapes of things, their colours, lights, and shades; these I saw. Look ye also while life lasts."

—from a plaque over the fireplace at the Murie cabin in Moose, Wyoming

the society, whose headquarters were in Washington, D.C. Murie agreed—with the stipulation that he be allowed to continue living in Wyoming. In 1950 he was elected president of the Wilderness Society, a position he held for seven years.

As an international authority on wildlife, Murie traveled to Norway, South America, and New Zealand to advise governments on preserving habitats and saving species from extinction. At home in Wyoming he completed the text and illustrations for a book he had been working on for many years, *A Field Guide to Animal Tracks*, which was published in 1954. Two years later he and Mardy led an expedition to the Brooks Range in northern Alaska to report on ecological changes in the region. Warning that the area's plants and animals were being harmed by settlement and exploitation, they led an effort to create the Arctic National Wildlife Refuge, which was established in 1960. The Muries are also credited with leading successful efforts to save substantial wilderness areas throughout the western states from development and dam construction.

Murie received numerous honors, including an honorary doctorate from Pacific University (1949), the Wildlife Society's Aldo Leopold Memorial Award (1952) for *The Elk of North America*, the American Forestry Association's Conservation Award (1954), and the Audubon Medal from the National Audubon Society (1959). In his last years, he campaigned for passage by the U.S. Congress of the Wilderness Act, making preservation official government policy, but he died in 1963, a year before President Lyndon Johnson signed it into law.

After Olaus's death, Mardy finished writing a book she and her husband had been working on for years; *Wapiti Wilderness* was published in 1966. Another book about her experiences, *Island Between*, appeared in 1978. Mardy Murie remained active on behalf of environmental causes as a paid staff member of the Wilderness Society, and was eventually elected a vice president and member of the governing council. Due largely to her efforts, North Cascades National Park was established in Washington State in 1968.

Like her husband, Mardy has received a number of awards for her work, including an honorary doctorate from the University of Alaska (1976) and recognition from the U.S. Department of the Interior and the Rocky Mountain Center on the Environment. In 1980 she received the National Audubon Society Medal, which Olaus had won 21 years earlier, and in 1983 she was presented with the Sierra Club's John Muir Award for outstanding service on behalf of the environment.

FURTHER READING

Curry, Peggy Simson. "Portrait of a Naturalist." *Audubon*, November-December 1963, 359-63. [About Olaus Murie.]

"1889 . . . Olaus J. Murie . . . 1963." *The Living Wilderness*, Summer-Fall 1963, 3-14.

LaBastille, Anne. "Margaret Murie." In *Women and Wilderness*. San Francisco: Sierra Club Books, 1980.

Murie, Adolph. *A Naturalist in Alaska*. Garden City, N.Y. Doubleday, 1963. [About Olaus Murie.]

Murie, Margaret. *Island Between*. Fairbanks: University of Alaska Press, 1978.

———. *Two in the Far North*. New York: Knopf, 1962.

Murie, Margaret, and Olaus Murie. *Wapiti Wilderness*. New York: Knopf, 1966.

"Murie, Margaret." In *Contemporary Authors*. Vol. 110. Detroit: Gale, 1984.

Murie, Olaus. *The Elk of North America*. Harrisburg, Pa.: Stackpole, 1951.

———. *A Field Guide to Animal Tracks*. Boston: Houghton Mifflin, 1954.

Weddle, Ferris M. "Wilderness Champion: Olaus J. Murie." *Audubon*, July-August 1950, 224-33.

Wild, Peter. "Science and Sympathy: Olaus Murie and the Fight for Wildlife." In *Pioneer Conservationists of Western America*. Missoula, Mont.: Mountain Press, 1979.

Marjory Stoneman Douglas

THE VOICE OF THE "RIVER OF GRASS"

The Florida Everglades, 1.8 million acres of tropical marshland in south Florida extending from Lake Okeechobee to the Gulf of Mexico, have been called many names over the centuries. To Native Americans they were "Grassy Water." Spanish mapmakers in the 17th century designated the region "The Lagoon of the Blessed Spirit"; English maps in the early 18th century identified it as "River Glades." Some time after the United States acquired Florida from Spain in 1819, the Everglades became known by their present name.

To Marjory Stoneman Douglas, who first saw the Everglades nearly 80 years ago, they are an endless "river of grass," a "green and brown expanse of saw grass and water" glittering in the bright sunlight. For most of her adult life, Douglas has fought for the preservation of the Everglades and its rich abundance of wildlife, which includes alligators, diamondback rattlesnakes, black bears, deer, numerous wading- and songbird species, and panthers.

Douglas, now more than 100 years old, is one of Florida's best-known residents, but she is not a native Floridian. She was born in Minneapolis, Minnesota, in 1890 to Frank and

Marjory Stoneman Douglas with one of her cats at her home in Coconut Grove, Florida, in the late 1920s.

Ninety-five-year-old Douglas acknowledges the applause at a ceremony in Tallahassee, Florida, in 1985 marking the dedication of the state's new Department of Natural Resources building, which was named in her honor.

Lillian Stoneman. Her father was an attorney, her mother a concert violinist who died when Marjory was a small child. Her father moved to Miami and Marjory was sent to Taunton, Massachusetts, to be raised by her maternal grandmother, who was French and a gifted storyteller.

Marjory majored in English at Wellesley College, and after graduation in 1912 moved to New Jersey to work for a department store. In 1914 she married Kenneth Douglas, a newspaper editor 30 years her senior, but the couple sepa-

rated a year later, after Kenneth was arrested for forging checks. Marjory Stoneman Douglas moved to Miami, to live with her father and his new wife.

Miami was then a frontier town, with a population of less than 5,000. Frank Stoneman had built a house in a rural area several miles south called Coconut Grove, which is now a Miami suburb. Douglas had not seen her father since she was six years old, but they found that they had a great deal in common, especially a love of books. Stoneman had practiced law for a decade in Orlando, then moved to Miami to found the city's first morning newspaper, which became the *Miami Herald*. Douglas worked for several years as a reporter and columnist for the paper. One of her proudest achievements was a series she wrote exposing the terrible living and working conditions of migrant laborers, which led to reforms by the state government.

In the last years of World War I Douglas served as an American Red Cross volunteer in Europe, then returned to the *Herald* to become assistant editor. Many of her editorials focused on the increasing development of Florida and the necessity for preserving its unique character. In 1923 she resigned from the paper to launch a successful career writing short stories for the *Saturday Evening Post* and other national magazines, using Florida—then little known to the rest of the country—as a setting.

In the late 1920s Douglas built her own house in Coconut Grove, across the street from her father's residence; this became her permanent home. Her fascination with the nearby Everglades began shortly after her move to Florida, and as the state's population increased she looked with increasing dismay at threats to the region's flora and fauna. The egret and spoonbill population had been virtually destroyed by hunters who sold the birds' plumes to hatmakers. Developers were draining some of the land to make it productive agriculturally. In 1927 she joined a group of local residents to campaign for the creation of Everglades National Park, giving speeches and writing articles to publicize their cause during the following decades.

In 1942 a New York publisher invited Douglas to write a book about the tiny Miami River, as part of a series on the rivers of America. Douglas was not convinced that the subject was worth pursuing. Why not a book about the Everglades, which could be considered a river? The publisher agreed, and Douglas devoted nearly five years to the project. Much of that time was spent doing library research, although she did venture into the marshland on a series of field trips to observe it firsthand.

Nineteen forty-seven was a special year for Douglas. President Harry S. Truman formally dedicated Everglades National Park, comprising three-quarters of the region, and Douglas's book *The Everglades: River of Grass* was published to

"In Florida . . . the people are being called on to choose between a blind obedience to the sheer increasing pressure of population and the vital necessity for building finer cities in a balanced and preserved natural background which alone can give them meaning and value. The future lies in them and in the strength with which man himself can set his powers of creation against his impulses for destruction. Perhaps this is the unending frontier."

—from Florida: The Long Frontier *(1967)*

Marjory Stoneman Douglas

BORN

April 7, 1890
Minneapolis, Minnesota

EDUCATION

B.A., Wellesley College

MAJOR INTEREST

Conservation

ACCOMPLISHMENTS

Longtime advocate of protection of the Florida Everglades; led efforts to establish Everglades National Park (dedicated in 1947); author of *The Everglades: River of Grass* (1947), *Hurricane* (1958), *Florida: The Long Frontier* (1967), and an autobiography, *Marjory Stoneman Douglas: Voice of the River* (1987)

HONORS

More than 50 awards for her efforts to save the Everglades, including honorary doctorates from the University of Miami and Florida Atlantic University; named Floridian of the Year (1983)

instant acclaim. Concern for the preservation of the region increased across the country as successful programs to renew the egret and spoonbill population were undertaken and opposition to further development mounted. Douglas continued her active support through an organization she founded called Friends of the Everglades.

Marjory Stoneman Douglas pursued her writing career as well as her crusade for the Everglades, publishing more short stories, several books for young adults, and *Hurricane* (1958), a history of tropical storms in the Southeast and the Caribbean. In 1967 Douglas published a history of her state called *Florida: The Long Frontier*. Her autobiography, *Marjory Stoneman Douglas: Voice of the River*, appeared in 1987, when Douglas was 97. She still works every day on a project that has occupied her for many years, a biography of the English naturalist W. H. Hudson, and attends meetings of the state legislature in Tallahassee as an advocate of the Everglades.

Douglas knows that the battle for their protection will never be over, for the well-being of the Everglades is essential to the entire ecosystem of south Florida. Rainfall in that part of the state is dependent upon evaporation from the Everglades, whose marshlands cannot be reduced further without serious environmental consequences. Development in

the rest of the state in the form of an interlocking system of pumps and canals has made possible Florida's successful agricultural industry, but more and more waste runoff has been allowed to enter the Everglades, and animal and plant species continue to be threatened.

Marjory Stoneman Douglas remains Florida's most well-known advocate of environmental protection, and during nearly half a century has won more than 50 awards for her efforts. She still works tirelessly with Friends of the Everglades, and despite setbacks she is optimistic about the future. "I've seen the ruin," she has said. "Now I see hope for the restoration."

FURTHER READING

Douglas, Marjory Stoneman. *The Everglades: River of Grass*. 1947. Reprint. Englewood, Fla.: Pineapple Press, 1988.

———. *Florida: The Long Frontier*. New York: Harper & Row, 1967.

———. *Hurricane*. New York: Rinehart, 1958.

Douglas, Marjory Stoneman, with John Rothchild. *Marjory Stoneman Douglas: Voice of the River*. Englewood, Fla.: Pineapple Press, 1987.

Gladstone, Valerie. "Marjory Stoneman Douglas." *Ms.*, January-February 1989, 68-71.

Louis Bromfield

THE MASTER OF MALABAR FARM

In 1939 an American novelist named Louis Bromfield returned to his home in Ohio after 14 years of living abroad. The opulent, frenzied 1920s had been succeeded by a decade of economic depression. Europe, where Bromfield had spent most of those years, was on the eve of World War II as German dictator Adolf Hitler threatened to invade Poland. Although Bromfield's books had won honors and acclaim, he longed for the simple rural life of his childhood. Louis Bromfield decided it was time to come home.

Bromfield bought 600 acres of run-down farmland near Mansfield, Ohio, his birthplace, and settled there with his family, which included three young daughters. He immediately set to work creating a model farm, which he named Malabar after the coast in India where he had lived for a while. Within three years Malabar Farm became a showplace, a testimonial to the possibilities of renewing worn-out land through crop rotation, soil conservation, and organic farming methods. Louis Bromfield had become the most well-known farmer in America.

Bromfield was no stranger to agriculture. Born on a farm in 1896, he grew up at a time when the majority of the American population still lived in rural areas. His family had farmed in Ohio for much of the 19th century, but by the 1890s the farm was a residence rather than a principal means of livelihood. Bromfield's father, a banker, encouraged his son's childhood dream to restore the family farm to full productivity, while his mother wanted him to become a writer. Eventually he would fulfill the aspirations of both parents.

In high school Bromfield worked as a part-time reporter for a local newspaper, but in 1914, following graduation, he enrolled at Cornell University to study agriculture. After a year there, he returned home to take more agriculture courses at Ohio Northern University, but after a few months withdrew and enrolled at Columbia University's School of Journalism. He enjoyed his classes, but World War I was raging in Europe, and early in 1917 he left college to join the French army as an ambulance driver.

For two years Bromfield saw service on almost every sector of the European front and was subsequently awarded the star of the French Legion of Honor and the Croix de Guerre. Because of his distinguished war record, Columbia University later awarded him an honorary bachelor's degree.

After returning to the United States in 1919 Bromfield worked as a newspaperman, music critic, and advertising director of a publishing company. In his spare time he began writing fiction and in 1924 his first novel, *The Green Bay Tree*, was published. Like most of his later books, it drew upon his

In his study at Malabar Farm, Louis Bromfield works on his writing while his pet boxers doze nearby.

Ohio background and reflected his dislike of industrialism. It also expressed his strong support for the democratic ideals of Thomas Jefferson, which included a belief in the superiority of an agricultural economy and rural society. *The Green Bay Tree* was well received and sold enough copies to allow Bromfield to become a full-time writer.

In 1925, shortly after the publication of his second novel, Bromfield, his wife, and their infant daughter moved to France, a country that attracted many American writers during the 1920s. His third novel, *Early Autumn*, was published in 1926 and won the Pulitzer Prize,

establishing him as a leading American writer. Henceforth Bromfield published a new novel nearly every year; *The Farm*, which appeared in 1933 and traced the lives of four generations on an Ohio farm, was strongly autobiographical. During the 1930s he made several extended visits to India, which became the background for *The Rains Came* (1937) and *Night in Bombay* (1940).

Bromfield never completely abandoned his interest in agriculture, however, and as he saw much of the world move to the brink of war, farming began to seem increasingly appealing. As he later wrote, explaining his decision to

Bromfield waters plants in the terraced ornamental gardens outside "the big house," the family residence at Malabar Farm. Bromfield also grew a variety of food crops on Malabar's thousand acres, which included several wildlife preserves.

return to Ohio, "After twenty-five years of witnessing revolutions, inflations, and the ruin of whole nations, I knew that the nearest thing to security that unstable man could still have was the land."

Much of America's farmland was no longer lush and productive, though. More than a century of intensive crop growing had worn out the soil, leaving it barren of essential nutrients needed to produce an ample harvest. Further depletion occurred during the 1930s,

when heavy winds created enormous dust storms that eroded millions of acres of topsoil across the nation.

Using his knowledge of modern agricultural science, Bromfield began restoring the arid fields of Malabar Farm, which eventually grew to a thousand acres with the acquisition of adjacent farmland. Erosion control was introduced through new techniques for soil conservation, including contour plowing, and the creation of ponds for proper drainage. (Contour plowing is a method

"Nature is still unconquered by man, and when he attempts to upset or circumvent her laws, he merely courts disaster, misery, low living standards, and eventual destruction."

—from *Malabar Farm* (1948)

of plowing along the natural lines of the land to retain water and prevent erosion.) Natural fertilizers were fed to the hungry soil, and crop rotation kept the replenished land from being overworked.

In addition to growing a variety of crops, Bromfield also raised poultry and cattle at Malabar Farm, which he ran as a cooperative. A dozen tenant farmers and their families shared in its abundant vegetables, meats, eggs, and dairy products, and yearly profits were divided among them. Some of the farm's acreage was set aside for reforestation, and natural springs that had been dammed were allowed to resume their normal flow. Natural wildlife preserves were created as birds and animals that had once been abundant in the area began to return.

Malabar Farm became known throughout the country for demonstrating that successful farming could be accomplished by cooperating with nature. Numerous visitors came to observe the farm's operation, and Bromfield wrote and lectured on the practices that had made Malabar's tranformation possible. His efforts attracted the attention of professional ecologists as well as agricultural scientists, and he received awards from several conservation organizations, including the National Audubon Society and Friends of the Land.

Bromfield wrote seven books about his second career as a farmer, and three

specifically about Malabar: *Pleasant Valley* (1945), which many regard as a 20th-century *Walden*; *Malabar Farm* (1948); and *Out of the Earth* (1950). During his years at Malabar Farm Bromfield also continued to write novels—"out of habit," he said—but readers were more interested in his nonfiction accounts of rural life.

Bromfield died in 1956, at the age of 59, but Malabar Farm lives on. Friends of the Land managed the farm until 1961, when the Malabar Farm Foundation was created to oversee its day-to-day operations as an experimental and model farm. In 1972 the state of Ohio took over the property, renaming it Malabar Farm State Park. Thousands of visitors come every year to the spot near the small town of Lucas where Louis Bromfield created a luxuriant garden out of a thousand acres of dust.

FURTHER READING

Bromfield, Louis. *Animals and Other People*. New York: Harper, 1955.

———. *From My Experience*. New York: Harper, 1955.

———. *Louis Bromfield at Malabar: Writings on Farming and Country Life*. Edited by Charles E. Little. Baltimore: Johns Hopkins University Press, 1988.

———. *Malabar Farm*. New York: Harper, 1948.

———. *A New Pattern for a Tired World*. New York: Harper, 1954.

———. *Out of the Earth*. New York: Harper, 1950.

———. *Pleasant Valley*. New York: Harper, 1945.

"Bromfield, Louis." In *Dictionary of American Biography*. Supplement 6. New York: Scribners, 1980.

Geld, Ellen [Bromfield]. *The Heritage: A Daughter's Memoir of Louis Bromfield*. New York: Harper, 1962.

EARTHKEEPERS

Louis Bromfield

BORN

December 27, 1896
Mansfield, Ohio

DIED

March 18, 1956
Columbus, Ohio

EDUCATION

Attended Cornell, Ohio Northern, and Columbia universities

MAJOR INTERESTS

Agriculture; ecology; writing

ACCOMPLISHMENTS

Advocate of restoring farmland through ecologically sound agricultural practices; established Malabar Farm (Ohio); prolific novelist who also wrote nonfiction, including *Pleasant Valley* (1945), *Malabar Farm* (1948), and *Out of the Earth* (1950)

HONORS

Awarded Légion d'Honneur and Croix de Guerre from the French government; Pulitzer Prize for fiction, 1926; Audubon Society Medal; Friends of the Land Medal; elected to American Institute of Arts and Letters

Katharine Ordway

SAVING THE PRAIRIES

Katharine Ordway was always interested in nature. From an early age, she studied plants and used her considerable artistic talent to create many botanical drawings and watercolors. As an adult she became interested in conservation and devoted her attention and considerable wealth to the preservation of nature. But the woman whom we remember today as "the lady who saved the prairies" did not begin her greatest life's work until she was more than 70 years old.

Katharine Ordway was born on April 3, 1899, in St. Paul, Minnesota, the fourth of five children and the only girl. Her father, Lucius Pond Ordway, was a business executive who made his fortune from plumbing supplies and real estate investments. Ordway went on to become a multimillionaire as the founder of the Minnesota Mining and Manufacturing Company, the manufacturer of Scotch tape, sandpaper, and other products. At his death in 1948, he left a trust fund for his children valued at $350 million.

Katharine Ordway was educated privately and then at the University of Minnesota, from which she graduated with honors, taking courses in both botany and art. In the early 1920s she attended Yale Medical School but decided against a medical career. As a young woman from a well-to-do family, she was free to pursue her interest in art, and she traveled all over Europe studying the work of the masters while she drew and painted. She also continued a hobby begun as a young girl, collecting important works of art, mostly by modern European and American artists. Today that valuable collection is part of the Yale University Art Gallery.

Despite her passion for art, Katharine Ordway's love of nature did not languish. At her homes in the woods of southwestern Connecticut, along the marshy shore of Long Island, and at the edge of the Arizona desert, she created beautiful gardens from native plants and flowers, working at the same time to preserve the natural landscape. In the early 1950s she began to take courses in biology and land-use planning at Columbia University, in New York City, and joined a study group, the Conservation Round Table, sponsored by the American Museum of Natural History.

Katharine Ordway's growing interest in conservation was encouraged by a cousin, Samuel H. Ordway, Jr., a lawyer who had cofounded (1947-48) and later headed the Conservation Foundation, an early environmental organization. In 1959 she used some of the money from her inheritance to create the philanthropic Goodhill Foundation. At first the foundation was supposed to make donations not only in the field of conservation but also for population control, art, and pure

scientific research, but Katharine Ordway soon focused her charitable interest on the preservation of open land, with an emphasis on keeping it wild and undeveloped.

With the help of Samuel Ordway and Richard Pough, cofounder of The Nature Conservancy (1950), the Goodhill Foundation gave the Conservancy money in 1966 to purchase a large wilderness tract in southwestern Connecticut known as Devil's Den, near Miss Ordway's home in Weston. According to the written agreement between Katharine Ordway and The Nature Conservancy, the land was to be "pre- served or maintained in its natural state and used solely for conservation of its natural beauty and resources, research…and nature study." The sanctuary, which now includes 1,565 acres and 15 miles of hiking trails, was named the Lucius Pond Ordway Pre- serve-Devil's Den, in memory of Katharine Ordway's father. It includes more than 500 species of plants, and its thick forest of trees dates back to the early 19th century.

The successful establishment of Devil's Den as a nature preserve encour- aged Katharine Ordway to acquire more open land. When Richard Pough told

Covering nearly 9,000 acres, the Konza Preserve in eastern Kansas is the largest protected tall-grass prairie in the United States. *Konza* is a variation of *Kansa,* the Indian tribe for which Kansas was named.

Katharine Ordway used her personal fortune to conserve prairies and other wilderness land throughout the United States.

the short- and tallgrass prairies lay regions of mixed-size grasses.

With the development of strong plows in the late 19th century to cut through the tough sod, most of the tallgrass prairie—once covering a quarter-billion acres— was eventually converted into prized farming land, what we now call the Corn Belt. Overgrazing of short- and mixed-grass prairies had led to their gradual disappearance as well. As early as the 1930s there had been private, state, and federal efforts to preserve surviving remnants of the original prairies, but farmers and ranchers had successfully opposed them.

Katharine Ordway had loved the prairies since her earliest childhood, so when Richard Pough suggested in 1970 that she finance the purchase by The Nature Conservancy of 310 acres of virgin tallgrass in western Minnesota, she readily agreed. Known as the Ordway Prairie Preserve, the tract is home to an abundance of bluestem, pasqueflower, prairie smoke, and numerous other wildflowers. She also gave the Conservancy funds to purchase three additional tracts of undeveloped prairie in the same area. One of these, the Chippewa Prairie Preserve, was used for the successful reintroduction of the nearly extinct greater prairie chicken to its natural habitat.

But Katharine Ordway was not satisfied with confining her conservation efforts to Minnesota, or to small tracts of land. What was needed, she believed, was an ambitious plan to save large expanses of tallgrass prairie wherever it existed. In 1971, at the age of 72, she embarked on her greatest life's work, creating the Ordway Prairie Reserve System as part of The Nature Conservancy.

In its first year alone, six new sanctuaries totaling nearly 2,000 acres of prairie were created within the new system, among them Konza, in the Flint Hills region of eastern Kansas. Konza Preserve, which has since grown to nearly

that the prairies of the United States were endangered, this prairie state native listened carefully. Natural grasslands, he explained, had once covered one-fifth of North America, from the foot of the Rocky Mountains to the edge of the eastern hardwood forests. In the high plains of the West the so-called short-grass prairie had flourished, comprising buffalo grass, wheat grass, and cacti. From the Dakotas down to the Texas-Louisiana border and in patches farther east stretched the tallgrass prairie, once as much as 10 feet tall and home to hundreds of different species of wildflowers, birds, mammals, and reptiles. Between

"Find me a prairie that goes on and on . . . "

—Katharine Ordway to Richard Pough of The Nature Conservancy (1971)

Katharine Ordway

BORN

April 3, 1899
St. Paul, Minnesota

DIED

June 27, 1979
New York City

EDUCATION

B.S., University of Minnesota; attended Yale Medical School; graduate study in biology and land-use planning, Columbia University

MAJOR INTERESTS

Land conservation; ecology

ACCOMPLISHMENTS

Created the Goodhill Foundation for the preservation of the natural environment (1959); established the Ordway Prairie Preserve System (1971); Katharine Ordway Endangered Species Conservation Program established posthumously (1984)

HONORS

Named the first "Land Guardian" by The Nature Conservancy (1978)

9,000 acres, is the largest protected tallgrass prairie in the United States. In 1979 the United Nations designated Konza as an International Biosphere Reserve, part of a global network of protected ecosystems.

Nearly all prairie reserves that she financed were, at Ordway's request, given Indian names—either of tribes native to the region or of plants, animals, or bodies of water found within their borders. One exception was the 7,500-acre Samuel H. Ordway, Jr., Memorial Prairie in north-central South Dakota, acquired in 1975 and named to honor the cousin who had sparked her interest in conservation and who had died four years earlier.

Ordway's financial resources made her impressive conservation efforts possible, but her contributions were not only monetary. She was personally involved in every acquisition, and insisted on visiting each proposed site before authorizing a purchase. Stooped and frail, sensibly dressed in pants and a long-sleeved shirt, carrying a large umbrella to shield her sun-sensitive skin, she always impressed those who accompanied her with her thorough knowledge of local birds, plants, and animals. As each preserve was acquired, she carefully oversaw its development, paying special attention to the reintroduction of species that had formerly flourished and were now virtually extinct. Among her many notable successes was the reemergence of the American bison on preserves she created in Kansas, the Dakotas, and Nebraska.

In 1978 Katharine Ordway extended her preservation efforts to include threatened coastal marshes, and made a major contribution to the Coast Reserve, a 40-mile-long chain of barrier islands off Virginia's Eastern Shore administered by The Nature Conservancy. In that year the Conservancy created a new award in her honor: she was the first person to be designated "The Land Guardian," a title conferred for life on only one recipient at a time.

At Katharine Ordway's death in 1979, her contributions to The Nature Conservancy totaled some $53 million and had enabled that organization to purchase some 1.4 million acres of land for preservation. In her name, the Goodhill Foundation continued its support of conservation until its dissolution in 1984—most notably through the creation of the Katharine Ordway Endangered Species Conservation Program, which has established sanctuaries in 32 states, from Hawaii to Florida. Today, Katharine Ordway, who began her true "career" at an age when most people have retired, is considered the greatest philanthropic supporter of conservation in the United States since John D. Rockefeller, Jr.

FURTHER READING

Blair, William D., Jr. *Katharine Ordway: The Lady Who Saved the Prairies.* Arlington, Va.: The Nature Conservancy, 1989.

Rachel Carson

IN DEFENSE OF NATURE

One day in the summer of 1958 a Massachusetts woman named Olga Huckins wrote a letter to an old friend, a biologist and noted science writer named Rachel Carson. The state had recently begun aerial spraying of DDT, a powerful pesticide, to control mosquitoes, and now Mrs. Huckins and her husband were finding dead birds scattered over the lawn of their home in Duxbury, where they had created a bird sanctuary. Moreover, harmless insects, including bees, had disappeared, yet the mosquito population was as strong as ever.

Could the DDT be responsible for these strange occurrences? Mrs. Huckins had called state authorities, who claimed that the spraying was a "harmless shower." Still, she was not convinced. Perhaps Rachel Carson, who had worked for many years for the federal government, could give her the name of an agency in Washington, D.C., that might be able to help her.

Carson, retired from government service and now a full-time writer, decided to look into the problem herself. A trained scientist, she began reading about pesticides in scholarly and technical journals, and the more she learned, the more frightened she became: the widespread use of DDT and other poisons was threatening the entire natural world. It was important, she believed, that the public be alerted to the dangers of pesticides.

At first, Carson planned to write a magazine article about the problem and approached a number of well-known periodicals to see if they would publish it. All but one turned her down, claiming that she had neither the authority nor the expertise to challenge the safety of pesticides. Only the *New Yorker* encouraged her, and suggested that she turn the project into a book, which she called *Silent Spring*. Its publication in 1962 immediately set off an enormous controversy.

Until then, the shy, hardworking Carson had known only success and acclaim in a professional life of more than 30 years' duration. Born the youngest of three children on a farm near Pittsburgh in 1907, she had been introduced in childhood to the delights of the natural world by her mother, who also made sure, despite the family's modest circumstances, that her children learned about books and music. Carson exhibited an early talent for writing, and one of her stories won an award from the national children's magazine *St. Nicholas* when she was 10.

After completing high school, Carson received a partial scholarship to the Pennsylvania College for Women, where she intended to study writing; to pay for the rest of her expenses, her mother sold the family's silver and good china. Carson changed her mind about her major when a biology teacher at the school rekindled an interest in science, and she graduated with a bachelor's degree in zoology in 1929. She received a graduate fellowship to Johns Hopkins University in Baltimore, where she earned a master's degree in the same field in 1932. Beginning in 1931, Carson taught part-time at the University of Maryland for five years; she spent summers on a teaching fellowship at the Marine Biological Laboratory in Woods Hole, Massachusetts, and also taught summer school classes at Johns Hopkins.

During this time Carson began contributing feature articles on scientific topics to the *Baltimore Sun* as a way to make extra money. The United States was mired in the Great Depression, and Carson was now helping to support her elderly parents, who had moved to Baltimore. In 1935 her father died, leaving Carson to look after her mother. Carson realized that she could not afford to continue teaching and began looking for a higher-paying job. In 1936 she took a test for the job of junior aquatic biologist at the U.S. Bureau of Fisheries. Outscoring other applicants—all male—she was hired, and became only the second woman ever employed by the bureau for a nonclerical position.

To be closer to her job in Washington, Carson and her mother moved to Silver Spring, Maryland, where they were soon joined by two grammar-school-age nieces. Carson now had the job of supporting three other people besides herself. Among her duties at the Bureau of Fisheries, Carson had to prepare scripts for radio programs about life in the ocean. When her supervisor rejected one of her scripts as "too literary," he suggested that she rewrite it into an article and submit it to the *Atlantic Monthly* for publication. "Undersea" was promptly accepted and appeared in the September 1937 issue.

The article impressed an editor in New York, who invited Carson to expand it into a book. In November

Rachel Carson conducts research for her book *The Sea Around Us* off Georges Bank, Newfoundland, in July 1949.

1941 *Under the Sea Wind* was published to excellent reviews, but a month later the United States was swept into World War II following the bombing of Pearl Harbor, and the book sold poorly as the public's attention turned to news of the war. One of those who did notice and applaud Carson's first book was the well-known writer and oceanographer William Beebe, who included excerpts from *Under the Sea Wind* in his collection of nature writing called *The Book of Naturalists* (1944).

In 1940 the Bureau of Fisheries merged with the U.S. Biological Survey to become the U.S. Fish and Wildlife Service. Carson moved up the ranks of the government bureaucracy as a

Carson explores a tidal pool along the Maine shoreline near her summer cottage in West Southport.

scientist-writer. During the war, when meat was rationed, she wrote pamphlets encouraging the public to eat fish. Later she produced a series of booklets about national wildlife refuges, visiting the Florida Everglades, Chincoteague Island, the Parker River Refuge in Massachusetts, and other sites to do research.

Financial pressure was still intense for Carson, and she decided to begin another book. Her work with the fishing industry had made her aware of vast amounts of top-secret research on

oceanography done by the U.S. government during the war. The research had now been declassified—made available to the public—and Carson made much of it the basis for her new work, a study of the geological formation of the oceans and the life they contained.

Every evening Carson returned home from the office to spend time on her second book. By 1949 Oxford University Press had agreed to publish it, and Carson embarked on field research during vacations. At William Beebe's

"The lasting pleasures of contact with the natural world are not reserved for scientists but are available to anyone who will place himself under the influence of earth, sea and sky and their amazing life."

—from *The Sense of Wonder* (1965)

Rachel Carson

BORN

May 27, 1907
Springdale, Pennsylvania

DIED

April 14, 1964
Silver Spring, Maryland

EDUCATION

B.A., Pennsylvania College for Women (now Chatham College); M.A., Johns Hopkins University

MAJOR INTERESTS

Marine biology; ecology

ACCOMPLISHMENTS

Alerted public to dangers of pesticides in *Silent Spring* (1962); author of four other books, including *The Sea Around Us* (1951) and *The Sense of Wonder* (1965)

HONORS

John Burroughs Medal and the National Book Award (for *The Sea Around Us*); National Audubon Society Medal; National Geographic Society Cullum Medal; elected to American Academy of Arts and Letters; honorary degrees from Chatham and Oberlin colleges

invitation, she did some undersea diving in Florida. She also spent 10 days aboard the *Albatross III*, the research vessel of the Fish and Wildlife Service, as it sailed along the Georges Bank south of Nova Scotia. Here, as she later wrote, she became fully aware for the first time that "ours is a water world dominated by the immensity of the sea." With the help of Beebe and naturalist-writer Edwin Way Teale, Carson received a Saxton Memorial Fellowship to continue her work on the book. Before publication, half of it was serialized in the *New Yorker*; to Carson's amazement, the amount she was paid by the magazine was equal to a year's salary at her government job.

The Sea Around Us was published in July 1951 and received instant acclaim. Carson was quickly transformed into a renowned literary personage, sought out for lectures and interviews. *The Sea Around Us* received that year's National Book Award, and its author was presented with the John Burroughs Medal for writing the outstanding natural history book of the year. Other honors poured in, including honorary degrees from her alma mater and from Oberlin College. *Under the Sea Wind* was reissued, and it, too, became a best-seller.

Carson now had enough money to retire from the Fish and Wildlife Service and write full-time. Research for her third book, *The Edge of the Sea,* a study of ecological relationships along the eastern seacoast of the United States, took her on extended field trips from Maine to Florida. It also became a best-seller following its publication in 1955, and Carson received more acclaim and awards. She next turned to a project that she had been thinking about for some time: a book that would help parents teach their children to appreciate nature. Carson wrote this book using her young grandnephew Roger as a focus; she later adopted the orphaned Roger after his mother's death.

Carson was hard at work on *The Sense of Wonder* when she received Olga Huckins's letter. Putting aside the manuscript, she began doing research on DDT, or dichlorodiphenyltrichlorothane. Based on a 19th-century German discovery, DDT had been reinvented as a pesticide in 1939 by a Swiss chemist, Dr. Paul Muller. During World War II the British and American governments used DDT to combat insect-borne diseases. In the South Pacific liquid DDT was sprayed to kill malaria-causing mosquitoes; in Europe DDT powder was dusted on troops and their clothing to destroy body lice, which spread the dreaded disease typhus.

DDT was hailed as a miraculous creation that would help mankind rid itself of pests that had plagued it throughout history. After the war, it came into common use. Americans sprayed or dusted it on their houses, their gardens, and even themselves to kill insects; state and local governments sprayed entire communities; the United Nations undertook a worldwide campaign to eliminate malaria, with DDT as its principal weapon. Occasionally people noticed dead birds and other wildlife after large applications of DDT, but no one seriously questioned the wisdom of its use. Dr. Muller was hailed as a scientific hero and in 1948 received the Nobel Prize in chemistry for his discovery.

Fourteen years later, Rachel Carson published her findings about the toxic effects of Dr. Muller's "miracle." Acknowledging that chemical pesticides were helpful if properly used, she marshaled clear, scientific evidence that they were being dangerously abused by a society "largely ignorant of their potentials for harm." DDT sprayed on home gardens, for example, found its way into rivers, where it was absorbed by plants that were eaten by fish. Fish in turn were eaten by humans, and residues of the poison were now being found in the fatty tissues of the entire population.

The "silent spring" that awaited us in the near future because the nation's songbirds were dying off from DDT contamination might be only the beginning of a wider disaster, Carson warned, for pesticides were also suspected of causing cancer and even genetic mutations. Furthermore, there were indications that pesticides were not eliminating harmful insects: on the contrary, stronger populations of chemical-resistant bugs were being produced, and mankind was struggling to keep a step ahead with stronger and stronger poisons.

Carson proposed biological controls—sterilizing and trapping insects; pitting one species against another—as sensible alternatives to our dependence on chemical annihilators. Such natural weapons were harmless to man. However, many readers focused on Carson's warnings rather than her proposed solutions. The once widely beloved author was now criticized in newspapers and popular magazines for being an alarmist, and the chemical and agriculture industries launched vicious personal attacks against her.

But there were also those who supported her, and praised her for her bravery in bringing such a controversial subject to public attention. Prodded by scientific groups and conservationists, President John F. Kennedy directed his Science Advisory Committee to study the problem. Carson began to be vindicated as the committee issued recommendations for further studies of the health hazards of pesticides and warned against their indiscriminate use. Eventually many pesticides, including DDT, were banned outright; others were brought under tighter control.

Carson did not live to see these later victories, however. Soon after starting to write *Silent Spring,* she was stricken with cancer. She battled the disease with radiation treatments and continued her work, not only on the new manuscript but on the preparation of a revised edition of *The Sea Around Us,* which was published in 1961. Prophetically, in her new preface she warned against the dangers of ocean pollution, particularly from nuclear waste. In her final years she completed *The Sense of Wonder,* published posthumously in 1965. She also campaigned vigorously for passage of the Wilderness Act, which President Lyndon Johnson signed into law five months after her death.

FURTHER READING

Bonta, Marcia Myers. "Rachel Carson." In *Women in the Field: America's Pioneering Women Naturalists.* College Station: Texas A&M University Press, 1991.

Brooks, Paul. *The House of Life: Rachel Carson at Work; with Selections from Her Writings.* Boston: Houghton Mifflin, 1972.

Carson, Rachel. *The Edge of the Sea.* 1955. Reprint. Boston: Houghton Mifflin, 1979.

———. *The Sea Around Us.* 1951. Reprint. New York: Oxford University Press, 1991.

———. *The Sense of Wonder.* 1965. Reprint. New York: HarperCollins, 1987.

———. *Silent Spring.* 1962. Reprint. Boston: Houghton Mifflin, 1987.

———. *Under the Sea Wind.* 1941. Reprint. New York: NAL/Dutton, 1991.

"Carson, Rachel." In *Dictionary of American Biography.* Supplement 7. New York: Scribners, 1988.

Wild, Peter. "Rachel Carson: The Issue Becomes Life Itself." In *Pioneer Conservationists of Eastern America.* Missoula, Mont.: Mountain Press, 1986.

Miriam Rothschild

A BORN NATURALIST

T raditionally, the eminent Rothschild family, which originated in Germany, has been associated with banking, but the branch of the Rothschilds that settled in Great Britain in the mid-18th century has also had its share of gifted naturalists. Charles Rothschild (who died in 1923) and his brother Walter (1868-1937), sons of England's first Lord Rothschild, dutifully worked at the family bank in London, but natural history was their real passion and both of them became noted amateur scientists and collectors.

Charles Rothschild was interested in entomology, the study of insects, and became an expert on butterflies and fleas. Early in the 20th century, on a trip to Egypt, he discovered the rat flea, which carries bubonic plague. Walter Rothschild, who had announced at the age of seven that he was going to "make a museum," spent most of his lifetime doing just that, amassing millions of butterflies, beetles, birds, tortoises, and other zoological specimens. The collection, housed at Walter Rothschild's estate in Tring, England, is now part of the British Museum.

Miriam Rothschild, the daughter of Charles Rothschild and his Hungarian wife, Rozsika, was drawn to the interests of

Miriam Rothschild is considered the world's leading authority on fleas, but her interests embrace all aspects of nature, including these rabbits bred at her estate.

Miriam Rothschild's uncle Walter Rothschild inspired her own interest in natural history. Walter assembled millions of specimens at Tring Park, his estate near London, which is now part of the British Museum. Part of his vast collection is exhibited in this room at Tring.

her father and uncle as a small child at Ashton Wold, the family estate near Peterborough, England, where she was born in 1908. Her earliest memories include taking a tame quail to bed with her, and by the age of four she was breeding ladybugs. She was educated at home; her family believed that formal academic training would stifle her zest for learning.

When her father died, 15-year-old Miriam began spending long periods with her uncle Walter at Tring and became absorbed in his collections. One day her brother, Victor, returned home on holiday from boarding school with a frog he had to dissect for biology class. He asked his sister to help, and the task was so fascinating to her that she decided to become a full-time naturalist.

Rothschild persuaded her family to allow her to attend evening classes at a technical institute in London. Then, through a family friend at the British Museum, she secured an appointment at the University of London's biological station in Naples, Italy, where she studied marine animals. Back in England, she spent most of the 1930s in Plymouth doing research on a primitive mollusk called *Nucula*, but to her dismay all of her work was destroyed during heavy German bombings of the city in 1940.

Unable to resume working in Plymouth because of the war, Rothschild returned to Ashton Wold and turned her attention to fleas. She continued her research after her marriage in 1943 to George Lane and the subsequent birth of six children, and began publishing scientific papers on her findings. Rothschild also had another, private occupation during World War II: she was recruited by the British secret service to work on the top-secret Enigma project, which cracked the German communications code, and later received a medal from the government for her participation.

In 1952 Rothschild's first book, *Fleas, Flukes and Cuckoos*, written for a nonscientific audience, was published. By now she had become recognized as the world's leading authority on bird fleas, and the popularity of her book quickly earned her the title of "Queen of the Fleas." During this time Rothschild also cataloged her father's collection of 30,000 flea specimens for the British Museum. The six-volume catalog was published over a 30-year period, beginning in 1953.

In addition to her research on fleas, Rothschild has studied mites and ticks as well as ladybugs, butterflies, and moths,

Miriam Rothschild

"If I had to wish one wish for my children, I would wish that they were interested in natural history, because I think there you get a spiritual well-being that you can get no other way."

—from an interview in *Smithsonian,* June 1985

and a large seabird called the skua. Butterflies hold a particular fascination for Rothschild, dating from her childhood familiarity with Uncle Walter's collection. Today she considers "watching butterflies" her favorite form of recreation. She has written two books about them for the general reader: *The Butterfly Gardener* (coauthored with Clive Farrell; 1983), and *Butterfly Cooing Like a Dove* (1990), a collection of illustrations, quotations, and her own commentary. Rothschild has also coauthored a scientific study of insect tissue and written a biography of her uncle Walter entitled *Dear Lord Rothschild* (1983). To date she has written more than 300 articles for scientific journals.

In recent years Rothschild, alarmed by the rapid disappearance of wildflowers from the countryside, has devoted her time to growing increasingly rare varieties. On the grounds of Ashton Wold she has created acres of flowering meadows. Seeds are painstakingly gathered and either sold or given away. Her goal is to reintroduce wildflower species on public lands throughout England.

Ashton Wold is a working farm, and Rothschild takes an active part in its management. She also continues as a leader of the Royal Society for Nature Conservation, which her father founded in 1912. Rothschild is a longtime advocate of animal rights, the subject of a lecture she delivered in 1985 at Oxford University and published the following year as *Animals and Man.*

Miriam Rothschild has been the recipient of numerous awards, including honorary doctor of science degrees from Oxford and other leading universities. In 1983 she was named a Commander of the British Empire (CBE) by Queen Elizabeth II and two years later was elected a fellow of the Royal Society of London. Despite her accomplishments in the field of natural history, Rothschild does not consider herself a scientist. "I am a naturalist," she insists, with "curiosity, a keen eye, a good memory, and boundless delight and enjoyment of the animal and plant world. . . . A scientist, up to a point, can be made. A naturalist is born."

FURTHER READING

Cowles, Virginia. *The Rothschilds: A Family of Fortune.* New York: Knopf, 1973.

Fraser, Kennedy. "Fritillaries and Hairy Violets." *New Yorker,* October 19, 1987, 45-74.

McCullough, David. "A Rothschild Who Is Known as the Queen of the Fleas." *Smithsonian,* June 1985, 139-53.

Rothschild, Miriam. *Animals and Man.* Oxford: Oxford University Press, 1986.

———. "A Born Naturalist's Keen Insights." *Scientific American,* August 1990, 116.

———. *Butterfly Cooing Like a Dove.* New York: Doubleday, 1990.

———. *Dear Lord Rothschild.* London: Hutchinson, 1983.

———. *Fleas, Flukes and Cuckoos.* London: Collins, 1952.

"Rothschild, Miriam." In *Current Biography,* October 1992, 47-52.

BORN

August 5, 1908
Peterborough, England

EDUCATION

Tutored at home

MAJOR INTERESTS

Natural history; entomology; conservation

ACCOMPLISHMENTS

Self-taught biologist and naturalist, considered the world's greatest authority on fleas; leading conservationist; author of more than 300 scientific papers and 12 books, including *Fleas, Flukes and Cuckoos* (1952), *Animals and Man* (1986), and *Butterfly Cooing Like a Dove* (1990)

HONORS

Honorary degrees from Oxford, Gothenburg, Hull, and Northwestern universities; Commander of the British Empire; fellow, Royal Society of London; member, American Academy of Arts and Sciences; honorary fellow, St. Hugh's College, Oxford

David Brower

FRIEND OF THE EARTH

T oday David Brower is a renowned environmentalist and accomplished mountaineer, but as a child he was terrified whenever he accompanied his family on their frequent excursions into California's Sierra Nevada range. Only in his 20s, while working as an office clerk at Yosemite National Park, did he finally overcome his fear of heights by deliberately ascending 33 surrounding peaks during a six-year period.

Brower believes that his phobia had its roots in an earlier childhood calamity. In 1913, near his home in Berkeley, California, one-year-old David fell from his baby carriage, knocking out his front teeth and severely damaging his gums. After that trauma, he had to wait for 11 years before a second set of teeth grew in. Schoolmates taunted him as "the toothless boob," and the shamed youth became extremely shy and afraid to smile.

Adversity continued to plague the Browers. When David was eight, his mother went blind and soon afterward his father lost his job as a mechanical drawing instructor at the nearby University of California. David and the other three Brower children pitched in to help the family, selling newspapers and helping to take care of two run-down apartment buildings that were their only steady source of income. In addition, David led his mother on long walks through the Berkeley Hills, becoming her "eyes" and describing in great detail their surroundings. As he noted many years later, "That looking for someone else may have sharpened my appreciation of the beauty in natural things."

Brower's frequent wanderings in the countryside led him to start a collection of rocks and minerals, and to become an expert at identifying flora and fauna, especially butterflies. At Berkeley High School, however, he felt that he had to hide his growing interest in entomology in favor of more "manly" pursuits, including managing one of the football teams. At 16 he enrolled at the University of California, unsure of what field of study to pursue, but dropped out in his sophomore year because of financial difficulties.

Brower went to work as a clerk at a local candy factory, still uncertain about his future. During a vacation in 1933 he took an extended trip through the Sierra wilderness—and was instantly enchanted by its beauty and freshness. "You could drink from any stream you saw and breathe any wind that came by," he later recalled. That same year he joined the Sierra Club, the conservation organization founded in 1892 by John Muir and his associates; his sponsor for membership was the renowned nature photographer Ansel Adams.

Brower returned to the wilderness frequently to hike and

camp, and was often late in returning to his job at the candy factory. Finally, in 1935, he was fired, and this time he decided to find employment in a more congenial environment. Hired as an office worker at Yosemite, Brower eventually worked his way up to publicity manager while conquering his fear of mountain heights by ascending every peak in the vicinity. His growing facility

for writing led to a new job in 1941 as an editor at the University of California Press; two years later he was married to a fellow editor, Anne Hus, and they subsequently had four children.

From 1943 until the end of World War II, Brower served with the U.S. Army's 10th Mountain Division in France and Italy. His duties included teaching climbing techniques to troops

Wearing a T-shirt featuring the emblem of the Earth Island Institute, a conservation organization he founded in 1982, David Brower rests during a hike in the wilderness.

> *"Progress is not the speed with which technology expands its control or the number of things a man possesses, but a process that lets man find serenity and grow more content at less cost to the earth."*
>
> —from the "Credo" of Friends of the Earth

and writing a manual on the subject, and his service earned him a Bronze Star. Brower returned to the University of California Press after the war and during his spare time began work on the *Sierra Club Handbook,* first published in 1947 and subsequently reissued in a number of revised editions.

In 1952 Brower was chosen by the Sierra Club's board to be its executive director. Although John Muir had founded the club to be an activist organization, campaigning for preservation, it had changed its direction markedly: in the 38 years since Muir's death, the Sierra Club had not won a single major environmental battle. Detractors called it nothing more than a "posey-picking hiking society" that sponsored outings for its well-to-do membership. Protests were now feeble at best; even veteran member Ansel Adams, who had photographed some of the most beautiful nature scenes in North America, had ultimately allied himself with the government in its successful effort to locate a nuclear reactor in Diablo Canyon.

David Brower was expected to continue the tradition that one member characterized as "friendly persuasion." "Don't be negative," he was told; demanding total capitulation by the "enemy"—government or business or individuals who wanted to exploit the environment—was unreasonable and would only hurt the organization in the long run. But Brower had other ideas. Preservation was going to be his watchword, and he set about attracting a new breed of environmental crusaders to join the club. Almost immediately, the U.S. Bureau of Reclamation provided him

with a cause when it announced that a dam would be built on the Green River, backing water into Dinosaur National Monument.

Brower decided to marshal the forces of the Sierra Club to fight the dam's construction. To help them do so, he published a book, *This Is Dinosaur,* which set forth in text and numerous illustrations the endangered preserve. This was the first in a series of best-selling volumes on scenic America, from the Maine coast to the Sierra Nevada, that were sponsored by the club. They not only reawakened the public's interest in the country's natural environment but also earned substantial amounts of money to pay for the Sierra Club's campaigns.

At the heart of Brower's activism was a strong belief in environmentalism as a political issue. The country could no longer afford to rely on "friendly persuasion" and hoped-for goodwill to save its precious natural legacy. Sierra Club members, whose numbers swelled from 7,000 to more than 70,000 under Brower's leadership, became politically active in defense of the environment: they wrote letters to congressmen, lobbied, demonstrated, and testified at government hearings. Their efforts paid off: Dinosaur National Monument was saved, and a subsequent effort by the government to create a dam in the Grand Canyon was also overcome.

Under Brower, the Sierra Club became the most effective organization of its kind as it led successful efforts to save the Giant Redwoods in California, the Great Smoky Mountains, Kentucky's Red River Gorge, Maine's Allagash wilderness, the Florida Everglades, and

Storm King Mountain in New York State. In addition, lobbying efforts led to the creation of two new national parks —North Cascades, in Washington State, and Canyonlands, in Utah—and the establishment of national seashores at Cape Cod, Massachusetts, and Point Reyes, California. The Sierra Club was active in the fight for passage of the 1964 Wilderness Act, which extended permanent protection to designated Wilderness Areas. During the late 1960s the Sierra Club blocked construction projects worth $7 billion that threatened the natural environment.

Despite these successes, not everyone on the Sierra Club's board of directors was happy with David Brower's aggressive leadership. Conservative and moderate members believed that he was alienating powerful government and business forces as he urged conservation for conservation's sake rather than trying to work realistically with industry. Board members accused him of working independently and spending large sums of money to publicize causes without their authorization. They were especially upset when, in an action directly traceable to Brower's activism, the Internal Revenue Service withdrew the Sierra Club's tax-exempt status, resulting in a huge financial loss for the organization. In the spring of 1969, disgruntled board members finally forced Brower to resign as executive director.

Brower promptly formed two organizations of his own, the John Muir Institute and Friends of the Earth. The institute, initially funded by a grant from the Atlantic Richfield oil company and later by support from the Ford Foundation, encourages and supports environ-

mental research and education. Brower directed the institute for two years, from 1969 to 1971. Friends of the Earth, which Brower served as president for 10 years, is a political activist group that lobbies for legislation and candidates favorable to environmental protection. In 1982 Brower founded another environmental action group, the Earth Island Institute, and he still serves as its chairman.

Brower continues as an active writer and lecturer on behalf of environmental concerns. The Sierra Club, the organization that Brower single-handedly rejuvenated, has continued to grow and remains a strong voice in the late-20th-century environmental movement, thanks largely to the course that he set it on unswervingly more than four decades ago. The club's board of directors belatedly recognized their indebtedness to Brower by giving him the prestigious John Muir Award in 1977. Over the years Brower has been the recipient of many honors from conservation organizations, but the Muir Award may well be the one he prizes most.

FURTHER READING

Brower, David. *For Earth's Sake: The Life and Times of David Brower*. Salt Lake City: Peregrine Smith, 1990.

————. *Work in Progress*. Salt Lake City: Peregrine Smith, 1991.

McPhee, John. *Encounters with the Archdruid*. New York: Farrar, Straus & Giroux, 1971.

Wild, Peter. "David Brower and Charisma: The Rebirth of the Conservation Movement." In *Pioneer Conservationists of Western America*. Missoula, Mont.: Mountain Press, 1979.

David Brower

BORN

July 1, 1912
Berkeley, California

EDUCATION

Attended University of California, Berkeley

MAJOR INTEREST

Environmentalism

ACCOMPLISHMENTS

Executive director, Sierra Club (1952–69); founder, president, Friends of the Earth (1969–79); founder, chairman, Earth Island Institute (1982–); editor of more than 50 books; author of two autobiographical volumes: *For Earth's Sake: The Life and Times of David Brower* (1990) and *Work in Progress* (1991)

HONORS

Bronze Star (U.S. Army); numerous honors from conservation groups, including the John Muir Award from the Sierra Club; honorary degrees from Claremont College and Hobart and William Smith College

Farley Mowat

PLEADING FOR AN END TO SENSELESS SLAUGHTER

In the spring of 1944, as war raged on the European continent, a young Canadian soldier riding inside an armored vehicle in Ortona, Italy, suddenly found himself in the midst of a combat zone. His unit had invaded Sicily the previous summer and had continued fighting its way northward on the Italian mainland, liberating the country from Fascist rule. The soldier had discovered in the course of the long campaign that he did not like war, although his father had often regaled him with accounts of his own service in World War I and encouraged him to fight for his country. In fact, the soldier was a member of his father's old regiment.

But the young soldier, Farley Mowat, had seen too many people die to believe that war was a glorious undertaking, and now, crouched inside the tank, he tried to quell the fear rising inside him. "I went back to the only safe place in my mind," he recalled many years later, "my childhood." Seizing a scrap of paper and a pencil, the soldier began writing down some of the comical misadventures of his family, focusing his concentration on an earlier, peaceful time in rural Canada.

Later, out of danger, Farley Mowat continued with his narrative and in letters home to his father, Angus, wrote about his experience of "escape" within the tank. Angus Mowat, who had long entertained dreams of becoming a novelist, passed on strong words of encouragement to his son and only child: Farley *could* and *should* be a writer; had he not inherited his father's gifts and aspirations?

Farley Mowat fulfilled his father's ambitions and more: he became one of his country's best-known writers, and his books have sold more copies than any other Canadian author of his time. Mowat credits both of his parents "for letting me go my own way, not interfering or interrupting or trying to direct me in ways of their choosing." His upbringing was far from conventional. Although his mother, Helen Thomson Mowat, came from a long line of bankers and clergymen, her husband seems to have been a jack-of-all-trades—sailor, hunter, builder, would-be writer, and finally a librarian—infected with a strong wanderlust. Shortly after Farley's birth in Bellevue, Ontario, in 1921, Angus Mowat moved his family to a series of other towns in the province. Finally, in 1928, he decided it was time to go west. He put together a small house on top of a Model T Ford and the Mowats traveled in this contraption across the country to Saskatoon, Saskatchewan.

Seven-year-old Farley had been introduced to the natural world back in Ontario, thanks to the influence of his great-uncle Frank, an amateur naturalist, and in his new home on the Canadian prairies he was more eager than ever to explore the countryside. By the age of 13 he was traveling 30 miles by

Farley Mowat

Trained as a biologist, Farley Mowat has written many books on nature and conservation. He has also defended the rights of the Inuits, whose hunting grounds have been plundered.

BORN

May 12, 1921
Belleville, Ontario, Canada

EDUCATION

B.A., University of Toronto

MAJOR INTERESTS

Nature writing; environmentalism

ACCOMPLISHMENTS

Author of more than two dozen books, including *Owls in the Family* (1961), *Never Cry Wolf* (1963), *A Whale for the Killing* (1972), *Sea of Slaughter* (1984), *Woman in the Mists: The Story of Dian Fossey and the Mountain Gorillas of Africa* (1987), and the autobiographical *My Father's Son* (1993)

HONORS

Numerous awards for writing, including the Governor General's Medal (1957) and the Hans Christian Andersen International Award (1958); Order of Canada (1981); honorary degrees from a number of colleges, including the University of Toronto

snowshoes into the wilderness. A year later Frank took him on a trip north to Fort Churchill, Manitoba, to study the bird life of the Arctic tundra and Farley was stunned by his first glimpse of a herd of caribou. As he later wrote of the journey, he became permanently infected with "virus arcticus"—Arctic fever.

Surrounded by books from earliest childhood, Farley Mowat also loved both reading and writing. As a teenager he published his own mimeographed magazine, called *Nature Lore*, and while still in high school sold weekly articles about nature to the local newspaper.

World War II broke out the year he graduated, and Mowat soon entered the Canadian army. It was a disillusioning and painful experience: at war's end he was the last surviving member of his regiment.

Following his discharge in 1946, Mowat put aside the book he had begun to write two years earlier and used his army educational benefit to enroll at the University of Toronto, where he eventually earned a bachelor's degree. After a year of full-time study, however, he was impatient to return to the wilderness. In the summer of 1947 he

Mowat's best-seller *Never Cry Wolf* (1963) included a strong plea for the preservation of wolves in the wild. Following publication of a Russian-language edition of the book, the Soviet government banned wolf killing throughout the U.S.S.R.

moved to the Northwest Territories, an area he came to call the Barrens, to work as a government biologist.

Mowat was assigned to find out why the caribou population was rapidly declining. Popular wisdom had it that wolves were responsible, and Mowat was supposed to make careful observations of what they ate. Camping out near a pack, Mowat discovered that their diet consisted mostly of field mice. Occasionally they ate a sick caribou, but the fact that they chose to prey on the weakest members of the population actually strengthened the herd. Human hunters, not wolves, were wiping out the caribou.

Mowat began work on a new book, an impassioned defense of wolves and a plea for their preservation, but before he could finish it, the plight of Inuits (Eskimos) in the Barrens captured his attention. Mowat became friendly with members of a tribe called the Ihalmiut and was impressed with how they lived in harmony with their environment. Nicknamed "People of the Deer" because of their dependence on caribou for food, clothing, and shelter, the tribe was dying out as the numbers of caribou rapidly declined. Mowat wrote to the Canadian government, asking them to save the Ihalmiut from starvation by enforcing conservation of Arctic mammals, but his pleas were ignored. To draw public attention to the Ihalmiut, he began writing articles for American and Canadian periodicals and in 1952 published a book about the tribe, *People of the Deer*.

Mowat's book made him the center of attention throughout North America and England. Government officials criticized his account and accused him of exaggeration and outright lying, but many readers applauded his courageous exposé. Mowat's defense of the Ihalmiut cost him his job, but he was now established as a full-time writer. While continuing to advocate the Inuit cause, he published an account of his World War II service called *The Regiment* (1955) and a highly praised juvenile novel, *Lost in the Barrens* (1956), about two boys who survive winter in the North by learning from nature and the Inuits.

The book Mowat had begun writing inside the tank in Italy back in 1944 was finally published 13 years later as *The Dog Who Wouldn't Be*; it became a best-seller and earned Mowat a number of honors, including the prestigious Hans Christian Andersen International Award. Another popular and award-winning book drawn from his childhood experiences was *Owls in the Family*, published in 1961.

Mowat has written several fictional works for children, as well as two volumes of autobiography and an account of conservationist Dian Fossey's work with gorillas in Africa, but he is most widely known for his nonfiction books about the Canadian Arctic. Although his advocacy of the Inuits was ultimately unsuccessful—a second book about them, called *The Desperate People,* appeared in 1959—his work on behalf of wolves has changed the attitudes of many toward these much-maligned animals. *Never Cry Wolf,* begun during his early days as a government biologist, was published in 1963 and became an immediate best-seller. An urgent plea to save the wolf, the book has been translated into many languages and was made into a movie in 1983.

During the 1960s Mowat moved to the small port town of Burgeo, Newfoundland, with his second wife, Claire Wheeler Mowat, also a writer. (Mowat has two sons by a previous marriage.) In Burgeo he wrote a sympathetic account of the local population, former seafarers who had been forced by the advent of large commercial fishing operations to abandon their traditional livelihood and work in a fish canning factory. His sympathy turned to horror, however, in 1967, when a pregnant whale became trapped in a local tidal pond and became the object of the townspeople's rage. The whale died slowly and painfully at the hands of tormentors who fired bullets at her and gashed her with speedboats. In great emotional pain, Mowat left Newfoundland and returned to Ontario, where it took him several years to write about the incident. The resulting account was *A Whale for the Killing,* published in 1972 and later made into a movie for television.

Mowat published half a dozen books about Arctic life and exploration during the 1970s. Later in the decade he moved to Cape Breton Island, in Nova Scotia, where he became increasingly aware of the fragility of the environment. In the early 1980s, he began a thorough study of the wildlife of North America's Eastern Seaboard since 1500, the year the first Europeans arrived. In *Sea of Slaughter,* which appeared in 1984, Mowat details the annihilation of hundreds of bird and animal species and concludes that in nearly 500 years Western man has destroyed between 80 and 90 percent of the wildlife on the Atlantic seaboard and its adjacent interior.

Farley Mowat continues to speak out on behalf of animal conservation, hoping that humankind will some day come to its senses and end the pointless killing that continues in much of the world today. Although he believes that his books have not had the impact he had hoped for, he is guardedly optimistic about a change in attitude. "More and more people are becoming fed up with the killer syndrome," he says, "and this is where the hope lies. We're not going to be able to reverse the killing process in the next decade, or perhaps two. But the indications are that in the very near future there will be such enormous pressure from the nonkilling members of the human species that the killers will be driven into a corner and disarmed. That's the hope."

"The living world is dying in our time."

—from *Sea of Slaughter* (1984)

FURTHER READING

Mowat, Farley. *And No Birds Sang.* Boston: Little, Brown, 1979.

———.*The Dog Who Wouldn't Be.* Boston: Little, Brown, 1957.

———. *My Father's Son.* Boston: Houghton Mifflin, 1993.

———. *Never Cry Wolf.* Boston: Little, Brown, 1963.

———. *Owls in the Family.* Boston: Little, Brown, 1961.

———. *Sea of Slaughter.* Boston: Atlantic Monthly Press, 1984.

———. *A Whale for the Killing.* Boston: Little, Brown, 1972.

———. *The World of Farley Mowat: A Selection from His Works.* Edited by Peter Davison. Boston: Little, Brown, 1980.

"Mowat, Farley (McGill)." In *Contemporary Authors.* New Revision Series, vol. 24. Detroit: Gale, 1988.

"Mowat, Farley (McGill)." In *1986 Current Biography Yearbook.* New York: H. W. Wilson, 1987.

Gerald Durrell

"NO CREATURE IS HORRIBLE"

On the island of Jersey, in the English Channel, is a most unusual zoo, home to some of the rarest creatures in the world. In fact, in order to be admitted to the Jersey Zoological Park, an animal must be considered an endangered species. The zoo and its administrative organization, the Jersey Wildlife Preservation Trust, are the creations of British naturalist Gerald Durrell.

When the 33-year-old Durrell opened his zoo in 1958, he was fulfilling a dream he had held since earliest childhood. His mother claims that his first clearly spoken word was "zoo," and not long after he learned to walk he began the lifelong habit of collecting animals, bringing them home to a family that was not always enthusiastic about Gerald's "treasures." There were owls, butterflies, mice, and turtles in Gerald's collections—but there were also snakes and spiders. Curious about every living thing, Gerald agreed that some animals were more endearing than others but claimed that he found nothing repulsive in nature. As an adult he believes this more strongly than ever: "No creature is horrible," he has said more than once, and that philosophy underlies his virtually lifelong commitment to wild animal conservation.

Born in India in 1925 to British parents, Gerald Durrell was the youngest of four children. His father, a civil engineer who supervised the construction of major railroads and bridges on the Indian subcontinent, died when Gerald was three. Shortly afterward the family returned to England, but Durrell still has memories of India and the animals he saw there on walks with his *ayah*, or nursemaid. For several years the Durrells divided their time between the British Isles and the European continent, then settled in 1933 on the Greek island of Corfu.

During his years on Corfu, Gerald's interest in natural history grew. Educated at home throughout his childhood by private tutors, he found ample time to go on collecting forays, turning the family home into a small zoo, much to the dismay of his mother, two brothers, and sister. His older brother Lawrence described the house as a "death-trap," filled with creatures "waiting to pounce"; for years afterward he vividly remembered the day he opened his matchbox and discovered a family of scorpions living inside. Despite his dislike of his younger brother's hobby, Lawrence served as a substitute father for Gerald and encouraged him to read widely.

Faced with the impending outbreak of war, the Durrells returned to London in 1939. Fourteen-year-old Gerald managed to bring most of his collection with him, but because their new home was a small apartment, he was not allowed to add any more specimens. The frustrated Gerald found solace by working in a pet shop, and also made frequent visits to the London Zoo. In 1945, much to his delight, he was hired as a student keeper at Whipsnade, a zoo in rural Bedfordshire run by the Zoological Society of London for the breeding and preservation of animals.

At Whipsnade Durrell fed and groomed the animals and cleaned their cages, but he also kept a detailed record of their behavior and compared it with accounts in the many books about wild animals and zoos that he was constantly reading. He began making a list of rare animals threatened with extinction and decided that the zoo he hoped to open someday would "act as a reservoir and sanctuary for these harried creatures."

In 1947 a substantial inheritance allowed Durrell to leave his job at the zoo and go on an animal-collecting expedition. He traveled first to the rain forests of the British Cameroons in Africa, and sent back more than 100 crates of mammals, reptiles, and birds to zoos in England. A year later he made another collecting trip, this time to the Cameroons grasslands, and in 1949-50 went to British Guiana, in South America, to gather rare specimens.

The three expeditions were a source of enormous pleasure to Durrell but nearly all of his inheritance was now spent. His older brother Lawrence, beginning to establish a career as a poet and novelist, suggested that he write a book about his travels in order to raise money for more expeditions. Gerald Durrell heeded his brother's advice and in 1953 published *The Overloaded Ark*, an account of his first trip to the Cameroons. The book was an enormous success and was quickly followed by equally popular accounts of his second Cameroons journey and his trip to British Guiana.

Proceeds from book sales enabled Durrell to go on three more expeditions during the 1950s, this time accompanied by his wife, Jacqueline, whom he had married in 1951. The first was a visit to Argentina and Paraguay in late 1953, where he again collected specimens for English zoos. The second, to the Cameroons in 1957, and the third, again to Argentina in 1958-59, were also collecting trips, but for his own zoo.

Durrell had always found it difficult to part with the animals he had collected and cared for, and he now decided that it was time to make his long-held

Gerald Durrell has been making friends with animals since the age of two, when he collected slugs from a ditch near his home in rural India.

Gerald Durrell

BORN

January 7, 1925
Jamshedpur, India

EDUCATION

Tutored at home

MAJOR INTERESTS

Zoology; nature writing; conservation

ACCOMPLISHMENTS

Author of more than 30 books about animals, including *The Overloaded Ark* (1953), *Birds, Beasts, and Relatives* (1969), and *The Amateur Naturalist* (1982); founder of Jersey Zoological Park and the Jersey Wildlife Preservation Trust; founder and chairman of Wildlife Preservation Trust International

HONORS

Order of the British Empire (1983); fellow, Royal Society of London and the Royal Geographic Society; honorary degrees from Yale and Durham universities

dream a reality. Borrowing from his publisher against earnings on future books, he acquired a 35-acre site, including a medieval manor house, on Jersey, the largest of the Channel Islands. The house became headquarters for the Jersey Zoological Park and during the next few years outbuildings were constructed for the animals.

The objectives of the nonprofit zoo, set forth by the Jersey Wildlife Preservation Trust, include the promotion of wildlife conservation throughout the world, the breeding of various species of animals threatened with extinction, the organization of special expeditions to rescue endangered species, and the collection of research data to protect threatened animals in the wild. The zoo attracts more than 200,000 visitors annually who come to view hundreds of rare mammals, birds, and reptiles bred on the premises.

Durrell continued to publish books about his experiences, including separate accounts of his third expedition to the Cameroons and two trips to Argentina. In addition, he wrote about his childhood, which he describes as "truly happy and sunlit," in three autobiographical volumes: *My Family and Other Animals* (1956), *Birds, Beasts and Relatives* (1969), and *The Garden of the Gods* (1978; published in the United States in 1979 as *Fauna and Family*). *Beasts in My Belfry* (1973; published in the United States as *A Bevy of Beasts*) tells the story of his "education" at Whipsnade.

Continuing the narrative of his life and work, Durrell's *Menagerie Manor* (1964) is an entertaining account of his early efforts to establish the Jersey zoo. *The Stationary Ark* (1976) is a more serious account of the zoo's scientific program and mission. Among the prolific Durrell's other books are fictional works for children—including *The Donkey Rustlers* (1968) and *The Talking Parcel* (1975)—and several novels with animal themes for adults. In 1982 he published *The Amateur Natural-ist: A Practical Guide to the Natural World*, coauthored with his second wife, Lee, an American zoologist. (Durrell's first marriage ended in divorce in 1979.) Lee and Gerald Durrell also collaborated on *Durrell in Russia* (1986), an account of their trip to the then-Soviet Union.

Durrell has traveled extensively in remote areas throughout the world on collecting or rescue missions for the zoo, where he continues to serve as honorary director. In addition to his writing, he has prepared radio and television broadcasts of his activities. Since 1972 Durrell has also directed the Wildlife Preservation Trust International, an organization he founded that year to promote conservation; the WPTI, which has its headquarters in Philadelphia, Pennsylvania, currently has thousands of members in countries throughout the world. Gerald Durrell continues to be as enthusiastic about natural history as he was in childhood, and apparently has no plans to retire. "A naturalist is lucky," he says. "He can indulge his hobby in any place at any time. . . . He can be equally interested and moved by the great herds on the African plains or by the earwigs in his back yard."

FURTHER READING

Durrell, Gerald. *The Amateur Naturalist: A Practical Guide to the Natural World*. New York: Knopf, 1983.

———. *The Ark's Anniversary*. New York: Arcade, 1991.

———. *Birds, Beasts and Relatives*. New York: Viking, 1969.

———. *My Family and Other Animals*. New York: Viking, 1956.

———. *The Overloaded Ark*. New York: Viking, 1953.

———. *A Zoo in My Luggage*. New York: Viking, 1960.

Durrell, Gerald, and Lee Durrell. *Durrell in Russia*. New York: Simon & Schuster, 1986.

Jane Goodall

"AN OLD-FASHIONED NATURALIST"

I n 1957 a 23-year-old former secretary and waitress boarded an ocean liner in England. Her destination was the port of Mombasa, on the eastern coast of Africa. The young woman had saved money for many months to make the trip, after receiving an invitation from a childhood friend who now lived on a farm in Kenya. The visit was supposed to be a vacation, an enjoyable break from a rather ordinary existence for Jane Goodall. She had no way of knowing, as she stood on the deck of the ship and watched the English coast recede, that this trip would dramatically change her life.

Jane Goodall had always liked animals—not just the usual household pets but all living creatures. As a small child, she even took earthworms to bed and hid them under her pillow. Her curiosity about animal behavior was also notable: she still remembers sitting in a chicken house for five hours one day waiting for a hen to lay an egg.

As a small child, Jane Goodall dreamed of going to Africa after reading Edgar Rice Burroughs's *Tarzan* and the Dr. Dolittle books by Hugh Lofting. Today she is the world's leading expert on chimpanzees and their behavior.

Jane Goodall

BORN

April 3, 1934
London, England

EDUCATION

Ph.D., Cambridge University

MAJOR INTEREST

Studying chimpanzees; conservation

ACCOMPLISHMENTS

World's leading authority on chimpanzees; revolutionized understanding of them by observing that their behavior closely mirrored that of humans; author of three books about her work in East Africa: *In the Shadow of Man* (1971), *The Chimpanzees of Gombe* (1986), and *Through a Window* (1990)

HONORS

Honorary member, American Academy of Arts and Sciences; awards from the New York Zoological Society and the National Geographic Society (including the Centennial Award); the J. Paul Getty Wildlife Conservation Prize

The older of two daughters of an engineer and his wife, a novelist, Jane Goodall was born in London but moved with her parents and sister to Bournemouth, on the English coast, in 1939, when she was five years old. She did well in school but always preferred playing outdoors. After graduating from secondary school in 1952, Goodall went to work as a secretary at Oxford University. In the back of her mind was the thought that she might eventually get a secretarial job in Africa: for a long time she had dreamed of one day traveling to the continent to see its numerous animals in the wild.

After several years at Oxford, Goodall moved to London and worked for a while as an assistant editor at a documentary film studio. Then she received a letter from her friend in Kenya, inviting her for a visit. Goodall promptly moved back to Bournemouth and got a job as a waitress in order to save money for the trip.

Goodall had often read about the work of Dr. Louis B. Leakey, a famous paleontologist who, with his wife, Mary, was searching for fossil remains of man's prehistoric ancestors in East Africa. She decided that while she was in Kenya she would make a trip inland, to the capital city of Nairobi, to visit the Coryndon Memorial Museum of Natural History. Leakey was the curator of the museum, and she might be able to meet him.

In fact, Goodall did manage to meet Leakey—and impressed him so much that he offered her a job on the spot as an assistant secretary. "Somehow he must have sensed that my interest in animals was not just a passing phase, but was rooted deep," she recalled some years later. Shortly after their first meeting, Goodall happily joined the Leakeys at their "dig" in Olduvai Gorge, in neighboring Tanganyika (now Tanzania).

For many years Louis Leakey had been trying to prove that man originated in Africa, and not in Asia or Europe, as was then commonly believed. Leakey believed that the study of the great apes, man's closest relatives, would help him understand the behavior of prehistoric man. He was especially interested in a colony of chimpanzees that lived on the shores of Lake Tanganyika, in the area of the Olduvai Gorge. Not long after Goodall had joined the Leakeys at the gorge, Louis Leakey asked her to undertake a long-term study of the chimpanzees, under his sponsorship.

According to Goodall, many of Leakey's colleagues told him he was "insane" to even think of sending an untrained young woman into the wild to do scientific research. But Leakey was insistent, and Goodall readily agreed, knowing that he valued the observations of a fresh mind "uncluttered by theories." She continued working with Leakey while he made preparations for her study, then returned to England for a while to do some intensive reading on chimpanzees and their behavior.

Leakey eventually obtained a grant for Goodall to spend six months at the Gombe Stream Game Reserve (now Gombe National Park) on Lake Tanganyika. Government authorities would not permit a foreign white woman to live alone in the African bush, so Goodall's mother agreed to accompany her. In the summer of 1960, both women arrived at Gombe. "It was a dry, beautiful day," Goodall recalled. "The hills were lush with green." After two African game scouts helped them set up tents, Goodall "slipped away and climbed up into the hills. I met a troop of barking baboons and knew then that my dream had come true."

Back in England Goodall had been told by zoologists that she would never be able to get close to chimpanzees unless she remained hidden. She ignored this warning, deciding that she would make the chimps aware of her presence. As they grew more familiar with her, she reasoned, they would become less wary. Every day she rose before dawn and

walked into the bush, climbing steep slopes in search of chimpanzees; predictably, the chimps fled as she approached. After two months she discovered a clearing some 1,000 feet above the lake, which she called "the Peak," from which she had a clear view of surrounding hills and valleys. This became her observation base, and she came here daily with binoculars and a notebook to record what she saw. Eventually, as she had

predicted, the chimpanzees overcame their fear of her and came closer and closer in the course of their daily activities.

Soon after her first visit to the Peak, Goodall made a revolutionary discovery about chimpanzees: they were very much like human beings in their expressions of affection to one another; they enjoyed prolonged physical contact—grooming, kissing, and

In recent years Goodall has become an ardent spokeswoman for the conservation and humane treatment of chimpanzees, and she travels around the world urging their protection.

> *"Because chimpanzees show intellectual abilities once thought unique to our own species, the line between humans and the rest of the animal kingdom, once thought to be so clear, has become blurred. Chimpanzees bridge the gap between 'us' and 'them.'"*

…from *Through a Window* (1990)

hugging. Further discoveries occurred in her fifth month at Gombe, when she learned that chimpanzees were meat eaters and that they made "tools" from twigs to poke into termite mounds and retrieve specimens of their favorite delicacy.

Goodall's originally planned stay of six months turned into a permanent residence at Gombe. She was able to make more detailed observations of the chimps' social behavior as they allowed her to follow them through the forest, and she began luring them to her camp by leaving bananas outside her tent. After several years she was fully accepted by the chimpanzees, who allowed her to groom them and hold their infants. Goodall sometimes stayed all night in the wild to observe the chimps' sleeping patterns. She saw them make "sleeping platforms" by interweaving branches in the forks of trees. They even made "pillows" of leafy twigs.

Because of her lack of formal training, however, Goodall's findings were at first not treated seriously by the scientific community. Louis Leakey therefore arranged for her to enter a doctoral program in ethology (the study of animal behavior under natural conditions) at Cambridge University in 1962. During the next three years Goodall worked toward a degree while continuing her research on the chimpanzees at Gombe. In 1965 she became the eighth person in the 700-year history of the university to receive a Ph.D. without having first earned an undergraduate degree.

In 1964 Goodall's camp became the Gombe Stream Research Center, an important site for research by ethologists. That same year Goodall married Hugo Van Lawick, a Dutch wildlife photographer who captured on film many scenes of his wife with the chimpanzees. Beginning in the mid-1960s television viewers in the United States and other parts of the world learned about Goodall's work through these films, which were made under the auspices of the National Geographic Society. Some of the films also showed Goodall and Van Lawick's small son, Hugo, nicknamed "Grub," playing with the animals he has known since birth. Goodall and Hugo Van Lawick were divorced in 1974; a year later she married the only white member of the Tanzanian parliament, but her second husband died in 1980.

During her first decade at Gombe, Goodall had come to believe that the chimpanzees were affectionate, gentle, and kind, but in the 1970s she learned to her dismay that they also "had a dark side to their nature." She saw displays of murderous violence and cannibalism by warring chimp communities and concluded that "they could be just as brutal" as humans.

Despite civil war in Tanzania, Goodall continued her work at Gombe, eventually earning the respect of other scientists around the world for observations gained by methods that had once been dismissed as amateurish. In recent years Goodall has become concerned about the decline in the number of chimpanzees as they become subjects for medical research. Many are also taken from the wild each year for zoos and circuses. In 1986 Goodall and several associates founded the Committee for the Conservation and Care of Chimpanzees, and she serves as the organization's chief spokesperson.

Goodall now spends extended periods away from Gombe, trying to alert the public to conservation issues in general and the plight of the chimps in particular. She has lectured extensively in the United States, written articles for American publications, and appeared on national television programs. She has also lobbied the U.S. Congress to give added protection to chimpanzees by reclassifying them as "endangered" rather than "threatened" species.

Goodall is the author of several bestselling books about her work in Africa, and she has received numerous awards from conservation and other wildlife organizations. Despite her undisputed distinction as the world's leading authority on chimpanzees, Goodall remains modest about her accomplishments. At heart, she says, she is "an old-fashioned naturalist."

FURTHER READING

Goodall, Jane. *The Chimpanzees of Gombe.* Cambridge: Harvard University Press, 1986.

———. *In the Shadow of Man.* 1971. Reprint. Boston: Houghton Mifflin, 1983.

———. *Through a Window: My Thirty Years with the Chimpanzees of Gombe.* Boston: Houghton Mifflin, 1990.

"Goodall, Jane." In *1991 Current Biography Yearbook.* New York: H. W. Wilson, 1992.

Montgomery, Sy. *Walking with the Great Apes: Jane Goodall, Dian Fossey, Birute Galdikas.* Boston: Houghton Mifflin, 1991.

Peterson, Dale, and Jane Goodall. *Visions of Caliban.* Boston: Houghton Mifflin, 1993.

Wendell Berry

"FARMING IS AN ART"

Farmer, writer, teacher, and ecology advocate Wendell Berry claims that he was born "with an aptitude for a way of life that was doomed"— farming without benefit of mechanization or modern technology. Growing up in rural Kentucky on land his ancestors had tilled since the 19th century, Berry learned to feel at one with the Earth as he worked a team of mules hitched to a plow.

This attachment to the land has been Berry's source of strength throughout his life, and he extols its value in his poems, novels, short stories, and essays. While celebrating human connectedness to the earth, his writings also deplore the destruction of the ecosystem and have made him a leading voice of the modern environmental movement. The abuse of the land and man's increasing separation from it in modern times—through the rise of farming by large corporations, often referred to as "agribusiness," and the corresponding decline of family farms—have led, Berry believes, to a loss of both personal identity and a sense of community, or "belonging."

Wendell Berry pauses outside his barn during farm chores. Because Berry may be inspired to write at any time, he always carries a pen in the pocket of his work shirt.

Berry has spent most of his life in rural Kentucky, where he teaches, farms, and invites his readers to appreciate "the peace of wild things."

When he was not plowing, or going to school, young Wendell Berry liked to spend time at a place called "the long-legged house," a cabin built by his great-uncle on a secluded bank of the Kentucky River near the Berry farmstead in Port Royal. The cabin became a retreat as he grew into rebellious adolescence, a place where he could find peace and "the dignity of solitude." Here he read Thoreau's *Walden* for the first time and became interested in poetry.

At the age of 18, in 1952, Berry entered the University of Kentucky, graduating four years later. Deciding to pursue a dual career as a writer and college teacher, he remained at the university for another year, earning a master's degree in English in 1957. That same year he married, and in the fall moved with his wife to California, where he studied creative writing for several years at Stanford University with novelist and conservationist Wallace Stegner.

Berry spent a year in Italy as a Guggenheim Fellow, then accepted a teaching position in the English Department at New York University. In 1960 he published his first book, a novel called *Nathan Coulter*, an account of a farm family in a fictional Kentucky village. After a few years in the city, Berry was ready to return home, and in 1964, the same year that he published his first book of poems, *The Broken Ground*, he left NYU to become an instructor at his alma mater, the University of Kentucky. He settled his family on a farm in Port Royal, not far from where he grew up, and rebuilt his great-uncle's "long-legged house" to use as a writing studio.

Berry's first collection of essays, appropriately entitled *The Long-Legged House*, was published in 1969 and includes reminiscences of his rural upbringing. His next nonfiction book was *The Hidden Wound* (1969), a meditative essay on racism and the exploitation of poor black farmhands. *The Unforeseen Wilderness* (1971) is an extended essay on Kentucky's Red River Gorge, heavily illustrated with photographs by his collaborator, Eugene Meatyard. A third nonfiction work, another essay collection called *A Continuous Harmony*, was published in 1972.

Berry became a focus of controversy in 1977, following the publication of *The Unsettling of America*, a nonfiction work that offers an extended criticism of modern agriculture. What Berry calls "the abstract values of an industrial economy preying upon the native productivity of the land and its people" has

> *"When despair for the world grows in me*
> *and I wake in the night at the least sound*
> *in fear of what my life and my children's lives may be,*
> *I go and lie down where the wood drake*
> *rests in his beauty on the water, and the great heron feeds.*
> *I come into the peace of wild things...."*

—from "The Peace of Wild Things," *Openings* (1968)

Wendell Berry

BORN

August 5, 1934
Port Royal, Kentucky

EDUCATION

B.A., M.A., University of Kentucky; studied creative writing at Stanford University

MAJOR INTERESTS

Farming; ecology; writing

ACCOMPLISHMENTS

Author of numerous volumes of nature poetry and fiction with an agrarian setting; has also published collections of essays that urge ecological awareness and respect for the natural life cycle, including *The Long-Legged House* (1969), *A Continuous Harmony* (1972), *The Unsettling of America* (1977), *The Gift of Good Land* (1981), and *Standing on Earth* (1991)

HONORS

Numerous awards include Vachel Lindsay Prize, *Poetry* magazine (1962); Jean Stein Award, American Academy of Arts and Letters (1977); Kentucky Governor's Award (1987); Lannan Foundation Award for Nonfiction (1989); Victory of Spirit Award, University of Louisville (1992)

resulted, he asserts, in personal, cultural, and ecological disaster. This point of view has been reasserted in subsequent essay collections, including *The Gift of Good Land* (1981), *What Are People For* (1990), and *Standing on Earth* (1991).

In a radio interview in 1986, Berry summarized his concern over the plight of the farmer, and its societal implications: "The technological evolution . . . hasn't been an agricultural evolution," he said. "The tune has been called by the agricultural scientists and the agricultural industrialists" who do not realize that "farming is an art . . . that grows out of a culture that belongs specifically to places, locations, kinds of soil, kinds of climate, those possibilities that are defined by natural circumstances, natural gifts." Technicians and economists see agriculture as quantifiable—capable of being measured—and as a result, "we are using numbers instead of practical questions and practical answers . . . deluding ourselves with the idea that practical reality is only economic or only technological." In fact, says Berry, practical problems like soil erosion require solutions that take quality, not quantity, into account.

Berry has published 13 works of nonfiction to date, as well as a collection of short stories and two novels, but he is also widely known as a poet. Since the appearance of *The Broken Ground* in 1964, nine additional volumes of Berry's poetry have appeared, including the anthology *Collected Poems: 1957-1982* in 1985. Most of his verses have rural themes and celebrate the peace and beauty of nature and its regenerative power.

After teaching at the University of Kentucky for 13 years, Berry resigned his professorship in 1977 to devote more time to farming, writing, and his family, which includes two children. However, a decade later he returned to the university faculty. Berry and his wife continue to live at their farm in Port Royal, where they work the land with horses and produce their own food and fuel.

FURTHER READING

Berry, Wendell. *A Continuous Harmony: Essays Cultural and Agricultural.* New York: Harcourt, Brace, 1972.

————. *The Gift of Good Land.* Berkeley, Calif.: North Point Press, 1981.

————. *The Long-Legged House.* New York: Harcourt, Brace, 1969.

————. *Recollected Essays.* Berkeley, Calif.: North Point Press, 1981.

————. *Standing by Words.* Berkeley, Calif.: North Point Press, 1983.

————. *The Unforeseen Wilderness.* Lexington: University Press of Kentucky, 1971.

————. *The Unsettling of America.* San Francisco: Sierra Club Books, 1977.

More Earthkeepers to Remember

American ornithologist **Margaret Morse Nice** (1883-1974) made pioneering studies of song sparrows at her home near Columbus, Ohio, and wrote about her work in *The Watcher at the Nest* (1939), considered a classic of ethology (the study of animal behavior in a natural setting). In the introduction to her autobiography, *Research Is a Passion with Me* (1979), Nobel Prize-winning Austrian ethologist Karl Lorenz (1903-89) called Nice the real founder of ethology, claiming that her work with sparrows was "the first long-term field investigation of the individual life of any free-living wild animal." The prolific Nice published more than 250 articles on birds in scientific journals and wrote more than 3,300 reviews of other ornithologists' books and monographs. In her later years she was an active conservationist, campaigning on behalf of the Indiana dunes, Dinosaur National Monument, and other endangered areas.

Fairfield Osborn (1887-1969), naturalist and conservationist, was the son of Henry Fairfield Osborn, longtime head of the American Museum of Natural History in New York City. Although young Osborn shared his father's enthusiasm for

As cohost of the 1992 television series "Realms of the Russian Bear," Nikolai Drozdov introduced wildlife from his native Russia to American audiences.

science, he was a businessman and banker for several decades until 1935, when he began working full time on behalf of animals. Osborn was the president of the New York Zoological Society for 28 years (1940-68) and made major contributions to the society's Bronx Zoo and New York Aquarium, including the development of natural habitats and the enlargement of educational and research facilities. A leading advocate of conservation, Osborn wrote two books about the Earth's resources— *Our Plundered Planet* (1948) and *The Limits of the Earth* (1953)—and during the 1950s and 1960s lectured and wrote numerous articles on what he viewed as the impending ecological crisis. Osborn established the Conservation Foundation within the Zoological Society and helped to create Wyoming's Jackson Hole Wildlife Park, a preserve where naturalists can conduct research on the plant and animal life of the Rocky Mountains.

French-born American microbiologist and environmentalist **René Dubos** (1901-82) was associated for most of his professional life with Rockefeller University (formerly the Rockefeller Institute for Medical Research) in New York City, where he pioneered research in antibiotics for medical use. During the 1960s he shifted his interest from the laboratory to man's relationship with the environment, and wrote and lectured on the harmful consequences of pollution. His many books include *So Human an Animal* (1968) and *Celebrations of Life* (1981).

American anthropologist and naturalist **Loren Eiseley** (1907-77) was a leading proponent of Darwin's theory of evolution and wrote numerous articles for both popular and scholarly publications on man's place in nature. His books include *The Immense Journey* (1957), *Darwin's Century* (1958), and *The Unexpected Universe* (1969).

American ornithologist, conservationist, and wildlife artist **Roger Tory Peterson** (1908-) has popularized the

study of birds in America and Europe through his illustrated handbooks, beginning with *A Field Guide to the Birds*, first published in 1934. The well-known Peterson Field Guide Series on nature was named after him and includes books by other naturalists as well as Peterson; his own contributions to the series include separate volumes on birds of eastern and western North America and Mexico, as well as a guide to the wildflowers of the eastern United States. In addition to the field guides, Peterson has written and illustrated several general books about nature, including *Wildlife in Color* (1951), *Wild America* (1955), and *The World of Birds* (with James Fisher; 1964). Active in the National Audubon Society and other conservation organizations, Peterson has received numerous awards for his efforts, including the World Wildlife Fund Gold Medal (1972).

Naturalist and wildlife painter **Sir Peter Scott** (1909-89), the only child of explorer Captain Robert Falcon Scott, founded The Wildfowl Trust in England in 1946. An association of seven bird sanctuaries throughout Great Britain, the trust is a nonprofit organization that

Chico Mendes attracted worldwide attention through his campaign to protect the rain forest in his native Brazil. His efforts have focused attention on conservation of tropical woodlands around the world.

John Walsh, an official of the World Society for the Protection of Animals, holds oil-soaked birds near the Gulf of Kuwait, casualties of the 1992 Gulf War. Walsh has directed wildlife rescue operations throughout the world for more than 30 years.

studies ducks, geese, swans, and flamingos from all over the world. It also conducts educational and conservation programs for schoolchildren in the British Isles. Scott, an internationally known conservationist, was the author of *The Eye of the Wind* (1961), an autobiography, and *Observations of Wildlife* (1980).

Joy Adamson (1910-80), an Austrian artist and naturalist, is best known for her book *Born Free* (1960), an account of the African lioness Elsa that she raised with her husband, game warden George Adamson (1906-89). Adamson went to Kenya in 1936 to photograph East African flora; for her work she received the Grenfell Gold Medal from the Royal Horticultural Society of London. Africa became Adamson's home for the rest of her life. She wrote many books and articles about anthropology, ethnography, and botany, and was an early advocate of wildlife

conservation on the continent. Two more books by Adamson continue the story begun in *Born Free: Living Free* (1961), an account of Elsa and her cubs, and *Forever Free* (1962), which describes the cubs' life after the death of Elsa.

Scottish writer, naturalist, and conservationist **Gavin Maxwell** (1914-69) gained international fame with the publication in 1960 of *Ring of Bright Water*, an account of his life with pet otters at Camusfearna, a remote cottage in the West Highlands of Scotland. The popularity of the book led Maxwell to write a children's version of the story called *The Otter's Tale* (1962). Maxwell wrote two more books about his otters in what became known as the Camusfearna Trilogy: *The Rocks Remain* (1962) and *Raven Seek Thy Brother* (1968). Maxwell's other books include a memoir of his childhood and adolescence entitled *The House of Elrig* (1965).

U.S. biologist and environmentalist

Garrett Hardin (1915-) is a longtime advocate of population control as the key to saving the Earth. Overpopulation, says Hardin, degrades the environment and lessens the quality of life for everyone. Hardin has written several books, including *Exploring New Ethics for Survival: The Voyages of the Spaceship Beagle* (1972) and *The Limits of Altruism* (1977). He is the editor of *Population, Evolution, and Birth Control* (1969).

Gaylord Nelson (1916-) first became interested in environmental protection in 1959, after reading forester Aldo Leopold's *Sand County Almanac*. During two terms as governor of Wisconsin (1959-63), Nelson concentrated on preserving the state's wetlands, and he also set aside thousands of acres as wilderness areas. Later, as a U.S. senator (1963-81), Nelson was a crusading environmentalist who sponsored a number of laws to combat pollution and protect natural resources, including the National Pesticide Control Act, the Water Quality Act, the Clean Air Act, the National Lakes Preservation Act, and the Wild Rivers Act. He also developed the National Hiking Trails System, a nationwide system of hiking trails protected by the U.S. government. Nelson is best known as the founder of Earth Day, first celebrated on April 22, 1970, and now a worldwide annual event that demonstrates concern for the environment.

Beginning in the late 1950s, American microbiologist and ecologist **Barry Commoner** (1917-) warned of the dangers of atmospheric contamination from nuclear explosions; for nearly three decades he has also campaigned against pollution of the Earth by detergents, insecticides, and carbon dioxide. Commoner, who has been called "the Paul Revere of ecology," is the author of *Science and Survival* (1966), *The Closing Circle: Nature, Man, and Technology* (1971), and other books and articles on the environmental crisis.

Earth, says U.S. biologist and ecologist **Paul Ehrlich** (1932-), is a spaceship with limited resources and an overburdened life-support system, and mankind is breeding itself "into oblivion." An outspoken critic of overpopulation, Ehrlich has written hundreds of papers and articles as well as the best-selling book *The Population Bomb* (1968).

Dian Fossey (1932-85), an occupational therapist from Kentucky, moved to Africa in 1966 to study mountain gorillas at the invitation of Dr. Louis Leakey, whom she had met three years earlier in Tanzania. Fossey began her investigations in the Congo (now Zaire), then established a new camp, the Karisoke Research Center, in 1968 in the Virunga Mountains of Rwanda. During the next 17 years she became an acknowledged authority on mountain gorillas and championed their preservation. Fossey related her experiences in the autobiographical *Gorillas in the Mist*, published in 1983.

Marine biologist and environmental activist **Sylvia Earle** (1935-) has devoted her life to studying what she calls "the deep frontier"—the oceans of the world. Trained as a botanist, Earle made history in 1970 when she led a five-woman team in an undersea project called Tektite II, sponsored by the U.S. government. Earle and her fellow scientists lived for two weeks beneath the coastal waters of the Virgin Islands, spending as much as 10 hours a day studying plant and animal life near their "home," a specially constructed habitat resting on the seafloor. Nine years later, Earle again made history when she dived 1,250 feet into the Pacific Ocean off the coast of Oahu, in the Hawaiian Islands, to explore the ocean floor and study marine life. This was the deepest solo dive ever made without a cable connecting the diver to a support system at the surface. An active environmentalist, Earle made extensive studies of the 1989 *Exxon Valdez* oil spill in Alaska's Prince William Sound and its effect on wildlife.

Kenyan environmentalist Wangari Maathai has won international recognition as the founder and director of the Green Belt Movement, a women's group that has planted more than 10 million trees in more than a dozen African nations.

Two years later, she was part of an international team that investigated environmental damage caused by the Persian Gulf War. In the early 1990s Earle served briefly as chief scientist of the National Oceanic and Atmospheric Administration (NOAA)—the first woman to hold that post. Several documentary films on Earle's work have been shown on television, including "Gentle Giants of the Pacific," a study of humpback whales. Earle is the coauthor, with Al Giddings, of *Exploring the Deep Frontier* (1980), an account of her career.

Russian naturalist **Nikolai Drozdov** (1937-) is known to millions of television viewers throughout the Commonwealth of Independent States (formerly the Soviet Union) as the host of the bimonthly program "In the World of Animals," which he began in 1969. Drozdov, a professor of biogeography at Moscow State University, has studied wildlife and habitats throughout the world. He has written two dozen books and nearly 200 research papers on topics concerning biology, geography, and conservation. His *Flight of the Boomerang* (1980, revised 1988), an account of a journey across Australia, has sold more than 200,000 copies in Russia. Drozdov has also made several award-winning films about wildlife, including the six-part series "Realms of the Russian Bear," which introduced him to American television audiences in 1992.

Trained in both criminal justice and wildlife biology, Boston-born **John Walsh** (1940-) has spent his entire career in the field of animal protection. Since the early 1960s, he has been associated with the London-based World Society for the Protection of Animals (formerly the International Society for the Protection of Animals) and now directs WSPA's field projects from an office in Boston. In 1964-65 Walsh headed Operation Gwamba, a massive wildlife rescue effort in Surinam. He and his coworkers saved some 10,000 jungle animals whose lives were threatened by the construction of a hydroelectric dam. Walsh later wrote a book about the operation, called *Time Is Short and the Water Rises* (1965), which has been translated into nine languages. Walsh pioneered the worldwide movement to save whales from commercial killing, led the drive to end the Canadian seal hunt, and established the first wildlife rehabilitation center in Costa Rica. Following the Persian Gulf War in 1991, Walsh was invited by the government of Saudi Arabia to help with the rescue and rehabilitation of birds and animals that were affected by the oil spill; he also saved many zoo animals in Kuwait. Walsh's efforts on behalf of animals have taken him to other troubled parts of the world, including war-torn Bosnia and Croatia in late 1992.

Environmentalist **Wangari Maathai** (1940-), the first woman in Kenya to earn a Ph.D. (in anatomy) and the first woman to become a professor at the University of Nairobi, launched the internationally acclaimed Green Belt Movement in 1977. The movement, composed mostly of women, is a grass-roots tree-planting project that counters deforestation and desertification. Volunteers have planted 10 million trees in more than a dozen African nations. Maathai was a featured speaker at the first Earth Summit, held in Rio de Janeiro, Brazil, in June 1992.

Chico Mendes (1944-88), a rubber-tree "tapper" in his native Brazil, led efforts to save the rain forests from destruction by both ranch owners (who cleared them for pasture) and loggers. Initially, Mendes hoped to protect the livelihood of tappers (who harvest latex from rubber trees by "tapping" the liquid from small incisions in the bark), but his crusade grew into a major environmental movement that focused on tropical woodlands around the world. Mendes was murdered in 1988 by Brazilian opponents of his campaign.

Appendix 1

Classifying Plants and Animals

The science of classifying groups of organisms is called *taxonomy*. The taxonomy of organisms is hierarchical—groups are ranked within other groups at different levels. A particular group is called a *taxon* (plural is *taxa*), and its level is called a *category*. Since the mid-19th century, scientists have used seven major categories to classify living things. From the most general to the most specific, they are *kingdom*, *phylum* (for animals; plural is *phyla*) or *division* (for plants), *class*, *order*, *family*, *genus* (plural is *genera*), and *species*.

The *species* is the basic unit of classification. A species is a group of organisms that breed only with others in their group; members of one species do not breed with other groups of organisms. Species are named in Latin with a binomial—two-name—system first devised by the naturalist Carl Linnaeus in the 18th century: the name of the genus is followed by an epithet—a brief descriptive word—that singles out the species within that genus. The species of modern humans is *Homo sapiens* —*Homo* (man) is the genus and *sapiens* (wise) is the epithet.

Genera are groups of similar species. Genera are grouped into families; families are grouped into orders, orders into classes, classes into phyla or divisions, and phyla or divisions into kingdoms. Until the mid-20th century only two kingdoms of organisms—plants and animals—were recognized by scientists. Today living things may be classified as belonging to one of five kingdoms: *Plantae* (plants), *Animalia* (animals), *Monera* (bacteria and blue-green algae), *Protista* (amoebas, paramecia, and single-cell algae), and *Fungi* (molds, yeasts, and mushrooms).

In Aristotle's time (ca. 350 B.C.) fewer than 1,000 species of organisms were known. In the late 20th century scientists estimate that there may be more than 5 million different species alive on the Earth. (Scientists also believe that as many as 16 billion species are extinct.) Today there are more than 1.5 million named species of Animalia (including 250,000 different beetles), some 265,000 species of Plantae, 2,700 Monera, 60,000 Protista, and 100,000 Fungi.

The table below illustrates the biological classification of two species: man and the white oak.

Man		**White oak**	
Category	**Taxon**	**Category**	**Taxon**
Kingdom	*Animalia*	Kingdom	*Plantae*
Phylum	*Chordata*	Division	*Magnoliophyta*
Class	*Mammalia*	Class	*Magnoliopsida*
Order	*Primates*	Order	*Fagales*
Family	*Hominidae*	Family	*Fagaceae*
Genus	*Homo*	Genus	*Quercus*
Species	*Homo sapiens*	Species	*Quercus alba*

Appendix 2

The Ages of the Earth

The exact age of the Earth has long been a subject of speculation. In the Western world, following the rise of Christianity, various scholars tried to arrive at an exact date for Earth's creation, using the Bible as their guide. In the 17th century an Irish clergyman, Archbishop Ussher of Armagh, announced after years of study that Earth had been created within six days in 4004 B.C. This date was printed in the Authorized Version of the Bible and was widely accepted by many scientists as well as the general public for nearly 200 years.

By the mid-19th century the sciences of geology and physics had progressed to such an extent that this figure seemed absurd: fossil evidence and a growing knowledge of how physical changes occur meant that Earth had to be millions of years old. The prominent English physicist Lord Kelvin claimed that the figure was 100 million, while Charles Lyell and other geologists—as well as naturalist Charles Darwin—believed that *hundreds* of millions was closer to the truth.

Following the discovery of radioactivity by Henri Becquerel in 1896, physicists were able to use radioactive elements as geological clocks to date the Earth's age more precisely. Their studies confirmed what Lyell and his followers had argued: the Earth was very, *very* old indeed. By the early 1930s, the age of the Earth was tentatively agreed to be 2 billion years. Since then, more scientific evidence has accumulated to produce a figure that most of the world's geologists and physicists agree upon in the late 20th century: 4.6 billion years. The Earth's solid crust is thought to be at least 3.8 billion years old.

The known history of Earth is divided into four long periods of time called *eras:* the Precambrian, which began 4.6 billion years ago and lasted 4 billion years; the Paleozoic, which began 590 million years ago and lasted 342 million years; the Mesozoic, which began 248 million years ago and lasted 183 million years; and our present era, the Cenozoic, which began 65 million years ago.

Eras are divided into *periods*, and periods into *epochs*. These various divisions are named according to the development of different forms of organisms—indicated by fossil remains—that occurred within them. An outline of Earth's history is shown on a chart that is called a *geological time scale*. Earth's earliest history is at the bottom, and its most recent history is at the top of the scale. This arrangement is similar to the formation of rock strata in the Earth.

Era/Period/Epoch/Length			Beginning (Years Ago)	Forms of Life
Cenozoic Era	Quaternary Period	Holocene Epoch 10,000 years	10,000	Planetary spread of human beings
		Pleistocene Epoch 2 million years (Ice Age)	2 million+	Development of modern human beings
	Tertiary Period	Pliocene Epoch 3 million years	5 million	Large carnivores (meat-eaters); first known appearance of hominids (humanlike primates)
		Miocene Epoch 20 million years	25 million	Whales, apes, grazing mammals
		Oligocene Epoch 13 million years	38 million	Browsing mammals; monkeylike primates; modern flowering plants
		Eocene Epoch 17 million years	55 million	Primitive horses; tiny camels; modern birds
		Paleocene Epoch 10 million years	65 million	First known primates and carnivores
Mesozoic Era		Cretaceous Period 79 million years	144 million	Extinction of dinosaurs at end of period; abundant marsupials, insectivores, flowering plants
		Jurassic Period 69 million years	213 million	Age of dinosaurs; flying reptiles, small mammals, fish, earliest birds, ferns, gymnosperms (especially cycads)
		Triassic Period 35 million years	248 million	First dinosaurs; earliest mammals; gymnosperm and fern forests
Paleozoic Era		Permian Period 38 million years	286 million	New varieties of reptiles; first conifers, cycads, and ginkgos; earliest flowering plants
	Carboniferous Period	Pennsylvanian Period 40 million years	330 million	Age of amphibians; first reptiles; abundant insects and sharks; large swamps; forests of gymnosperms, ferns, and horsetails
		Mississippian Period 30 million years	360 million	
		Devonian Period 48 million years	408 million	Age of fish; first amphibians; lunged fish; numerous mollusks; extinction of primitive vascular plants; first modern vascular plants
		Silurian Period 30 million years	438 million	Rise of fish and reef-building corals; abundant shell-forming sea animals; arthropods invade land; earliest vascular plants; modern algae and fungi
		Ordovician Period 67 million years	505 million	First primitive fish; invertebrates dominant; first fungi; plants invade land
		Cambrian Period 85 million years	590 million	First sea invertebrates with shells; abundant diversification of eukaryotic organisms (Protista)
Precambrian Era		4 billion years	4.6 billion	Origin of life: development of prokaryotic organisms (Monera); eukaryotic organisms (Protista) appear by end of era; earliest known fossils date from this era, including marine invertebrates without shells

Appendix 3

A List of Organizations Promoting Conservation and Nature Study

Membership in these organizations is open to anyone who shares their goals; write or telephone them for further information.

American Forestry Association
1516 P Street, N.W.
Washington, D.C. 20005
Telephone: 202-667-3300

Founded in 1875; 35,000 members; promotes "the intelligent management and use of forests, soil, water, wildlife, and all other natural resources"; publishes *American Forests* bimonthly and *The National Registry of Champion Big Trees and Famous Historical Trees*.

Appalachian Mountain Club
5 Joy Street
Boston, Mass. 02108
Telephone: 617-523-0722

Founded in 1876; 54,000 members; promotes "the protection, enjoyment, and wise use of the mountains, forests, open spaces, and rivers of the Northeast"; pub-lishes *AMC Outdoors*, a monthly magazine.

Applachian Trail Conference
Washington & Jackson Streets
P.O. Box 807
Harpers Ferry, W. Va. 15425
Telephone: 304-535-6331

Founded in 1925; 23,000 members; protects and maintains the Appalachian Trail; publishes *Appalachian Trailway News* five times yearly.

British Trust for Conservation Volunteers
36 St. Mary's Street
Wallingford, Oxon. OX10 OEU, England
Telephone: 491-39766

Founded in 1959; 12,000 members; "seeks to protect, manage, and improve global, national, and local environments through committed voluntary action"; publications include the quarterlies *BTCV in Action*, *Conserver*, *Local Action*, and *LifeClass*, and an annual, *Protecting the Environment*.

Citizens for a Better Environment
407 South Dearborn Street
Chicago, Ill. 60605
Telephone: 312-939-1530

Founded in 1971; 25,000 members; works for the reduction of toxic substances in air, water, and land; publishes *Environmental Review* quarterly as well as research reports and fact sheets.

Conservation International
1015 18th Street, N.W.
Washington, D.C. 20036
Telephone: 202-429-5660

Founded in 1987; 60,000 members; international group promoting environmental protection and conservation; publishes *Orion Nature Quarterly* and *Tropicus*, a quarterly.

Defenders of Wildlife
1244 19th Street, N.W.
Washington, D.C. 20036
Telephone: 202-659-9510

Founded in 1947; 88,000 members; works for the preservation of wildlife and their habitats; publishes *Defenders Magazine* bimonthly and the annual *Endangered Species Report*.

Ducks Unlimited
One Waterfowl Way
Memphis, Tenn. 38120
Telephone: 901-758-3825

Founded in 1937; 640,000 members in the United States, Canada, Mexico, and New Zealand; works for the conservation of migratory waterfowl and the protection of their habitats; publications include *Ducks Unlimited Magazine,* a bimonthly, and a book, *The Ducks Unlimited Story.*

Earth Island Institute
300 Broadway, Suite 28
San Francisco, Calif. 94133
Telephone: 415-788-3666

Founded in 1985; 33,000 members; works for environmental and wildlife protection; publishes *Earth Island Journal* quarterly.

Friends of the Earth
218 Street, S.E.
Washington, D.C. 20003
Telephone: 202-544-2600

Founded in 1969; 14,000 members; works for environmental protection; publishes *Not Man Apart* bimonthly, as well as books and pamphlets.

Friends of the Earth/Amis de la Terre (Canada)
701-251 Laurier Avenue, W.
Ottawa, Ontario, Canada K1P 5J6
Telephone: 613-230-3352

Founded in 1978; 25,000 members; works for responsible use of the environment; sponsors Ozone Protection Campaign and Campaign for Alternatives to Pesticides; offers the Rainforest Education Kit; publications include the quarterlies *Atmosphere* and *Earth-Words* and numerous books, pamphlets, and fact sheets.

Friends of the Earth…England
26-28 Underwood Street
London N1 7JQ, England
Telephone: 71-4901555

Founded in 1971; 180,000 members; works for the responsible use of environmental resources; publishes *Earth Matters,* a quarterly.

Friends of the Everglades
202 Park Street
Miami Springs, Fla. 33166
Telephone: 305-888-1230

Founded in 1969; 5,000 members; works for the protection of the Florida Everglades; publishes *Everglades Reporter* annually as well as reports, newsletters, and books.

Greenpeace
1436 U Street, N.W./P.O. Box 96128
Washington, D.C. 20090
Telephone: 202-462-1177

Founded in 1979; 1.5 million supporters; affiliated with Greenpeace International; works for the protection of the environment and wildlife through nonviolent protest; publishes *Greenpeace* bimonthly.

International Wildlife Coalition
634 N. Falmouth Highway/P.O. Box 388
North Falmouth, Mass. 02556
Telephone: 508-564-9980

Founded in 1982; 130,000 supporters; works for the preservation of wildlife and their habitats; publishes periodic information packets and a quarterly, *Whalewatch.*

Izaak Walton League of America
1401 Wilson Boulevard, Level B
Arlington, Va. 22209
Telephone: 703-528-1818

Founded in 1922; 50,000 members; works for the conservation and "wholesome utilization" of natural resources; publishes *Outdoor America* and *Outdoor Ethics Newsletter,* both quarterly; *League Leader* bimonthly; and reports and brochures.

Jersey Wildlife Preservation Trust
Les Augres Manor
Trinity
Jersey, Channel Islands JE3 5BF, England
Telephone: 534-864666

Founded in 1963; 12,500 members in 75 countries; breeds endangered species and promotes conservation in the wild; publications include the thrice-yearly *Dodo Dispatch* and *On the Edge* and the annual *Dodo Journal.*

National Audubon Society
950 Third Avenue
New York, N.Y. 10022
Telephone: 212-832-3200

Founded in 1905; 600,000 members; welcomes all persons "interested in ecology, energy, and the conservation and restoration of natural resources"; publishes *American Birds* and *Audubon,* both bimonthly, and *Audubon Adventures,* a bimonthly children's newspaper.

National Wildlife Federation
1400 16th Street, N.W.
Washington, D.C. 20036
Telephone: 202-797-6800

Founded in 1936; 6.2 million members; works for "the intelligent management of the life-sustaining resources of the Earth"; publications include *International Wildlife* and *National Wildlife*, both bimonthly, and monthly.

The Nature Conservancy
1815 North Lynn Street
Arlington, Va. 22209
Telephone: 703-841-5300

Founded in 1917; 550,000 members; "dedicated to the preservation of biological diversity through land protection of natural areas"; cares for 1,600 nature preserves throughout the country; publishes *The Nature Conservancy Magazine* bimonthly.

Rainforest Information Centre
c/o Ian Peter
P.O. Box 368
Lismore, New South Wales, Australia
Telephone: 66-218505

Founded in 1980; 20,000 members in 12 countries; works for the protection of tropical forests; publishes *World Rainforest Report* (in English, German, and Hindi) three times a year.

Ranger Rick's Nature Club
8925 Leesburg Pike
Vienna, Va. 22184
Telephone: 703-790-4000

Founded in 1967; 900,000 members; children's division of the National Wildlife Federation (see above); members receive *Ranger Rick's Nature Magazine*, a monthly for children.

Royal Society for the Protection of Birds
The Lodge
Sandy, Beds. SG19 2DL, England
Telephone: 767-680551

Founded in 1889; 442,000 members; encourages the protection and conservation of wild birds; produces and distributes films; publishes *Bird Life* bimonthly, *Birds* quarterly, and the annual *RSPB Conservation Review*.

Save-the-Redwoods Leagzue
114 Sansome Street
San Francisco, Calif. 94104
Telephone: 415-362-2352

Founded in 1918; 45,000 members; works for the preservation of redwoods, sequoias, and other trees, principally in California; publishes brochures and bulletins on tree conservation.

Sierra Club
730 Polk Street
San Francisco, Calif. 94109
Telephone: 415-776-2211

Founded in 1892; 565,000 members; promotes protection and conservation of natural resources in the United States and throughout the world; publishes *Sierra* bimonthly, as well as books on environmental issues.

World Wildlife Fund
1250 24th Street, N.W.
Washington, D.C. 20037
Telephone: 202-293-4800

Founded in 1961; 800,000 members; works for the preservation of endangered and threatened species throughout the world; publishes *Focus* bimonthly.

The Wilderness Society
900 17th Street, N.W.
Washington, D.C. 20006
Telephone: 202-833-2300

Founded in 1935; 390,000 members; works for "the establishment of the land ethic as a basic element of American culture and philosophy" by promoting wilderness preservation and protection; publishes *Wilderness* quarterly.

Wildlife Conservation International
c/o New York Zoological Society
Bronx, N.Y. 10460
Telephone: 212-220-5155

Founded in 1897; 40,000 members; supports international conservation projects that focus on habitat protection; publishes *Wildlife Conservation* bimonthly.

World Wide Fund for Nature
World Conservation Centre
Avenue du Mont-Blanc
CH-1196 Gland, Switzerland
Telephone: 22-3649111

Founded in 1961; 1.5 million members in 23 countries; "promotes conservation of the natural environment and ecological processes essential to life on Earth"; publications include the biennial *WWF Conservation Yearbook*; *The New Road* and *WWF Special Reports*, both quarterlies; and *WWF News* and *WWF Reports*, both bimonthlies.

Glossary

acid rain—precipitation (rain, snow, or sleet) harmful to the environment that contains high concentrations of acid-forming chemicals; the chemicals are released into the air from burning coal, chemical manufacturing, and other industrial processes.

artificial system of classification—any system of plant or animal classification that takes into account only partial characteristics of an organism. See also **Linnean system of classification** and **natural system of classification.**

biodegradable—capable of decaying through the action ocnisms.

biology—the science of life or living organisms and their origin, growth, reproduction, structure, and behavior.

biosphere—the part of the Earth's crust, waters, and atmosphere that supports life.

biotic—of or relating to life.

botanical garden—a garden for the culture, study, and exhibition of special plants, usually in association with a greenhouse and sometimes an herbarium.

botany—the branch of biology that deals with plant life.

chlorofluorocarbons (CFCs)—any of several compounds of carbon, fluoride, chlorine, and hydrogen used as refrigerants, foam-blowing agents, and solvents that deplete the ozone layer and allow harmful ultraviolet rays to enter Earth's atmosphere; chlorofluorocarbons were once commonly used as spray-can propellants. See also **ozone layer depletion.**

climatology—the science that deals with climates and their phenomena.

closet naturalist—a naturalist who works primarily indoors classifying specimens rather than going outdoors to collect them.

conservation—using resources carefully, without wasting them.

contour plowing—a method of plowing along the natural lines of the land in order to retain water and prevent soil erosion.

cosmos—the world or universe regarded as an orderly, harmonious system.

crop rotation—the system of varying successive crops on the same plot of land to avoid depleting the soil and to control weeds, diseases, and pests.

curator—a museum employee in charge of a collection.

deforestation—the process of clearing (cutting down) forests.

ecology—the branch of biology dealing with the relations and interactions of organisms with their environment.

ecosystem—a system formed by the interaction of a community of organisms with its environment.

endangered species—a species at risk of extinction (in the United States, it is an official U.S. government designation). See also **threatened species**.

entomology—a branch of zoology concerned with the study of insects.

environmentalism—a movement that calls for the protection of nature from pollution.

environmentalist—a person who supports environmentalism.

ethnography—the scientific study of individual cultures.

ethology—the study of animal behavior in natural environments.

evolution, Darwinian—the theory that species originate through the natural selection of those individuals best suited to reproduce their own kind; also called Darwinism. See also **natural selection.**

fauna—the animals of a given region or era considered as a whole.

flora—the plants of a given region or era considered as a whole.

fossil—a remnant, impression, or trace of an animal or plant from a past geologic age that has been preserved in a mineralized or petrified form in the Earth's crust.

game—wild animals hunted for sport or food.

genetics—a branch of biology that deals with the heredity and variation of organisms.

geography—a science that deals with the land, sea, air, and distribution of plant and animal life on Earth.

geology—a science that deals with the history of the Earth and its life, especially as recorded in rocks.

geophysics—the branch of geology that deals with the physics of the Earth and its atmosphere.

glacier—a large body of ice moving slowly down a slope or valley or spreading outward on a land surface.

global warming—the steady rise in global mean temperature during the past 100 years caused by the greenhouse effect; global warming will eventually lead to droughts, heat waves, and shifting climate zones that endanger crops and wildlife, and it may also cause coastal flooding as warming seas expand and rise. See also **greenhouse effect.**

greenhouse effect—the tendency of carbon dioxide and other gases in the atmosphere to trap heat and warm the Earth, similar to the way in which the glass panes of a greenhouse capture the sun's warmth; combustion from power plants, automobiles, and factories has accelerated the greenhouse effect: during the past 100 years the concentration of carbon dioxide alone in the atmosphere has increased by 22 percent.

habitat—the place where an animal or plant naturally lives and grows.

herbarium—a collection of dried plant specimens that are mounted and arranged for reference.

herbicide—an agent used to inhibit or destroy plant growth.

heredity—the transmission of characteristics from parents to offspring through genes.

herpetology—a branch of zoology dealing with reptiles and amphibians.

horticulture—the science and art of growing fruits, vegetables, flowers, and ornamental plants.

Ice Age—in geological time, the Pleistocene epoch, which began 2 million years ago and ended 10,000 years ago and was characterized by glacial ice over much of the Earth.

ichthyology—a branch of zoology that deals with fish.

isotherm—a line on a weather map or chart connecting points having equal temperature; also called isothermal line.

Linnean system of classification—an artificial system of classifying organisms according to the structure of their reproductive parts; also called sexual system of classification. See also **artificial system of classification** and **natural system of classification.**

meteorology—the science of weather and weather forecasting.

natural history—the study of nature and its plants, animals, and other phenomena.

naturalist—a person who studies nature.

natural selection—the process by which forms of life with traits that enable them to adapt to their environment survive and reproduce in greater numbers than others of their kind, leading to the perpetuation of those traits in succeeding generations.

natural system of classification—a system of classifying plants or animals that takes into account all characteristics of the organism. See also **artificial system of classification.**

organic farming—growing crops with fertilizers and pesticides of animal or vegetable origin rather than using manufactured chemicals.

ornithology—the branch of zoology that deals with birds.

overpopulation—an excessive number of people, which strains available resources and facilities.

ozone—a form of oxygen found in the atmosphere in minute quantities; in the upper atmosphere, ozone absorbs ultraviolet rays from the sun, preventing them from reaching the surface of the Earth. See also **ozone layer** and **ozone layer depletion.**

ozone layer—the layer of the upper atmosphere, about 8 to 30 miles above the Earth, where most ozone is concentrated.

ozone layer depletion—the formation of holes in the ozone layer by man-made chlorofluorocarbons (CFCs), which allows ultraviolet rays from the sun to penetrate Earth's atmosphere (ultraviolet rays can cause severe sunburn, skin cancer, and eye problems). See also **chlorofluorocarbons.**

paleontology—the scientific study of past geological periods through their fossil remains.

pesticide—an agent used to destroy pests; usually refers to chemical substances.

pollution—contamination of the environment, especially with man-made wastes.

predator—an animal that exists by preying upon other animals.

primatologist—a zoologist who studies primates, including monkeys, apes, and gorillas.

rain forest—a tropical forest having a high annual rainfall (100 inches or more) and composed of tall, broad-leaved evergreen trees that form a continuous canopy.

silviculture—the development and care of forest trees.

species—a group of organisms that breed only with each other; in taxonomy, the basic unit of classification. See **taxonomy**

taxidermy—the art of stuffing and mounting the skins of animals.

taxonomy—the orderly classification of plants and animals according to their natural relationship.

threatened species—a species whose existence is likely, in the near future, to become endangered. See also **endangered species**.

toxic wastes—poisonous substances created as a by-product of industrial processes.

watershed—the region drained by a river, stream, or other body of water.

wetlands—land that has a wet, spongy soil, such as a marsh, swamp, or bog.

zoology—the branch of biology that deals with animal life.

Further Reading

Each of the major entries in *Earthkeepers* includes a list of readings; refer to the index for page references.

The following reading list is intended as a supplement and is divided into three sections: More about Earthkeepers, Natural History, and Conservation and Ecology.

Although the following books vary in level of difficulty, none of them are technical; nearly all are written for a general audience. Books preceded by an asterisk (*) are especially appropriate for younger readers.

More About Earthkeepers

Aberbach, Alan D. *In Search of an American Identity: Samuel Latham Mitchill, Jeffersonian Naturalist.* New York: Lang, 1988.

Adams, Alexander B. *Eternal Quest: The Story of the Great Naturalists.* New York: G. P. Putnam, 1969.

Barber, Lynn. *The Heyday of Natural History: 1820–1870.* Garden City, N.Y.: Doubleday, 1980.

Bogue, Margaret Beattie. "Liberty Hyde Bailey, Jr., and the Bailey Farm." *Agricultural History,* Winter 1989, 26–48.

Bonta, Marcia Myers. *Women in the Field: America's Pioneering Women Naturalists.* College Station: Texas A&M University Press, 1991.

Boorstin, Daniel. *The Lost World of Thomas Jefferson.* Boston: Beacon Press, 1960.

Brooks, Paul. *Speaking for Nature: How Literary Naturalists from Henry Thoreau to Rachel Carson Have Shaped America.* Boston: Houghton Mifflin, 1980.

Carter, Harold B. *Sir Joseph Banks.* London: The British Museum, 1988.

Cohen, Bernard, ed. *Thomas Jefferson and the Sciences: An Original Anthology.* Salem, N.H.: Ayer, 1980.

Covel, Paul F. *Beacons Along a Naturalist's Trail: California Naturalists and Innovators.* Oakland, Calif.: Western Interpretive Press, 1988.

Cutright, Paul R., and Michael Brodhead. *Elliott Coues: Naturalist and Frontier Historian.* Urbana: University of Illinois Press, 1981.

Cutright, Paul R. *The Great Naturalists Explore South America.* 1940. Reprint. Salem, N.H.: Ayer, 1968.

————. *Lewis and Clark: Pioneering Naturalists.* Urbana: University of Illinois Press, 1969.

Eiseley, Loren. *Darwin's Century.* Garden City, N.Y.: Doubleday/Anchor Books, 1961.

Fein, Albert. *Frederick Law Olmsted and the American Environmental Tradition.* New York: Braziller, 1972.

*Fenton, Carroll Lane, and Mildred Adams Fenton. *Giants of Geology.* Garden City, N.Y.: Doubleday, 1952.

Fossey, Dian. *Gorillas in the Mist.* Boston: Houghton Mifflin, 1983.

Huxley, Thomas Henry. *Autobiography and Selected Essays.* Boston: Houghton Mifflin, 1909.

Iltis, Hugo. *Life of Mendel.* New York: Hafner, 1966.

Irvine, William. *Apes, Angels, and Victorians.* New York: McGraw-Hill, 1955.

Kastner, Joseph. *A Species of Eternity.* New York: Knopf, 1977.

LaBastille, Anne. *Women and Wilderness.* San Francisco: Sierra Club Books, 1980.

Lloyd, Clare. *The Traveling Naturalists.* Seattle: University of Washington Press, 1985.

Martin, Edwin T. *Thomas Jefferson, Scientist.* New York: Schuman, 1952.

Mowat, Farley. *Woman in the Mists: The Story of Dian Fossey and the Mountain Gorillas of Africa.* New York: Warner, 1987.

Newhall, Nancy. *A Contribution to the Heritage of Every American: The Conservation Activities of John D. Rockefeller, Jr.* New York: Knopf, 1957.

Nice, Margaret Morse. *Research Is a Passion with Me.* Introduction by Konrad Lorenz. Toronto: Consolidated Amethyst Communications, 1979.

Peattie, Donald Culross. *Green Laurels: The Lives and Achievements of the Great Naturalists.* New York: Simon & Schuster, 1936.

———. *The Road of a Naturalist.* 1941. Reprint. Boston: G. K. Hall, 1986.

Richardson, Edgar P., Brook Hindle, and Lillian B. Miller. *Charles Willson Peale and His World.* New York: Abrams, 1983.

Roosevelt, Franklin D. *Franklin D. Roosevelt and Conservation: 1911–1945.* 2 vols. 1957. Reprint. Salem, N.H.: Ayer, 1972.

St. John de Crèvecoeur, J. Hector. *Letters from an American Farmer.* 1782. Reprint. New York: Penguin, 1981.

Schwartz, William, ed. *Voices for the Wilderness.* New York: Ballantine Books, 1969.

Scott, Peter. *The Eye of the Wind.* Boston: Houghton Mifflin, 1961.

Sellers, Charles Coleman. *Charles Willson Peale.* 1947. Reprint. New York: Scribners, 1969.

———. *Mr. Peale's Museum.* New York: Norton, 1980.

Smith, Edward. *The Life of Sir Joseph Banks.* 1911. Reprint. New York: Arno, 1975.

Stineman, Esther Lanigan. *Mary Austin: Song of a Maverick.* New Haven: Yale University Press, 1989.

Teale, Edwin Way. *Dune Boy: The Early Years of a Naturalist.* 1943. Reprint. New York: Dodd, Mead, 1957.

Tomalin, Ruth. *W. H. Hudson: A Biography.* London: Faber & Faber, 1982.

Tracy, Henry Chester. *American Naturalists.* New York: Dutton, 1930.

Tree, Isabella. *The Ruling Passion of John Gould: A Biography of the Bird Man.* New York: Grove Weidenfeld, 1992.

*Vandivert, Rita. *To the Rescue: Seven Heroes of Conservation.* New York: Frederick Warne, 1982.

Von Hagen, Victor Wolfgang. *South America Called Them: Explorations of the Great Naturalists.* New York: Knopf, 1945.

Watkins, T. H. "A Department of Conservation." Part 7 in *Righteous Pilgrim: The Life and Times of Harold Ickes.* New York: Holt, 1990. [Ickes was Secretary of the Interior during the Presidency of Franklin D. Roosevelt,1933–45.]

Wild, Peter. *Pioneer Conservationists of Western America.* Missoula, Mont.: Mountain Press, 1979.

———. *Pioneer Conservationists of Eastern America.* Missoula, Mont.: Mountain Press, 1986.

Wilkins, Thurman. *Clarence King: A Biography.* New York: Macmillan, 1958.

Natural History

Ackerman, Diane. *The Moon by Whale Light and Other Adventures Among Bats, Penguins, Crocodilians, and Whales.* New York: Random House, 1991.

Adamson, Joy. *Born Free.* 1960. Reprint. New York: Pantheon,1987.

———. *Forever Free.* New York: Harcourt, Brace, 1962.

———. *Living Free.* New York: Harcourt, Brace, 1961.

Andrews, Roy Chapman. *Across Mongolian Plains: A Naturalist's Account of China's "Great Northwest."* New York: Appleton, 1921.

Atlas of Plant Life. New York: Crowell, 1973.

Austin, Mary Hunter. *Earth Horizon.* Boston: Houghton Mifflin, 1903.

———. *The Land of Little Rain.* 1903. Reprint. Albuquerque: University of New Mexico Press, 1974.

*Bailey, L. H. *How Plants Get Their Names.* New York: Dover, 1963.

Baker, R. Robin. *The Evolutionary Ecology of Animal Migration.* New York: Holmes & Meier, 1978.

Bates, Henry Walter. *The Naturalist on the River Amazonas.* 1863. Reprint. New York: Dover, 1975.

Beebe, William. *The Book of Naturalists: An Anthology of the Best Natural History.* 1944. Reprint. Princeton, N.J.: Princeton University Press, 1988.

Beston, Henry. *Especially Maine: The Natural World of Henry Beston, from Cape Cod to the St. Lawrence.* Edited by Elizabeth Coatsworth. Brattleboro, Vt.: Stephen Greene, 1970.

———. *The Outermost House: A Year of Life on the Great Beach of Cape Cod.* 1928. Reprint. New York: Holt, 1992.

*Burton, Maurice, and Robert Burton, eds. *International Wildlife Encyclopedia.* 25 vols. London: Marshall Cavendish, 1990.

Campbell, David G. *The Crystal Desert: Summers in Antarctica.* Boston: Houghton Mifflin, 1992.

Carlquist, Sherwin. *Island Life: A Natural History of the Islands of the World.* Garden City, N.Y.: Natural History Press, 1965.

Carr, Archie. *So Excellent a Fishe: A Natural History of Sea Turtles.* 1967. Reprint. New York: Scribners, 1984.

———. *The Windward Road: Adventures of a Naturalist on Remote Caribbean Shores.* 1957. Reprint. Gainesville: University Press of Florida, 1979.

Cassin, John. *Illustrations of the Birds of California, Texas, Oregon, British and Russian America.* 1856. Reprint. Dallas: Summerlee Foundation/Texas State Historical Association, 1992.

Cheesman, Evelyn. *Insect Behaviour.* 1933. Reprint. London: Royal Entomological Society, 1966.

*——— *Insects: Their Secret World.* New York: Sloane, 1953.

Cooper, Susan. *Rural Hours.* 1854. Reprint. Syracuse, N.Y.: Syracuse University Press, 1968.

Cousteau, Jacques, and Yves Paccalet. *Whales.* New York: Abrams, 1988.

Curtis, Helena, and N. Sue Barnes. "Evolution." Section 7 in *Biology.* 5th ed. New York: Worth, 1989.

Daniel, J. C., ed. *A Century of Natural History.* New York: Oxford University Press, 1988.

*Dennis, Jerry. *It's Raining Frogs and Fishes: Four Seasons of Natural Phenomena and Oddities of the Sky.* New York: HarperCollins, 1992.

*Duan, Margery G., and Barbara A. Payne, eds. *Forgotten Edens: Exploring the World's Wild Places.* Washington, D.C.: National Geographic Society, 1992.

Eiseley, Loren. *The Immense Journey.* New York: Random House, 1957.

———. *The Unexpected Universe.* New York: Harcourt, Brace, 1969.

Eldredge, Niles, ed. *The "Natural History" Reader in Evolution.* New York: Columbia University Press, 1987.

Endangered Wildlife of the World. London: Marshall Cavendish, 1992.

Evans, Howard Ensign, and Mary A. Evans. *Australia: A Natural History.* Washington, D.C.: Smithsonian Institution Press, 1983.

*Fenton, Carroll Lane, and Mildred Adams Fenton. *The Fossil Book.* Rev. ed. New York: Doubleday, 1992.

Finch, Robert, and John Elder, eds. *The Norton Book of Nature Writing.* New York: W. W. Norton, 1990.

Frisch, Karl von. *Animal Architecture.* Translated by Lisbeth Gombrich. 1974. Reprint. New York: Van Nostrand Reinhold, 1983.

Galston, Arthur W., Peter J. Davies, and Ruth L. Satter. *The Life of the Green Plant.* 3rd ed. Englewood Cliffs, N.J.: Prentice Hall, 1980.

Gould, Stephen Jay. *Bully for Brontosaurus: Reflections in Natural History.* New York: W. W. Norton, 1992.

———. *Ever Since Darwin: Reflections in Natural History.* New York: W. W. Norton, 1977.

———. *The Flamingo's Smile: Reflections in Natural History.* New York: W. W. Norton, 1985.

———. *Hen's Teeth and Horse's Toes: Further Reflections in Natural History.* New York: W. W. Norton, 1983.

———. *The Panda's Thumb: More Reflections in Natural History.* New York: W. W. Norton, 1980.

Griffin, Donald. *Listening in the Dark: The Acoustic Orientation of Bats and Men.* 1958. Reprint. Ithaca, N.Y.: Cornell University Press, 1986.

*Grzimek, Bernhard. *Grzimek's Animal Life Encyclopedia.* 13 vols. New York: Van Nostrand Reinhold, 1972–75.

Halle, Louis J. *The Sea and the Ice: A Naturalist in Antarctica.* Ithaca, N.Y.: Cornell University Press, 1989.

Hawkes, Jacquetta. *A Land.* New York: Random House, 1952.

Hawkins, R. E., ed. *Encyclopedia of Indian Natural History.* New York: Oxford University Press, 1987.

Heywood, Vernon H., ed. *Flowering Plants of the World.* Englewood Cliffs, N.J.: Prentice Hall, 1985.

Hudson, W. H. *The Book of a Naturalist.* 1923. Reprint. New York: AMS Press, n.d.

Huxley, Julian. *Evolution in Action.* New York: Harper, 1953.

Illustrated Encyclopedia of Wildlife. 15 vols. Lakeville, Conn.: Grey Castle, 1991.

King, Carolyn M., ed. *The Handbook of New Zealand Mammals.* New York: Oxford University Press, 1990.

Krutch, Joseph Wood. *The Desert Year.* 1952. Reprint. Tucson: University of Arizona Press, 1985.

———. *The Forgotten Peninsula: A Naturalist in Baja California.* 1961. Reprint. Tucson: University of Arizona Press, 1986.

Lack, David L. *Darwin's Finches.* 1947. Reprint. Cambridge: Cambridge University Press, 1983.

———. *The Life of the Robin.* 4th ed. London: Witherby, 1965.

Lewin, Roger. *Bones of Contention.* New York: Simon & Schuster, 1988.

———. *Thread of Life: The Smithsonian Looks at Evolution.* New York: W. W. Norton, 1982.

Lopez, Barry. *Arctic Dreams.* New York: Scribners, 1986.

———. *Of Wolves and Men.* New York: Scribners, 1978.

Lorenz, Konrad. *King Solomon's Ring.* 1952. Reprint. New York: Harper & Row, 1979.

Lyon, Thomas J., ed. *This Incomparable Land: A Book of American Nature Writing.* Boston: Houghton Mifflin, 1989.

Matthiessen, Peter. *African Silences.* New York: Random House, 1991.

*Maxwell, Gavin. *The Otter's Tale.* New York: Dutton, 1962.

———. *Raven Seek Thy Brother.* New York: Dutton, 1969.

———. *Ring of Bright Water.* 1960. Reprint. New York: Penguin, 1987.

———. *The Rocks Remain.* New York: Dutton, 1962.

Mech, L. David. *The Wolf: Ecology and Behavior of an Endangered Species.* Minneapolis: University of Minnesota Press, 1983.

Mertens, Robert. *The World of Amphibians and Reptiles.* Translated by H. W. Parker. New York: McGraw-Hill, 1960.

Morrison, Reg, and Maggie Morrison. *Australia: The Four-Billion Year Journey of a Continent.* New York: Facts on File, 1990.

Moss, Cynthia. *Portraits in the Wild: Animal Behavior in East Africa.* 2nd ed. Chicago: University of Chicago Press, 1982.

Mountfort, Guy. *Wild India: The Wildlife and Scenery of India and Nepal.* Cambridge: MIT Press, 1991.

Osborn, Henry Fairfield. *Naturalist in the Bahamas: October 12, 1861–June 25, 1891.* 1910. Reprint. New York: AMS Press, n.d.

Owen, Denis. *Camouflage and Mimicry.* Chicago: University of Chicago Press, 1982.

The Oxford Dictionary of Natural History. New York: Oxford University Press, 1985.

Peattie, Donald Culross. *A Natural History of Western Trees.* 1953. Reprint. Boston: Houghton Mifflin, 1991.

Peck, Robert M. *Land of the Eagle: A Natural History of North America.* New York: Summit, 1991.

Perrins, Chris, and Alex L. A. Middleton. *The Encyclopedia of Birds.* New York: Facts on File, 1986.

Perry, Donald. *Life Above the Jungle Floor.* New York: Simon & Schuster, 1986.

Peterson, Roger Tory. *A Field Guide to the Birds East of the Rockies.* 4th ed. Boston: Houghton Mifflin, 1980.

———. *A Field Guide to Western Birds.* 3rd ed. Boston: Houghton Mifflin, 1990.

———. *A Field Guide to Wildflowers of Northeastern and North-Central North America.* Boston: Houghton Mifflin, 1968.

*———. *First Guide to Wildflowers.* Boston: Houghton Mifflin, 1986.

Pliny the Elder. *Natural History.* Translated by John F. Healy. New York: Penguin, 1991.

Punch, Walter T. *Keeping Eden: A History of Gardening in America.* Boston: Little, Brown, 1992.

Romer, Alfred. *The Vertebrate Story.* 4th ed. Chicago: University of Chicago Press, 1971.

Schaller, George B. *The Deer and the Tiger: A Study of Wildlife in India.* Chicago: University of Chicago Press, 1967.

———. *The Giant Pandas of Wolong.* Chicago: University of Chicago Press, 1985.

———. *Golden Shadows, Flying Hooves.* 1973. Reprint. Chicago: University of Chicago Press, 1983.

———. *The Last Panda.* Chicago: University of Chicago Press, 1993.

———. *The Serengeti Lion: A Study of Predator-Prey Relations.* Chicago: University of Chicago Press, 1976.

Schmidt-Nielsen, Knut. *Desert Animals.* New York: Oxford University Press, 1964.

Scott, James A. *The Butterflies of North America*. Palo Alto, Calif.: Stanford University Press, 1992.

Scott, Peter. *Observations of Wildlife*. Oxford, England: Phaidon Press, 1980.

Simpson, George Gaylord. *Fossils and the History of Life*. New York: W. H. Freeman/Scientific American Library, 1983.

———. *Horses*. New York: Oxford University Press, 1951.

———. *Splendid Isolation: The Curious History of South American Mammals*. New Haven: Yale University Press, 1983.

Sparks, John. *Realms of the Russian Bear: A Natural History of Russia and the Central Asian Republics*. Boston: Little, Brown, 1992.

Stanley, Steven M. *Extinction*. New York: W. H. Freeman/Scientific American Library, 1986.

Teale, Edwin Way. *Autumn Across America*. 1956. Reprint. New York: St. Martin's, 1990.

———. *Exploring the Insect World*. 1944. Reprint. New York: Grosset & Dunlap, 1953.

———. *North with the Spring*. New York: Dodd, Mead, 1951.

*Thackray, John. *The Age of the Earth*. London: Institute of Geological Sciences, 1980.

Waterton, Charles. *Wanderings in South America*. 1825. Reprint. New York: Century/Hippocrene Books, 1984.

Wauer, Roland H. *Naturalist's Mexico*. College Station: Texas A&M University Press, 1992.

The Way Nature Works. New York: Macmillan, 1992.

White, Gilbert. *The Natural History of Selbourne*. 1788. Reprint. New York: Penguin, 1977.

Whole Earth Quiz Book: How Well Do You Know the Planet? New York: Lothrop, 1991.

Wickler, Wolfgang. *Mimicry in Plants and Animals*. London: World University Library, 1968.

Wild Animals of North America. Rev. ed. Washington, D.C.: National Geographic Society, 1988.

*Williamson, Henry. *Salar the Salmon*. 1935. Reprint. Boston: David Godine, 1990. [Fiction]

*———. *Tarka the Otter*. 1927. Reprint.: Beacon Press, 1990. [Fiction]

Wilson, Edward O. *The Insect Societies*. Cambridge: Harvard University Press, 1971.

World Wildlife Habitats. 3 vols. London: Marshall Cavendish, 1992.

Yates, Steve. *The Nature of Borneo: A Natural History*. New York: Facts on File, 1992.

Zhao Ji, ed. *The Natural History of China*. New York: McGraw-Hill, 1990.

Zimmermann, Martin H., and Claude L. Brown. *Trees: Structure and Function*. New York: Springer-Verlag, 1975.

Conservation and Ecology

*Atwood, Margaret. *For the Birds*. Buffalo, N.Y.: Firefly Books, 1991.

Commoner, Barry. *The Closing Circle: Nature, Man, and Technology*. New York: Knopf, 1971.

———. *Science and Survival*. New York: Viking, 1966.

Curtis, Helena, and N. Sue Barnes. "Ecology." Section 8 in *Biology*. 5th ed. New York: Worth, 1989.

Davis, Richard C., ed. *Encyclopedia of American Forest and Conservation History*. 2 vols. New York: Macmillan, 1983.

Douglas, William O. *The Three Hundred Year War: A Chronicle of Ecological Disaster*. New York: Random House, 1972.

Dubos, René. *Celebrations of Life*. New York: McGraw-Hill, 1981.

———. *A God Within*. New York: Scribners, 1972.

———. *So Human an Animal*. New York: Scribners, 1968.

Dubos, René, and Barbara Ward. *Only One Earth: The Care and Maintenance of a Small Planet*. New York: W. W. Norton, 1972.

Durrell, Lee. *State of the Ark: An Atlas of Conservation in Action*. New York: Doubleday, 1986.

Ehrlich, Paul R. *The Population Bomb*. San Francisco: Sierra Club Books, 1968.

Ehrlich, Paul R., and Anne Ehrlich. *Extinction*. New York: Random House, 1981.

Ehrlich, Paul R., and J. Roughgarden. *The Science of Ecology*. New York: Macmillan, 1987.

Forsyth, Adrian, and Ken Miyata. *Tropical Nature: Life and Death in the Rain Forests of Central and South America*. New York: Scribners, 1984.

Fox, Stephen. *The American Conservation Movement*. Madison: University of Wisconsin Press, 1985.

Frome, Michael. *Battle for the Wilderness*. New York: Praeger, 1964.

————. *Whose Woods These Are: The Story of the National Forests*. Garden City, N.Y.: Doubleday, 1962.

Gore, Al. *Earth in the Balance: Ecology and the Human Spirit*. Boston: Houghton Mifflin, 1992.

Graham, Frank, Jr. *Audubon Ark: A History of the National Audubon Society*. New York: Knopf, 1990.

————. *Man's Dominion: The Story of Conservation in America*. New York: M. Evans, 1971.

Hardin, Garrett. *Exploring New Ethics for Survival: The Voyages of the Spaceship Beagle*. New York: Viking, 1972.

————. *The Limits of Altruism*. Bloomington: Indiana University Press, 1977.

————. *Nature and Man's Fate*. New York: New American Library, 1961.

*Javna, John. *Fifty Simple Things Kids Can Do to Save the Earth*. Kansas City, Mo.: Andrews & McMeel, 1990.

The Living Wilderness, Spring-Summer 1964. [Special issue on the history of the Wilderness Act of 1964; includes complete text of the law.]

McKibben, Bill. *The End of Nature*. New York: Random House, 1989.

Nash, Roderick. *Wilderness and the American Mind*. 3rd ed. New Haven: Yale University Press, 1982.

Osborn, Fairfield. *The Limits of the Earth*. Boston: Little, Brown, 1953.

————. *Our Plundered Planet*. Boston: Little, Brown, 1948.

Ponting, Clive. *A Green History of the World*. New York: St. Martin's, 1991.

Rathje, William. *Rubbish!* New York: HarperCollins, 1992.

Reiger, John F. *American Sportsmen and the Origins of Conservation*. New York: Winchester Press, 1975.

Revkin, Andrew. *Global Warming: Understanding the Forecast*. New York: Abbeville Press, 1992.

Ricklefs, Robert E. *Ecology*. 3rd ed. New York: Chiron Press, 1987.

Schell, Jonathan. *The Fate of the Earth*. New York: Knopf, 1982.

Smith, Michael L. *Pacific Visions: California Scientists and the Environment, 1850–1915*. New Haven: Yale University Press, 1987.

Smith, Robert L. *Ecology and Field Biology*. 4th ed. New York: Harper & Row, 1989.

Storer, John H. *The Web of Life*. New York: New American Library, 1966.

Trefethen, James B. *Crusade for Wildlife: Highlights in Conservation Progress*. Harrisburg, Pa.: Stackpole, 1961.

Udall, Stewart L. *The Quiet Crisis and the Next Generation*. Rev. ed. Layton, Utah: Gibbs Smith, 1988.

van den Bosch, Robert. *The Pesticide Conspiracy*. Garden City, N.Y.: Doubleday, 1978.

Wilson, Edward O. *The Diversity of Life*. Cambridge: Harvard University Press, 1992.

World Resources Institute. *The 1993 Information Please Environmental Almanac*. Boston: Houghton Mifflin, 1992. [Published annually]

Wyant, William K. *Westward in Eden: The Public Lands and the Conservation Movement*. Berkeley: University of California Press, 1982.

Index

Acknowledgments

Special thanks are owed to Claire Quigley, director of interlibrary loan services at the Westport (Connecticut) Public Library, for locating so many of the books necessary for the preparation of *Earthkeepers*, and to Thomas Bartunek, for his invaluable assistance.

Thanks also to Mary Ellen Chijioke, curator, Friends Historical Library, Swarthmore College; the Department of English, University of Kentucky, Lexington; Joan Parks, *Farm Journal* magazine; Clarise Roberts, administrative assistant, the Goldman Environmental Foundation, San Francisco; Deborah Schildkraut, Boston; Maria Voles, director of publications, The Nature Conservancy; Jane Wilkins, World Society for the Protection of Animals, Boston; and Beth Zebrowski, Conservation Center, American Association for Zoological Parks and Aquariums, Bethesda, Maryland.

Picture Credits

Ann T. Keene is a freelance writer and editor of nonfiction for both children and adults. She is the author of *Children's Literature: A Study Guide*; *Historic Americans: Scholars and Educators*; and the forthcoming *Willa Cather*, a new young adult biography of Cather. Ms. Keene has also published reviews and essays on American culture. She has taught at George Mason University and Indiana University, where she is a doctoral candidate in American studies. Ms. Keene lives in Westport, Connecticut.

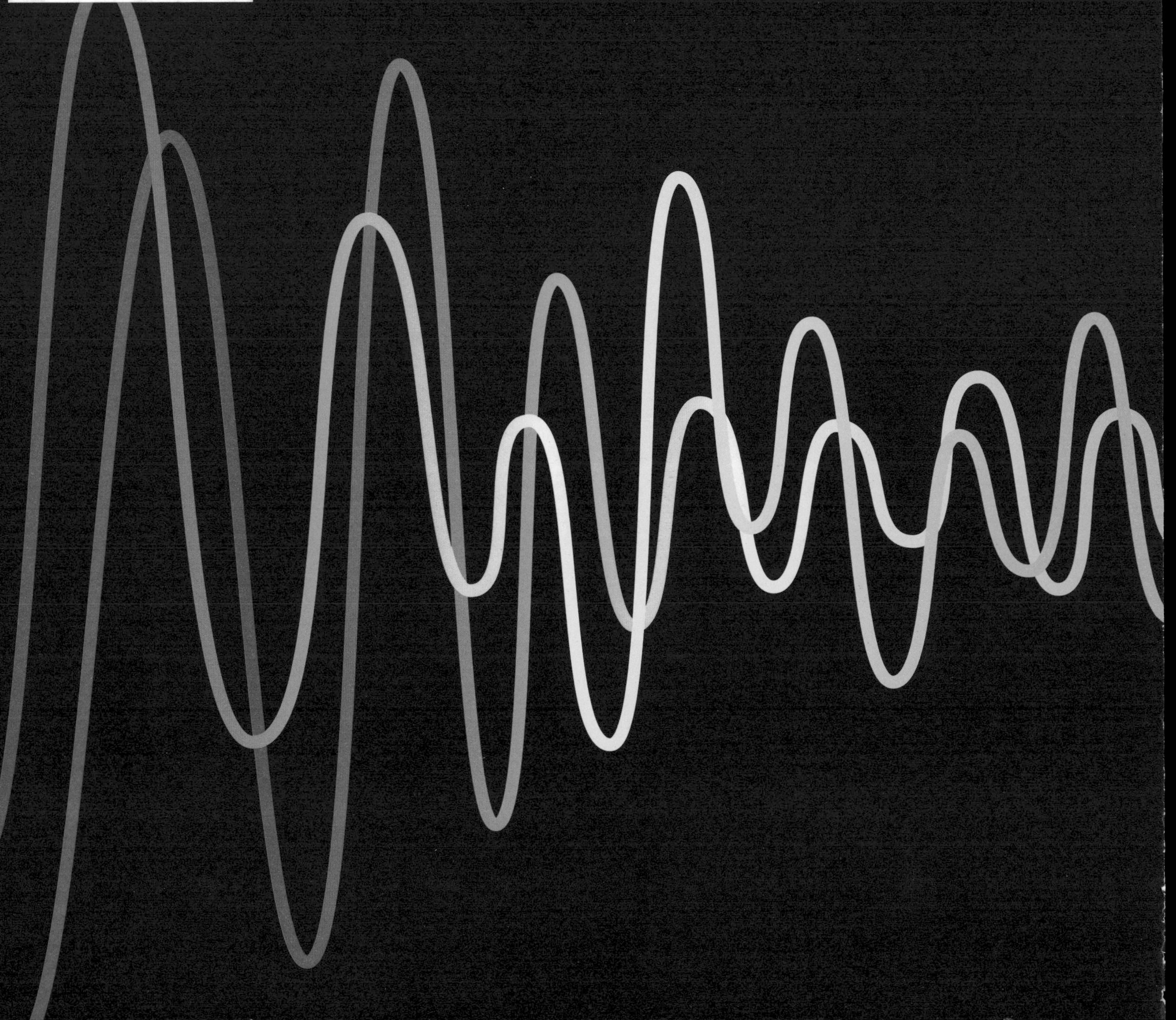

...your laughter!

...an alarm going off

...a train roaring by

...waves crashing

...a plane humming

...footsteps crunching

...drums banging

...a balloon popping

...a child crying

...your heart beating

...a branch snapping

...high notes

...low notes

...thunder crashing

...slurping

...a bird singing

...a bee buzzing

i HEAR...

PatrickGeorge

In the same series by PatrickGeorge:

© PatrickGeorge 2012
First published in the United Kingdom in 2012
This edition first published for the U.S.A. and Canada in 2013 by PatrickGeorge

Illustrated, designed and published by
PatrickGeorge
46 Vale Square
Ramsgate
Kent CT11 9DA
United Kingdom

www.patrickgeorge.biz

ISBN 978-1-908473-07-3

British Library Cataloguing in Publication Data.
A catalogue record for this book is available from the British Library.

Printed in China by Gagu International Trade Limited,
415 Room Jian mao Building, 1# Road Tianbei Luo Hu, Shenzhen.

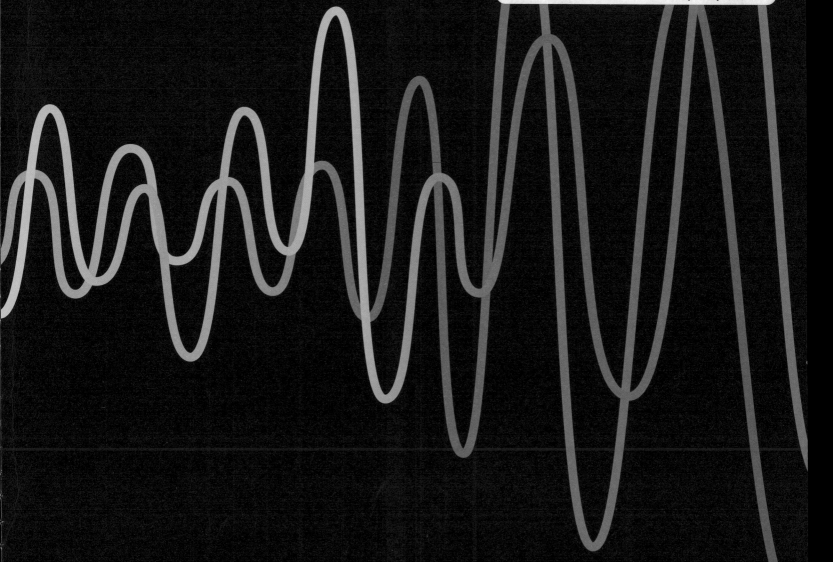